Southern Illinois University Press

Carbondale & Edwardsville

Singular Texts/Plural Authors:
Perspectives on Collaborative Writing

Edited by Patricia St. John

Designed by David Ford

Production supervised by Natalia Nadraga

93   92   91   90   4   3   2   1

Library of Congress Cataloging-in-Publication Data

Ede, Lisa
Singular texts/plural authors : perspectives on
collaborative writing / Lisa Ede and Andrea Lunsford
p.   cm.
Includes bibliographical references
Includes indexes.
1. Authorship—collaboration.   I. Lunsford, Andrea
II. Title.
PN145.E34   1990
808′.02—dc20   89-19712
ISBN 0-8093-1447-9   CIP

The paper used in this publication meets the minimum requirements of
American National Standard for Information Sciences
—Permanence of Paper for Printed Library Materials, ANSI Z39.48-1984 ∞

For our parents

Contents

Preface

In his essay "Terministic Screens," Kenneth Burke enjoins his readers to "pick some particular nomenclature, some one terministic screen . . . that you may proceed to track down the kinds of observations implicit in the terminology you have chosen, whether your choice of terms was deliberate or spontaneous" (*Language* 47). For us, the "nomenclature" of writing together, which began spontaneously, evolved quickly into just the kind of tracking down—as Burke could have told us— that led to ever-widening circles of investigation.

Why write . . . together? Our involvement in collaborative writing grew out of the personal, the homely, the concrete. We wrote together as an extension and an enrichment of our long friendship. In the process of making each of us present to the other, of hearing our "selves" echoed back and forth, of constituting and reconstituting, forming, transforming, and reforming voices to speak our texts, we came ineluctably to hear within ourselves a large polyphonic chorus rather than just a duet. And so we set out to chart our own experience of collaborative writing and to view that experience through the "nomenclatures" of work-related writing, of history, theory, technology, and pedagogy.

The experience and the study of collaboration have been for us in some ways acts of subversion and of liberatory significance. We began collaborating in spite of concerned warnings of friends and colleagues, including those of Edward P. J. Corbett, the person in whose honor we first wrote collaboratively. We knew that our collaboration represented a challenge to traditional research conventions in the humanities. Andrea's colleagues (at the University of British Columbia) said so when they declined to consider any of her coauthored or coedited works as part of a review for promotion. Lisa's colleagues (at Oregon State University) said so when, as part of her tenure review, they supportively but exhaustively discussed how best to approach the problem of her coauthored works.

These professional impediments to our collaboration strengthened, rather than weakened, our resolve to work together. We are each, in our different ways, very stubborn. We are also committed to working to change the academy so that others can, without penalty, experience the satisfactions and challenges of collaborative inquiry. One hindrance to academic collaboration in the humanities, we believe, is the practice of insisting on the concept of primary and secondary authorship. By crediting the first author as primary and the second and following authors as secondary, this practice denies the reality of collaboration such as ours. Whenever we write together, however we list our names, our collaboration is equal. When we first began working together, we thought that presenting our names in alphabetical order would indicate our shared responsibility for and participation in our texts. Quickly disabused of that notion, we have since alternated the order of our names. We have even considered publishing major projects such as this book under coined neologisms, such as Annalisa Edesford or LisaAnn Lunede. Our ultimate recognition of the problems this practice might cause our colleagues and readers forced us to abandon this plan. The visual presentation of our names on the title page, then, is yet another attempt to indicate how seamless is the weaving of our ideas, words, and responsibilities in this book.

The years that we have worked on this project have been difficult ones for both of us. This book bears the mark of our struggle—one that has emboldened us to take risks, to write more personally than we have in the past. Not the least of this personal struggle has been our attempt to question each other's assumptions and to recognize, to really hear, and to appreciate the questions of others. For this book about collaboration reflects not only our personal exploration of collaborative writing but an extraordinarily wide range of co-collaboration.

The research project with which this book began was funded in 1984 by the Fund for the Improvement of Post-Secondary Education, under the auspices of the Mina Shaughnessy Scholars Program. The meetings we shared with the project directors and with other Shaughnessy Scholars helped us refine not only our research design but our thinking about collaboration as well. In the course of carrying out that research, we received invaluable critiques and help from Linda Flower, Lynn Troyka, Pamela Bodenroeder, and from Helen Berg, who steadfastly insisted that we could understand and use the statistical manipulations she was carrying out for us. We owe an early and continuing debt to Bob Connors, who has patiently listened to us talk through this book, and also to Theresa Enos, who has supported our work by allowing versions of some of it to appear in *Rhetoric Review*. We are also enormously grateful to those respondants to our early surveys who allowed us to conduct extended interviews with them: Albert Bernstein, Eleanor Chiogioji, James Goodling, Chris Kuhn, Lyle Matznick, Dick Miller, Bill Qualls, Scott Roser, Allan Warrior. Some of their stories animate and make concrete the research story we tell in chapter 2.

From our CCCC community, we have drawn support and insight throughout the long process of writing. Many colleagues have graciously and generously shared their own work with us: Nancy Allen, Diane Atkinson, Charles Bazerman, Deborah Bosley, Mary Beth Debs, Stephen Doheny-Farina, Janis Forman, Anne Gere, Dixie Goswami, Jeanne Halpern, Sharon Hamilton-Weiler, Tori Haring-Smith, Shirley Brice Heath, Mara Holt, Karen LeFevre, Hallie Lemon, Meg Morgan, Lee Odell, Ann Piternick, Jim Reither, Mike Rose, Craig Snow, Susan Stevenson, Jan Swearingen, John Trimbur, Steve Witte. We are grateful to them all.

Kenneth Bruffee, Anne Gere, Tom Hilgers, Karen LeFevre, Elaine Maimon, Barbara Nodine, and Harvey Wiener put together CCCC sessions with us, and out of those sessions and our other presentations came criticism and response that enriched and broadened our understanding. At one such meeting, Lisa Albrecht challenged us to probe more fully the questions of power and of gender raised by the data we were gathering, and she showed us ways we might do so. And many, many other women in our profession, by the example of their works and lives, have contributed to the making of this book. We especially wish to note Suzanne Clark, Sharon Crowley, Janet Emig, Beth Flynn, Phyllis Franklin, Cheryl Glenn, Shirley Brice Heath, Janice Lauer, Susan Miller, the late Mina Shaughnessy, and C. Jan Swearingen.

As we worked toward a final draft, we had the benefit of particularly strong readings from John Trimbur, Karen LeFevre, Charles Cooper, Suzanne Clark, and Chris Anderson, whose criticisms were in every case constructive. And we have had the luxury of two incredibly helpful departments. At Oregon State, Bob Frank and Bill Potts offered strong support throughout this project. Anterra Beyerl, Lois Gangle, Anne Wilson, and Marjorie Kickert provided much-needed help with copying, mailing, and other chores, while Diane Slywczuk demonstrated absolutely magical abilities to negotiate the rough terrain of grant budgets and administrative documentation. And without the friendship, assistance, and support of Barb Hogg and Lex Runciman, much of the work of this book simply would not have been possible. At Ohio State, Murray Beja, Ed Corbett, and David Frantz provided encouragement and always found time to listen; Jim Phelan and the students in our spring 1989 graduate seminar sparked new ideas every day; Cindy Cox, Carole Papper, Melinda Bako, Kelly Vezdos, Jane Ashby, and Nader Ayish worked tirelessly to document all those voices we wanted to include in the bibliography; Beverly Bruck and Lorraine Carlat produced meticulous copy for us and kept the express mail meters humming; Heather Graves developed two workable and complete indexes for the book; and Gerald Nelms and Roger Graves added so much to the process of producing this book that we scarcely know where to begin in listing their contributions.

Finally, we owe a particularly strong debt to the dedicated staff at Southern Illinois University Press. We wish to thank Patricia St. John, Susan Wilson, and Natalia Nadraga, who worked with us as we prepared the final manuscript for publication. And we can never adequately thank Kenney Withers, who not only supported, encouraged, and (when we needed it) goaded us during the years we worked on this project, but who has, in his role of editor, done so much to encourage the revival of rhetoric in English studies.

We do not mean by this lengthy list of acknowledgments to eschew responsibility for the text that follows. Indeed, we are eager to assume that responsibility: to *author* this book. But we are acutely aware of the extent to which our ability to author anything at all is anchored in our experiences with others. Even as we drew up this list of those who most directly supported and influenced our work, we were aware of the scores of others upon whom we indirectly relied, and we realized that we could never make this list complete, never compile a definitive set of acknowledgments. With this text, we have entered the crowded parlor of which Burke speaks, and we have joined the multiplicitous conversation in progress there. But we have not arrived alone. Instead, we have been accompanied by a whole chorus of voices which have also entered into that conversation—a chorus that we have attempted to evoke in the Intertexts preceding each chapter. For all the voices we are most particularly grateful, for they have taught us to listen even as we try to speak.

Singular Texts/Plural Authors

INTERTEXTS

In collaborating on writing this book we searched for a single voice—a way of submerging our individual perspectives for the sake of the collective "we." Not that we denied our individual convictions or squelched our objections to one another's points of view—we argued, tried to persuade, even cried at times when we reached an impasse of understanding—but we learned to listen to each other, build on each other's insights, and eventually to arrive at a way of communicating as a collective what we believe. Hence, this book is not separated into parts that we wish to attribute to one or the other of us, even though each of us took the primary responsibility for different parts. There may be stylistic differences from one section to the next, but the book as a whole is the product of our joint efforts and interchange of ideas.—Mary Field Belenky, Blythe McVicker Clinchy, Nancy Rule Goldberger, Jill Mattuck Tarule, Women's Ways of Knowing

*   *   *   *   *

A Kinsey Institute sex survey that could help researchers understand how AIDS spreads was delayed for almost a decade because two of its authors fought over whose name should appear first on the title page. . . . Publication was scheduled in 1980, when an intense dispute broke out about whose name should appear on the title page. . . . The survey languished for years, unavailable to most researchers, until [an Institute Director] persuaded the authors to settle their differences.—"What Revolution?"

*   *   *   *   *

The authorship or compilership of a dictionary . . . is, indeed, a question like that of the identity of the darned and redarned stockings

with the original pair.—Spectator 14 December 1867, quoted in
Oxford English Dictionary

*   *   *   *   *

In film, theater, and dance, collaboration among creative individuals
is taken for granted. Even when dominated by one person—writer,
director, or choreographer, for example—the ensemble is integral
to the realization of the work. Similarly, joint authorship of books
and articles occurs frequently, and teamwork in scientific research is
standard.

In the visual arts, too, there is a rich collaborative tradition, which,
however, has been overlooked until recently. From medieval workshops and Renaissance ateliers through the nineteenth-century
Beaux-Arts studios, projects were created by pairs or teams of
painters, sculptors, and printmakers. In our own time, collaborators
also include photographers, filmmakers, and video and performance artists. Since the period of artistic as well as political ferment
preceding the outbreak of World War I, most avant-garde movements have had significant collaborative components.—Artistic Collaboration in the Twentieth Century, Hirshhorn Museum Exhibit,
Smithsonian Institute

*   *   *   *   *

As most young scientists learn in the early stages of their careers, the
key to success is to master a nettlesome paradox. To thrive in
science, you must be both a consummate collaborator and a relent-
less competitor. You must balance, with an almost gymnastic precision, the need to cooperate against the call to battle. Modern science has become too broad and complex a venture for any one researcher to go it alone; scientists need other scientists. At the same
time, those scientists who avoid the often vitriolic squabbles and
races that are such prominent features of doing science risk professional failure. By a generally accepted rule of thumb, if you don't
publish your results before your opponent does, you may as well not
publish at all. And in science, if you don't publish, you don't survive.

Casual and sentimental observers may wish that society could
somehow encourage scientists to cooperate more. There's an old
stereotype of the selfless scientist who seeks to solve the puzzles of

nature for the joy of helping humanity, and that stereotype dies hard. Besides, doesn't extreme competition lead to all sorts of problems—name-calling, data stealing, even scientific fraud? Wouldn't science be more efficient and productive if scientists could devote themselves entirely to research and leave political warfare behind?—Natalie Angier, "Nice Guys Don't Win Nobel Prizes"

* * * * *

"People said [The Talisman, a novel written collaboratively with Peter Straub] would be like a teenage marriage," says Stephen King, who first proposed a collaboration . . . six years ago. "They said we'd ruin a good thing and wind up hating each other for life." The writing, however, went almost completely according to plan. —Charles Leerhsen, Review in Newsweek

* * * * *

Nancy Mitford's best-seller, The High Cost of Death, was co-authored with her lawyer husband; however, her publisher said that two authors would mean fewer sales, and only her name appears on the title page.—Alleen Pace Nilsen, "Men and Women: Working Together in Changing Times"

* * * * *

"Increasingly in recent years we do write together very much more than we used to. In working on the sequel to Madwoman, there are something like five enormous chapters in the opening sections, and we've been writing every word together."—Sandra M. Gilbert, quoted in Laura Shapiro, "Gilbert and Gubar"

* * * * *

If the old boys' network in psychiatry has a code of discretion, Jesse O. Cavenar, Jr., has offended it. He says he had cause. Cavenar, a 47-year-old professor of psychiatry at Duke, sued in December for recognition as top editor of a major textbook whose cover gives first credit to someone else.

The other person is Robert Michels, 51, chairman of Cornell University's Department of Psychiatry and director of the prestigious Payne-Whitney Clinic in New York City. Cavenar says the publisher considered Michels' name more marketable and gave it first rank, even though Michels did not edit the book.

The court decided that Cavenar had been wronged . . . [and] Cavenar is satisfied. He also claims to have struck a blow for scientific integrity, and his case sets out in grimy detail the way in which publishers, editors, and academics carve up the rewards in multi-authored texts. The credit goes mostly to those who are already prominent, and the labor is done by those who are not.
—Eliot Marshall, "Textbook Credits Bruise Psychiatrists' Egos"

*   *   *   *   *

Can it be that the notion of individualism, so sacred to the United States, also is its fatal flaw—the basic strength that works against itself to reduce strength? —Andrew Polack, "Scholars Reconsider Role of Trendy High-Tech Entrepreneurs"

What we want is not terms that avoid ambiguity,
but terms that clearly reveal the strategic spots at
which the ambiguities necessarily arise.—Kenneth
Burke (*Grammar* xviii)

1 / Old Beginnings

QUESTIONING ASSUMPTIONS

In his essay "Common Sense as a Cultural System," Clifford Geertz argues that one of the most effective ways an anthropologist can begin to understand another culture is to study what that culture takes to be commonsense wisdom—the knowledge in our advanced Western society, for instance, that "rain wets and that one ought to come in out of it, or that fire burns and one ought not play with it" (75). Such analysis can, Geertz notes, reveal how a "culture is jointed and put together" much better than traditional functionalist accounts (93). Not that such analysis is easy. "There is something," Geertz comments, "of the purloined-letter effect in common sense; it lies so artlessly before our eyes it is almost impossible to see" (92).

The research that led to this book began when we caught a glimpse of a purloined letter in our own field: the pervasive commonsense assumption that writing is inherently and necessarily a solitary, individual act. What caused us, six years ago, to look not through this assumption but at it, to see the purloined letter? (In Edgar Allan Poe's mystery of that name, detective C. Auguste Dupin locates a very important missing letter that has been "hidden" in plain view "upon a trumpery fillagree card-rack of pasteboard" and thus prevents a major political crisis [49].) The answer to our mystery is simple and even perhaps predictable: our own experience as coauthors. Most succinctly, our interest in collaborative writing grew out of the dissonance generated by the difference between our personal experience as coauthors and the responses of many of our friends and colleagues.

Though we began writing together almost by accident—deciding on the spur of the moment to write an article together for a volume of essays to be published in honor of our mutual friend and mentor Edward P. J. Corbett—we found the experience so natural and so productive that we continued to write together. What seemed natural to us, however, seemed anything but natural to our English department colleagues. Some in our field cautioned us, for instance, that we would never receive favorable tenure decisions or promotions if we insisted on publishing coauthored articles. Even those who did not caution us about the dangerous consequences of our habit professed amazement at our ability to write together, questioning us in detail as though we had just returned from a strange new country. Our own experience as coauthors, then, provided the lens through which we initially took a new and intensely curious look at work in our own field of composition studies. What view of writing was inscribed there? On the occasions when writing teachers have attempted to describe writing in the most straightforward or commonsensical terms, the solitary nature of writing has emerged.

In his essay "Writing/Speaking: A Descriptive Phenomenological View," Loren Barritt attempts to define this relationship through phenomenological analysis, a method that has as its goal "'naive' looking, which is achieved by 'bracketing' popular beliefs, be they doubts or theories" (125). Consequently, a phenomenological study of speaking-writing relationships, Barritt adds, "involves a direct exploration and description of these language phenomena *as they are experienced*." Barritt then presents five statements that, he argues, "seem to me to be at the heart of the experience of written composition" (127):

> When I write, I sit down, pick up my pen,
> and begin to write words on paper. (127)

> When I write, I have some idea what I
> intend to say. (128)

> I write for someone, with a purpose in
> mind. (129)

> When I write, my thoughts tumble over one
> another. I have trouble moving my pen to keep
> up with my thoughts. (129)

> *You are alone when you write.* (130, our emphasis)

Interestingly, Barritt goes on to connect this inevitable solitariness with the difficulties many writers experience: "Because writing is a solitary . . . activity, I find it easy to avoid getting started on a writing task. Writing means going off somewhere to be alone with my thoughts and plans" (130).

We found this generally unspoken and commonsensical assumption that "writers work in solitude, where they address absent persons virtually all of whom are and always will be totally unknown to them" silently informing both the theory and the practice of the teaching of writing (Ong 184). James Moffett's theory and method in his influential *Teaching the Universe of Discourse* rest largely on the assumption that "the most critical adjustment one makes [in learning to write] is to relinquish collaborative discourse, with its reciprocal prompting and cognitive cooperation, and go it alone" (87). Much research on the composing process, such as the early work of Flower and Hayes (1981, 1984) or Bereiter and Scardamalia (1982), examines writers in the act of writing alone, using the data thus collected as the basis of proposed models of the composing process. Even most of the early work on collaborative learning in composition classes, such as the pioneering efforts of Kenneth Bruffee (1978, 1981, 1983, 1984), limited collaboration in practice to peer responses to a text already drafted by an individual student. As Donald Murray notes in "Writing as Process: How Writing Finds Its Own Meaning," "*Once the writing is produced,* it is shared" (27, our emphasis). For Murray and many others, we discovered, the writing process itself inevitably occurs in isolation.

SETTING A RESEARCH AGENDA

Yet our own experience as coauthors and our growing awareness that at least some work-related writing is highly collaborative belied the commonsensical view of writing as an individual act. So in 1984, with the help of a grant from the Fund for the Improvement of Post-Secondary Education (FIPSE) Shaughnessy Scholars program, we set out to investigate this anomaly. The following research questions, first articulated in our grant proposal, guided our early explorations:

1. What specific features distinguish the processes of co- or group authorship? Is it possible to locate from the range of potential co- and group authorship situations (which can vary from intensive collaboration between two individuals to large and often loosely organized group-writing efforts) a corpus of shared models and strategies?

2. How frequently and in what situations are members of representative professions called upon to write collaboratively?

3. Is the emphasis on or weight of various cognitive and rhetorical strategies different when writing collaboratively than when writing alone?

4. How do computers and other technologies, such as dictating, affect the process of co- or group authorship?

5. What epistemological implications do co- and group authorship hold for traditional notions of creativity and originality?

6. How might the ethics of co- or group authorship be defined?

7. What are the pedagogical implications of co- and group authorship? Can we develop ways to teach students to adjust readily to co- or group writing tasks?

Readers of this volume will note that our interest in co- and group authorship grew directly out of pragmatic, practical concerns. Did the view of writing implicit in composition theory and practice conflict with the view of writing emerging from work experience? How supportable and accurate was the view of writing we were presenting to our own students? Why were our coauthored articles received with alarm by many of our colleagues? Should writing teachers be encouraged to prepare their students for on-the-job collaborative writing? With such pragmatic questions in mind and with a set of research questions articulated, we devised a multilevel research project designed to provide some baseline data and preliminary answers, particularly to questions regarding the incidence and kinds of collaborative writing utilized on the job.

For the first stage of this research, we developed a questionnaire to survey 1,400 randomly selected members (200 from each group) of the American Institute of Chemists, the American Consulting Engineers Council, the International City Management Association, the Modern Language Association, the American Psychological Association, the Professional Services Management Association, and the Society for Technical Communication. Our goal in this initial survey: to determine the frequency, types, and occasions of collaborative writing among members of these associations.

After analyzing the results of this first survey—especially the problematic or anomalous results—we developed a second questionnaire, a longer, more open-ended instrument to be completed by twelve members of each of these seven professional associations who had responded to our first survey. This second questionnaire explored such issues as the kinds of documents respondents most typically write as part of a group; the way in which respondents and fellow group members divide such writing activities as brainstorming, information gathering, and editing; their use of organizational patterns or set plans to assign duties for completing a project; the assignment of authorship or credit; and the advantages and disadvantages of collaborative writing. In the third stage of this research, we held on-site interviews with at least one collaborative writer from each of these seven associations in locations as diverse as Lexington, Kentucky; Medford, Oregon; Columbus, Ohio; and Washington, D.C. These interviews—nonquantifiable as they are—have proven particularly valuable resources because they were informed by our analysis of the first and second surveys and because the open-ended format of the interviews allowed us to explore issues and problems at much greater length.

Chapter 2 reports the results of these surveys and follow-up interviews—results that play an important role in this book's argument; for they indicate that, in these seven professional associations at least, collaborative writing is a frequent activity. Perhaps even more importantly, these results provide insights into those social processes and contexts that can make collaborative writing a productive and satisfying—or an unproductive and frustrating—experience.

SURVEYING LITERATURE ON COLLABORATION:
EARLY ATTEMPTS

When we began to prepare for this research on collaborative writing in the professions, we found little research within the discipline of composition studies that directly addressed our concerns and questions. An early computer ERIC search and a review of all issues of the *Education Index* from 1975 to 1983 unearthed only a few scattered essays. Alleen Pace Nilsen's "Men and Women: Working Together in Changing Times" (1980), for instance, discusses the unusually high number of husband and wife teams currently writing books for children. Two other essays, L. Ray Carry's "Dissertation Publication: The Issue of Joint Authorship" (1980) and Cheryl M. Fields' "Professors' Demands for Credit as 'Co-Authors' of Students Research Projects May Be Rising" (1983), review the ethical issues potentially involved with joint publication by graduate students and their professors. While we could find very little information or research on collaborative writing, the late seventies and early eighties did produce calls for a collaborative pedagogy in writing classes. Bruffee's early essays and textbook (1972, 1973, 1978, 1980, 1983) called for such a pedagogy, as did studies by Hawkins (1976), Coe (1979), Gebhardt (1980), and Clifford (1981). Though these studies emphasize the importance of collaborative learning, all assume single authorship as a model. Peers can work collaboratively in every stage of the writing process except for drafting. In these and other early models of collaborative learning, students inevitably draft alone.

At the start of our project, then, we had little indication of interest or support in composition studies for research on collaborative writing. While Lester Faigley and Thomas P. Miller's 1982 article indicated that "the majority (73.5%) [of their respondents] sometimes collaborate with at least one other person in writing" (567), such observations provoked little response from those teaching and studying expository writing. The purloined letter—the assumption that writing is inevitably a solitary activity—had not yet come into view.

Because so little research in our field directly addressed our concerns and questions, of necessity we cast a wide net in our effort to locate studies that could help us better understand the phenomenon of collaborative writing. Our early inquiries produced surprisingly diverse leads. We discovered, for instance, a substantial (indeed overwhelming) body of research in sociology, psychology, speech communication, education, and business on group processes and decision making. As Bobby

R. Patton and Kim Griffin note in *Decision-Making Group Interaction,* research in these areas on "the study of groups is largely a twentieth-century phenomenon" (3). From its start in the 1920s, this research has been largely empirically based; the emphasis, however, has shifted from a concern with productivity (the dominant concern from the 1920s to World War II) to the group process itself.

It is not possible here to survey the efforts of researchers involved in the study of group processes. This research is so diverse that it is difficult to develop a sufficiently broad perspective to enable integration, much less evaluation, of these multidisciplinary efforts. In the introduction to his 1982 study *Creativity in Small Groups,* A. Paul Hare notes the difficulties that inevitably arise when individuals in a variety of fields conduct research on a related problem or subject. In commenting on "the sources of research for . . . [his] analysis of social interaction and creativity in small groups," Hare observes that "psychologists dominate the field, followed by sociologists, and then by persons in the applied fields of psychotherapy, education, social work, and business." Inevitably, given these diverse disciplinary affiliations, not only methods but crucial definitions can vary considerably. "In some cases those who are part of the 'group dynamics school' are concerned with groups much larger than the typical 'small' group of five to twenty members. On the other hand, many of the social-psychologists who have made contributions to the understanding of social interaction in small groups were not studying groups as such but rather individual behavior in a social situation" (16). Finally Hare adds, "For all the research in this area, relatively few persons work in a general theoretical context that provides a way of integrating the various research results" (16).

If a researcher such as Hare, whose *Handbook of Small Group Research* is considered a basic resource for those studying small group processes, finds synthesis and application difficult, so inevitably will researchers in composition. In our unavoidably incomplete review of research on small group processes, we have nevertheless located researchers who have drawn a number of useful preliminary conclusions on the characteristics of effective and ineffective groups (Beebe and Masterson 1982, Hall and Williams 1970), the determinants of productivity (Steiner 1972, Jewell and Reitz 1981), and the role that pressures toward conformity, sometimes called groupthink, play in group interactions (Fisher 1980, Forsyth 1983, Janis 1983). These references might most fruitfully be viewed as starting points— places to begin exploring research in this area.

Investigations beyond our own disciplinary boundaries also revealed a related body of research in education on what is variously called cooperative learning (Johnson and Johnson 1974, 1985; Johnson and Johnson 1987; Sharan and Sharan 1976; Sharan 1980; Slavin 1980; Slavin et al. 1985; O'Donnell et al. 1985) or active learning (Bouton and Garth 1983). Although this research does not comment specifically on collaborative writing, it does contribute to our understanding of how teachers can more effectively encourage collaborative learning and writing in their classrooms. As was the case with studies of small group processes, the focus of this research is diverse. Bouton and Garth note in the introduction to *Learning in Groups* that those engaged in research on collaborative learning groups often have a variety of purposes, including: "overcoming student passivity in large classes . . . , developing liberal education skills and abilities . . . , teaching writing . . . , developing competent professionals . . . , improving scholarly ability among graduate students . . . , and encouraging learning beyond the classroom" (2). The studies cited by Bouton and Garth (1983), as well as the extensive research projects reviewed by Slavin (1980) and Sharan (1980), provide substantial evidence that, when effectively structured and guided, learning groups can help students improve their mastery not only of particular subject areas or academic skills, such as writing, but also increase their general cognitive skills and their engagement with and interest in learning.

Research in the sociology and history of science on the nature and impact of scientific collaboration also provided useful information about collaborative writing in the sciences. As Derek J. de Solla Price notes in *Little Science, Big Science,* such studies, whether statistical or interpretive, focus on "general problems of the shape and size of science and the ground rules governing growth and behavior of science-in-the-large" (viii). Price calls the growth of multiauthored over single-authored scientific papers "one of the most violent transitions that can be measured in recent trends of scientific manpower and literature" (89). And because of this trend, much attention is paid to the collaborative writing practices of scientists.

Typically in this research the focus is not on the process of collaborative writing but on its effect, particularly on the impact of collaborative practices on scientific productivity. As Mark Oromaner has noted, to this end "sociologists and historians of science have increasingly relied upon examinations of citations as a means of analysis. These analyses have been concerned with (1) the rate of growth and obsolescence of scientific literature; (2) the identification of the most important, eminent, influential, or visible scholars, publications, departments, invisible colleges and schools in particular disciplines or sub-disciplines; and (3) the sociometric networks among scholars, publications, departments, invisible colleges and schools among disciplines or within a particular discipline or sub-discipline" (98–99).

This research is of interest, obviously, for its detailed support of the collaborative practices—including collaborative writing—of modern scientists (Price 1963, Meadows 1974). But it also reveals that even in disciplines where collaboration is the norm, problems remain. Since the late seventies, a number of sociologists, such as Porter (1977), Long, McGinnis, and Allison (1980), and Lindsay (1980), have begun to argue against the established practice of noting only first authors in citation counts. Lindsay asserts that the practice of "count[ing] both publications and citations with procedures that take no account of multiple authorship" represents perhaps "one of the most serious errors in empirical judgment made in the sociology of science" (145).

A number of researchers in psychology and sociology explore what Meadows calls "one of the more arcane areas of scientific communication—the ordering of authors' names on research papers" from a somewhat different perspective, that of attempting to establish the fairest, most equitable means of attribution (197). These efforts include detailed analyses of the effects of name-ordering among authors of scientific papers (Zuckerman 1968, Nudelman and Landers 1972); proposals for the development of a coding system that would "provide more complete information on which author is responsible for what" (Simon 265); analyses of the causes and effects of collaborative research and publication in these disciplines (Over 1982, Over and Smallman 1973, Mitchell 1961); and discussions of the ethical standards governing the assignment of publication credit (Spiegel and Keith-Spiegel 1970).

As we analyzed responses to our surveys, we also continued to collect rich and varying sources on many issues surrounding collaborative writing. But despite their usefulness, our early reading and research, including our own surveys and interviews, could only answer some of the questions that continued to command our attention. They could not tell us why prohibitions against collaborative writing in the humanities have remained so strong or why the assumption that writing is a solitary activity has been so deeply and broadly accepted by English teachers. Nor could they help us probe larger issues, such as the nature of authorship or of knowledge, the essence of the latter brought into question most prominently by the growing influence of social-constructivist arguments in a variety of disciplines, including that of composition studies. As a result, at the time when we had planned to have our research project finished, we found ourselves shifting focus, no longer satisfied simply to report our results and have done with it. We were, in fact, at a new beginning.

REVISING OUR RESEARCH AGENDA

The third chapter of this book charts the course of that new beginning, examining a number of theoretical questions raised by our research. This discussion, which is far from conclusive, ranges from the general (an analysis of those forces which together encouraged the identification of writing as inherently an individual activity in Western culture) to the specific (the consequences of electronic media for copyright and patent laws). Inevitably, we have drawn on research from a number of related disciplines—philosophy, history, anthropology, sociology, psychology, and literary theory. Such interdisciplinary explorations are always dangerous; one must be careful not merely to pick and choose that evidence which best supports one's own views, ignoring important disciplinary constraints. But the risk is, we feel, justified: only such a broad interdisciplinary approach can begin to suggest the implications of interrogating fully our traditional notions of what it means to be an author.

While our exploration of historical and theoretical dimensions of collaborative writing raised myriad questions, we hoped that our research would eventually yield answers to some important practical pedagogical questions. If men and women in the work force frequently write collaboratively, should not writing teachers help prepare them for an important part of their job? Our own experiences as coauthors have been both personally and professionally satisfying. Might students find writing more enjoyable and less alienating if they collaborated occasionally? How might such opportunities best be embedded in the curriculum? How are attacks on the subject in psychology and sociology and the destabilization of the author in literary studies reflected in our pedagogy? What would an effective collaborative assignment look like? Chapter 4 attempts to deal with such pedagogical issues and offers, where possible, tentative guidelines and suggestions for teachers who wish to include collaborative writing in their classes. But the more we worked with our materials in this chapter, the harder it became for us to devise a set of clear-cut, pragmatic recipes for collaboration. In fact, our subject proved as problematic pedagogically as it had theoretically and historically. Issues of power and authority, of consensus and conflict, of gender, race, and class raised questions about a pedagogy of collaboration that we could not ignore. And our growing awareness of and sensitivity to such issues made us particularly cautious in recommending any one kind of collaborative writing activity.

As this introduction suggests, the research odyssey on which we embarked six years ago has changed us, as we have changed it, as it has in turn changed us again. That first deceptively simple-sounding question we posed—is writing necessarily an individual activity?—did not plunge, straight and swift, toward safe answers but rather drifted in and out of currents and eddies, sending forth a rippled series of secondary and tertiary questions. Our attempt throughout this volume is to render our own sounding of these currents, our own processes of discovery and change. Though we originally strove to make it so, what you will read in the ensuing chapters is not and could not finally be cast in the traditional patriarchal academic mode: a distanced, seamless, logical process, marching inexorably from proof to demonstration to conclusion. Our lived experience of this book's story has been filled with personal struggle and pain, false hopes and starts, rich rewards, even richer uncertainties. Thus we arrive, in chapter 5 of this volume, not at a conventional set of proven conclusions but, as has most often been the case in our collaborative efforts, at a new beginning.

A NOTE ON DEFINITION

Before turning to chapter 2, which reports the results of our FIPSE-funded study of collaborative writing practices in seven professional associations, we must address one particular site of uncertainty—term definition. The meaning of the term *collaborative writing* is far from self-evident. Like other aspects of this study, our understanding of this term and the role of definitions shifted as our research progressed.

Our first efforts to define the phenomenon we wished to study were motivated primarily by pragmatic considerations. We needed to identify, and then to describe, this phenomenon in such a way that the members of the associations we were studying could understand and respond to the questions in our survey. Rather than use the term *collaborative writing* in our first two surveys, we referred to *group writing*—a term that we believed respondents to our surveys would more easily identify and understand. Once we had decided upon a name for our object of inquiry, we needed to define it. After considerable reflection, we decided that we would do so in the broadest possible terms. Consequently, we posited the following series of definitions as an introduction to Survey 2:

> This survey explores the dynamics and demands of group writing in your profession. For the purposes of this survey, writing includes any of the activities that lead to a completed written document. These activities include written and spoken brainstorming, outlining, note-taking, organizational planning, drafting, revising, and editing. Written products include any piece of writing, from notes, directions, and forms to reports and published materials. Group writing includes any writing done in collaboration with one or more persons.

We chose such a broad-based strategy for several reasons. First, as those who study the history of invention are aware, modern students, writers, and teachers of writing have traditionally ignored or undervalued the numerous complex intellectual and social processes that constitute an important part of most writing activities. Despite the possible danger of collapsing distinctions between writing and all related intellectual activities, we wanted to explore the full range of processes our survey respondents might identify as related to their on-the-job writing. Finally, given the paucity of our knowledge of collaborative writing and the ways it might function in the seven professional associations we intended to study (or in society in general, for that matter), we did not want to restrict participants by defining either writing or group writing too rigidly. Our attempt at a broad definition rested, then, on the very pragmatic desire to get as much information as possible about our subject.

The analysis presented in chapter 2 will demonstrate, we hope, the benefits derived from choosing such a broad lens through which to view our subject. Others interested in collaborative writing, however, have chosen more delimited definitions of the term. A group of researchers at Purdue University, for example, derived a definition from the descriptions provided by experienced collaborators, one that features three distinguishing features: (1) production of a shared document; (2) substantive interaction among members; and (3) shared decision-making power over and responsibility for the document (Allen, Atkinson, Morgan, Moore, Snow "Experienced").

The focus in this definition on the document directs their gaze in particular ways and leads to an efficient, pragmatic—though less broad—definition of both collaborative writing and writing. A similarly focused definition appears in the work of Deborah Bosley: "Collaborative writing is defined as two or more people working together to produce one written document in a situation in which a group takes responsibility for having produced the document" (6).

In practice, the term *collaborative writing* appears in many different settings and in fairly narrow—and often conflicting—definitions. In expository writing classes and in composition theory, which we will discuss more fully in chapter 4, the term has until recently most often described peer evaluation of individually written drafts. As Bosley's work demonstrates, researchers in professional and technical communication have also referred to any number of specific configurations as "collaborative writing" (4):

> supervisor's assignment of a document that is researched and drafted by a staff member, but carefully edited by the supervisor (Paradis, Dobrin, Miller)
>
> collaborative planning of a document that is drafted and revised by an individual (Odell)
>
> individual planning and drafting of a document that is revised collaboratively (Doheny-Farina)
>
> a peer's critiquing a co-worker's draft (Anderson) (4)

Countering these more specific implicit definitions are those of Jim Reither and other scholars, who tend to conflate writing and collaborative writing. For them, all writing is collaborative.

This unstructured and unsettled debate over definitions points up, most notably, just what is at stake in definitions in general and in definitions of collaborative writing in particular. We name in order to know, but that naming inevitably limits our knowing. Furthermore, these differing interpretations illustrate the problematic nature of defining terms. Each conception rests on a necessary but usually unstated definition of writing, a term that has of late proven highly resistant to simple or pat definitions. And definitions of writing, of course, reflect a set of ideological assumptions that we ignore only at our peril. Thus while we continue to use our broad definition—"any writing done in collaboration with one or more persons"—as a way of orienting our data and guiding readers through our study, we view this definition as largely unsatisfactory and just as problematic as any other. Indeed, the shifting and conflicting nature of the definitions revolving around the term *collaborative writing* seems to us to call not for simplification or standardization but for a Burkean complexifying—a series of perspectives by incongruity. By exploring such perspectives, we hope this book will contribute to an increasingly complex and enriched conversation about what it can mean to write collaboratively.

INTERTEXTS

Ever since the 16th century, scientists have been pursuing more and more of their research in cooperation with other scholars. But only in recent years have they stopped fearing potential dangers in collaboration, according to Karl Hufbauer, professor of history at the University of California at Irvine, who spoke at the 17th International Congress of History of Science.

Today, Mr. Hufbauer said, "no longer do most scientists work alone." But even into the 20th century, he said, many scientists still were afraid that "cooperation would endanger science by stifling individual orginality."—"Fears of Collaboration Among Scientists Examined"

*   *   *   *   *

Successful teams, like Tolstoy's happy families, may all seem alike, friendly and intimate, with partners easily accessible to each other, but the failures prove how hard collaboration can be. The most typical obstacle is the inability to discuss and resolve conflict. —Gloria Jacobs, "Work/Life: Going into Business—Have You Considered a Partnership?"

*   *   *   *   *

Although our cultural stereotype of "the writer" is highly individualistic, the real social tendency is toward collective writing. This is especially true of progressive writings. A union leaflet is rarely the work of one person. A political pamphlet or position paper usually represents a collective position and often does so because it has been written collectively. On the left, political writers often go out of their way to work collectively.—Richard M. Coe, "Writing in Groups"

*   *   *   *   *

The almost total lack of research specific to the question of the technical writer as collaborator underscores the first paradox writers face: they have been working for years at a profession still defining itself. The problem is not that the questions of professional identity confronting the technical writer are insignificant but that no one has thought of asking the questions.—Elaine Eldridge, Solving Problems in Technical Writing

*   *   *   *   *

The role collaboration plays in the writing done by writers working in different contexts points to the fundamental interdependence of all the language arts during the act of writing. Writing for these individuals, while sometimes accomplished in physical isolation from others (e.g., students separated from one another and from the teacher and textbook during an examination, the engineer alone in his office drafting a letter to a lawyer about necessary changes in a contract), never occurred in a social vacuum. The writing of each . . . depended in important ways on both prior and ongoing socially circumscribed "conversations" with others, "dialogic events" which themselves presupposed speaking, listening, reading, and "seeing" skills as preconditions for participation.—Stephen P. Witte, "Some Contexts for Understanding Written Literacy"

*   *   *   *   *

What happens when a doctoral student in, say, clinical psychology has done a good piece of research but then enters private practice and doesn't have the time or the inclination to publish? Is the research director going to let a good piece of research disappear? So he writes it up, and then what does he do about authorship? —Cheryl M. Fields, "Professors' Demands for Credit as 'Co-Authors' of Students' Research Projects May Be Rising"

*   *   *   *   *

In literature . . . feminism has had an impact on theory and practice, but resistance continues because the disciplinary practice of focusing on single authors, themes, genres, and theories facilitates avoidance of feminist scholarship.—Mary Anne Ferguson, "Review: Feminist Theory and Practice, 1985"

*   *   *   *   *

Thus, in answer to the questions which prompted this study [To what extent are physicists engaged in collaborative research? How does such collaboration compare with that of researchers in other disciplines? Does faculty involvement in this type of research affect the nature of graduate education?], physicists do a great deal of collaborative research, collaboration is more prevalent among physicists than among scholars in all other fields considered, and collaboration potentially has a very positive effect upon graduate education. Our study suggests that how physicists interact as a team is worthy of attention.—J. D. Memory, J. F. Arnold, D. W. Stewart, and R. E. Fornes, "Physics as a Team Sport"

*   *   *   *   *

In the future, no computer will be an island. . . . "Most work is collaborative in science and industry," says Wayne Rosing, vice president of advanced development for Sun Microsystems. "It's a waste to have hundreds of computers in a building that share nothing but AC power." But that won't be the case for long, and once computers are connected, experts predict a new class of software: "groupware." Groupware will permit an officeful of people to collaborate on, for example, a magazine advertisement, with artists, copywriters and sales people all contributing, via computer, to the project.—Michael Rogers with Richard Sandza, "Computers of the '90s: A Brave New World"

*   *   *   *   *

There are probably as many ways to go about collaborating as there are reasons for getting the idea in the first place.—Keith Laumer, "How to Collaborate Without Getting Your Head Shaved"

The ethical values of work are in its application of
the competitive equipment to cooperative ends.
—Kenneth Burke (*Philosophy* 316)

2 / Collaborative Writers at Work

SCENES OF COLLABORATION: FOREGROUNDINGS

In this chapter, we will contrast the conventional image of writers at work—an image that privileges the solitary writer working in isolation—with a different picture, that of writers planning, gathering information, drafting, and revising collaboratively. We know the first image well; the "reigning trope" for writing is, as Linda Brodkey observes, that of "the solitary scribbler" (55). In *Academic Writing as Social Practice,* Brodkey captures this image of the writer with rich specificity.

> Writing is a social act. People write to and for other people, yet when we picture writing we see a solitary writer. We may see the writer alone in a garret, working into the small hours of the morning by thin candlelight. The shutters are closed. Or perhaps we see the writer in a well-appointed study seated at a desk, fingers poised over the keys of a typewriter (or microcomputer). The drapes are drawn. Or we may even see the writer hunched over a manuscript in a magnificent public or university library, the walls and walls of books standing between the writer and the world. Whether the scene of writing is poetic or prosaic, the writer above the madding crowd in a garret, only temporarily free from family and friends in a study, or removed from the world in a library, it is the same picture—the writer writes alone.

> We do not easily picture writers in social settings. On those rare occasions when we do, we are likely to see a writer who is not writing. Maybe we see F. Scott Fitzgerald carousing, or Henry James dining out, or Tolstoy teaching peasants. Whether it is a picture of Virginia Woolf speaking to undergraduate women at Oxford or Ernest Hemingway on the Left Bank, these are not images of writers at work. However caught up they may be by the details of their social lives, these are pictures of writers playing or working at something other than writing. The image we hold of the writer places social life on the other side of

20

writing, that which occurs before or after writing, something or someone that must not be allowed to enter the scene of writing. (54–55)

Because images or pictures have such power, we wish to begin this report of our FIPSE-funded research project not with statistics but with descriptions of the writers we interviewed in order to discover more about collaborative writers at work. These descriptions are just that: descriptions. They should not be taken as generalizations or as representing ideal models for effective collaborative writing—though many of those we interviewed seemed to us to write quite effectively with others. Nor do our interviewees represent a comprehensive range or typology of collaborative writers. They are simply people who generously agreed to share their work and time with us. We have much to learn from them, both in terms of what these snapshots record about the everyday, commonsense collaboration that characterizes writing in the workplace and what these snapshots leave out or obscure. As this chapter progresses, then, we will attempt not only to report on collaborative writers at work but to problematize and to complicate that "report."

Collaborative Writing in a Large Consulting Engineering Firm

Bill Qualls describes himself as a city planner, but when we interviewed him for several days in the spring of 1985, he struck us as a modern Renaissance individual. His undergraduate degree is in architecture; his M.A., in city planning; and his Ph.D., in higher education with an emphasis on curriculum development. When we asked Qualls to explain his varied educational background, he indicated that he had moved from architecture to city planning because "I had more interest in complete city design as opposed to the design of individual buildings." His reasons for choosing a Ph.D. in higher education suggest a great deal about his interests and character:

> After I had been out of school a number of years practicing as a city planner, I had become concerned about why we could develop a good plan for a community and try to explain it to people and they wouldn't seem to understand it. They wouldn't support it for one reason or another. And time and time again we would see a good plan go down the drain because people didn't agree with it or for some reason didn't actively support it. So I decided I needed more education. At first, I was going to get a Ph.D. in planning. But finally it occurred to me that, no, that was not what I wanted. I wanted to know more about the learning process—the educational process.

Bill Qualls works in a large consulting engineering firm in the south, and he is obviously successful in his work—he is a vice president of his firm. Qualls has the pragmatism characteristic of many engineers: "Once we get a job we've got to do it and generally we find a way to do it." But in several respects Qualls struck us as different from many of his peers. When we asked him how his varied education had influenced his approach toward his work, Qualls responded that the "major differ-ence is that we [Qualls and his team members] feel hurt if we can't get the client to understand what we are doing. Often, the professional doesn't really care about that as long as he gets paid for what he's done." This concern for understanding, for true communication, acts as a primary motivating force: "What motivates me is how I can help my clients—how I can help them comprehend what I am talking about . . . in order that they can better participate in the decision-making process. I will do whatever I can to help them understand."

As his own words indicate, Bill Qualls is a self-reflective and systematic collabora-tive writer. When we first arrived at his office, Qualls had a carefully prepared pre-sentation of the methods he and his co-workers use in their work-related writing ready for us—complete with charts and examples. As later discussion will indicate, Qualls possesses a particularly clear, detailed, and highly articulated representation of his task, and he has developed innovative means of responding to its demands.

In these and other respects, Bill Qualls is not typical. He is not a typical member of his firm, most of whom are engineers. He is not a typical member of the Ameri-can Consulting Engineers Council (ACEC), one of the seven professional associa-tions whose members we surveyed. In fact, we learned when we visited him, he is not a member of the ACEC at all. Our original survey had been received by another member of the firm who had passed it on to Qualls, who is unofficially considered his firm's writing expert. (Although in planning our research we intended to inter-view at least one member from each of the seven professional associations we sur-veyed—certainly a logical and tidy pattern for our interviews—this expectation was confounded in this and several other instances.)

Why highlight such an atypical individual? In the first place, we choose to do so because we discovered in this and other interviews that the "typical" individual is more than an apparent contradiction in terms. Each of the collaborative writers with whom we spoke was, in some sense, unique. There are several other reasons why we chose to begin our description of scenes of collaborative writing with a dis-cussion of Bill Qualls. One consideration was practical. We were able to spend the longest amount of time (two and one half days versus two to three hours) with Qualls and his colleagues. We thus have the clearest, most complete view of collab-orative writing as it is practiced by these individuals. (Most of our interviews were with single individuals or, in one case, with two persons who worked together regu-larly. We were able not only to interview Bill Qualls several times but to conduct in-terviews of from one to two hours with several of his co-workers.)

Finally, as noted earlier, Bill Qualls was one of the most self-consciously reflec-tive collaborative writers we interviewed. When we first chose those we hoped to in-terview, we determined that we would attempt to talk with individuals who were satisfied, productive, and articulate collaborative writers (as indicated by their responses to our first two surveys). Bill Qualls is such an individual. He is no more typical of all collaborative writers than the protagonist of a novel is typical of all humans. But just as we can learn a great deal about the human condition by describing and analyzing characters in a play or a novel, so too can we learn about collaborative writing by studying—and listening to—thoughtful and effective collaborative writers.

At the time of our interview, Qualls and his co-workers had most recently worked on several master plans for military installations. As Bill Qualls described it, such a project for a large army post may take three to five years to complete and involves planning for "a city of 60,000 or 70,000 people, a specialized city." As anyone who has dealt with the federal government can imagine, those preparing master plans for a new military base necessarily encounter numerous bureaucratic constraints. Bill and his team must, for instance, "come up with proposals for new buildings, new streets, other types of needs, based on what the army says a unit is due. . . . [We must always] estimate needs according to their regulations."

The most immediate difficulty posed by a project of this magnitude is simply comprehending precisely what their clients want. Though clients initiate the process by developing a scope of work, or statement of requirements for a project, Qualls generally finds these difficult to interpret. "I think to a great extent the people who put the scope of work together don't understand it. The people who respond to it [consulting firms such as Qualls'] don't know anything either, so they wander around in each other's ignorance and come up with something neither is satisfied with."

In response to these and other problems characteristic of the large projects which he typically manages, Qualls has developed a sophisticated method for analyzing and organizing all activities connected with a project. Over time, co-workers began affectionately to call Qualls' techniques the Critical Qualls Method—referred to in-house as the CQM—after the Critical Path Method sometimes used in their field to organize complicated activities.

We first learned of the CQM when we unfolded the large (30″ × 32″), intricate chart that accompanied Bill Qualls' second survey. (We had asked respondents to send any information that they thought might help us understand collaborative writing better.) We studied this chart carefully, but even though its seven major sections were clearly labeled, as were subsections, we could not fully understand it. Only when we visited Bill Qualls and were able to question him and his colleagues about the chart and the method that it exemplifies were we able to understand the purpose and the function of the chart's seven major sections:

I.   Contract Data and Progress Bars
II.   Report Outline and Phases

This chart serves multiple functions. Qualls uses it initially as a means of clarifying the often vague or confusing language of the scope of work. The following excerpt is from a longer description of the ways in which the CQM "translates" the information in the scope of work into concrete objectives, responsibilities, and deadlines:

> We show [in the CQM] all the end products you the client want—in terms of the master plan report, mapping, etc. The number of times products are to be submitted is shown here. Some you want submitted just once, some twice, and some three times. . . . Here we indicate end products for maps and reports. These are the headings and chapters for your report, and we use this same organization for our cost proposal. Here I'll place the names of every person working on the report and how many days or hours they will be working on each chapter. We summarize these to develop many of our cost estimates.

Qualls and his team thus use this information, carefully organized according to the CQM format, "to explain to the client how we are translating their statement of work into something else that we think is a lot more understandable." If the client selects his firm, Qualls and his team develop a final CQM that reflects their negotiations and modifications. "When we sign a contract, the CQM becomes part of it, and it is used daily throughout the project."

Once Qualls' firm has signed a contract for a project, the CQM functions in different—and much more dynamic—ways. It is the means by which Qualls coordinates the efforts of team members. (The ten persons working on a recent project included the following: project manager [Qualls], project engineer, hydrology and sanitary engineer, mechanical engineer, architect, telecommunications engineer, electrical engineer, cartographer, planner, and secretary.) Although some of Qualls' staff, such as his planning technician and secretary, are permanently assigned to him, others vary depending upon the project.

One of Qualls' co-workers explained that as they work on a project the CQM "becomes a sort of homing point for everything that we are doing." Qualls and his co-workers use the CQM to monitor their progress: "Each month we select a color and we color in everything completed in that month. Visually, that tells you how much you have completed and what's left to be done. And if you have to check roughly when you did something, [you can] just go back to the CQM and look at the colors. . . . We also send copies of the CQM to each of our staff members . . . so they can redline what they are assigned to do as a reminder of what needs to be done."

The last two sections of the CQM, "End Products Submittal Record" and "Submittal Time Sequence," also enable team members to keep track of responsibilities and meet deadlines. Finally, because the CQM also includes all of the products the group must produce—the report in full outline form, and the numerous maps that will illustrate their plan—it also functions as a style guide, one that is particularly helpful in insuring that group members (most of whom are responsible for drafting the part of the report that involves their area of expertise) adhere to the same format. The CQM thus plays a role in every aspect of this group's efforts. The form itself maps every stage of the process—from their original analysis of the scope of work through the information-gathering and technical stages (including preparation of maps and other graphics) and through pencil, preliminary, and final drafts—relating each stage to the organizational format or outline of the final document.

At first glance—or even at second or third glance—the CQM looked formidably uninviting to us, more a maze in which to get lost than a map by which to find the way. We were surprised, therefore, when not only Qualls (its originator) but other team and firm members as well spoke of its wide-ranging usefulness. One of the team's cartographers said, "It helps as far as due dates and submittals and exactly what is needed—the title of each map and the tab number. We may have to refer back to the contract to get specifics, but this helps you see right away which maps you have done, which maps you have yet to do." An engineer who usually heads up another team in the firm has adopted the CQM for his projects. "It is," he says, "a very good concept." For his projects, the team "agree on the CQM, which essentially sets our outline and our process. . . . The bigger the job the more critical it is. We use it to the letter."

Not every team in this large firm uses the CQM; smaller projects especially seem to proceed efficiently without it. But this complex form, which is modified and tailored to each individual project, is more widely used—and praised—than we would ever have expected. The Qualls team member responsible for visiting the project site and gathering local background information said, "Oh, the big Qualls method: *everyone* respects it."

We have dwelt on the CQM at such length for several reasons. As is already obvious, this chart functions as a crucial part of the team's collaboration. It orchestrates the collaborative process—from the time it is conceived in response to a scope of work; through the team visit to the project site; through the contract negotiations; through the research and drafting of the plan (which team members carry out individually according to area of expertise); through the series of revisions, deadlines, and submittals. By the time the team leader—usually Qualls—checks off the blocks for the executive summary and the letter of transmittal (which he always writes), the CQM looks like a Klee painting—its bars ablaze with color. The CQM provides a visual representation of collaboration, a vivid picture of a job well done.

When one of the team members used the phrase "pride of authorship," we asked for elaboration. "We take great pride in doing these things, and we really help each other. Bill's knowledge expands our horizons and ours expands his. We all have a sense of pride in the [CQM and resulting report], because it makes us all shine more. An individual engineer—me included—would never put the time in to produce that quality. You look at a standard engineer's report, and you won't see anything like this." For members of this collaborative team, the final CQM serves as a symbol for this pride.

A second notable characteristic of the CQM also became apparent. Although its formality struck us as static and rigid, in practice it is a dynamic tool that intricately binds process and product. Although in one sense a product, the CQM drives the research, planning, writing, and illustrating processes forward; and they are in turn encoded in the complete report and charted on the CQM—an elegant enactment of the symbiotic relationship between product and process in any written discourse.

Finally, we have focused on the CQM because it demonstrates the way in which collaborative writing is highly goal oriented and context bound. An engineer in another firm reading about the CQM, for instance, might be tempted to import it and impose it on his or her own writing situation. Doing so might work but probably would not because the CQM was developed in response to a particular set of circumstances and needs. In addition, as a number of his colleagues' remarks indicated, the CQM is very much a product of Bill Qualls' personality and style. In that particular rhetorical situation, both CQM and his personal style are accepted and appreciated. "I have never met a professional more committed than Qualls," says one co-worker. Another elaborates, "Most engineers can't put their pragmatism into words, can't write it out so somebody can understand it or accomplish it. That is what makes Bill so rare and valuable."

Qualls' abilities include not only a gift for systematization but the tendency to see the project as a whole. Over and over again in our interviews with him, he came back to the importance of this way of perceiving reality—what he called "matrix thinking": "If you read a book or document, like a scope of work, what you may miss is the matrix that holds it all together. That to me is what is so important. Is there something that brings this all together so that when we finish we have something that holds water, that helps us understand the situation better?"

One of his colleagues describes this tendency to see the whole or the matrix as "thinking in terms of function *and* form." Bill puts it more graphically: "It is as though I am an overeater. I want to eat as quickly, enjoyably, and efficiently as I can, so I like to have the whole dinner laid out in front of me. I don't want people bringing me individual servings. Give me the whole buffet and let me go at it. I like to see everything at once when I am making certain decisions." And that is just what Qualls and his colleagues have developed in the CQM: a tool that brings them together (they often meet where it is posted to check on the phase of a project) and allows them to see "the whole thing at the same time."

A Clinical Psychologist Who Writes in a Variety of Collaborative Settings

Unlike most of the writers we interviewed, American Psychological Association member Albert Bernstein works independently, rather than for business or industry. Bernstein is a clinical psychologist in private practice, and he describes himself as very satisfied with his professional situation: "I would say that I am doing with my profession precisely what I want to do. I thought about what would be the ideal job for me and made it happen." In addition to his private clinical practice, Bernstein also presents workshops, acts as a consultant, develops videotapes, and writes a variety of documents. At the time that we interviewed him, for example, Bernstein had recently worked with a group of psychologists to draft a brochure describing the Oregon Psychological Association; met with administrators at a local college to draft guidelines for students who are disruptive because of mental health problems; consulted with businesses who wished to develop stress management programs and drafted brochures advertising these programs; and begun writing a popular psychology book in collaboration with a professional writer, who will help him transform his case studies into "stories that will interest people." All of these writing situations involve frequent collaboration with others.

These examples do not cover all of the collaborative writing that Bernstein has done and continues to do in his career. Bernstein has extensive grant-writing experience for example: "For years I worked for a mental health center. I was clinical director and had to write hundreds of grants, budget narratives, policies, and procedures." And he has worked with committees of the Oregon Psychological Association to draft laws dealing with such subjects as the rights of schizophrenics to treatment. More than any other individual we interviewed, Bernstein regularly wrote a wide variety of documents in an equally diverse range of situations. (According to Bernstein, the variety of writing he regularly works on is not typical of most clinical psychologists, many of whom primarily write clinical evaluations.)

Bernstein's answers to the open-ended questions in our second survey also indicated that he had thought a great deal about communication—and that he had a nice sense of wit. In response to the question "Please comment on how your high school or college English classes might have better prepared you for professional group writing tasks," Albert Bernstein had dryly responded: "My English teachers taught me how to scan poems and diagram sentences. Need I say more?"

Like Bill Qualls, Albert Bernstein is a particularly self-conscious and reflective writer. This interest in communication undoubtedly derives in part from his academic training: as a Ph.D. student he emphasized research in communication, and the popular psychology book he was working on at the time of our interview focused on the same subject. Bernstein also conveyed a strong sense of the importance of effective communication for his career. "If you want to achieve something you have to promote yourself. The good things go to people who promote themselves, whether we like it or not. And one of the ways you can promote yourself is to know how to write. If people ask me to write something or make a speech somewhere I never turn them down. That is my advertising." Bernstein was also conscious of the ways in which he varied language to suit different audiences. Early in our interview, for example, he informed us that "I write only English but I write six kinds of English: psychobabble, management jargon, formal psychology (journal article style), educationese, a little bit of hype (but not much), and everyday English." Finally, Bernstein cares about style. He told us that he prided himself "on never having used the word *utilize* in my life."

Unlike most of the individuals we interviewed, Bernstein had not consistently described collaborative writing as productive and satisfying in the answers to our first two surveys. He answered a question on the first survey that asked "How productive do you find writing as part of a team or group?" by indicating that he found such collaboration "not too productive." (The possible responses included: "very productive," "productive," "not too productive," and "not at all productive.") Thus we were not surprised when at the start of our interview Bernstein emphasized many of the problems he had encountered in collaborative writing situations.

One of the most difficult of all his group writing experiences occurred when he was charged with the task of writing a brochure for a statewide organization of which he was an active member. "This particular brochure took me four months to write, and it is not because I am a slow writer. It was because I had to go to board meetings and hear 'Well, I don't know about using this word, and this sentence might offend somebody.' "

Despite these problems—familiar to all who have engaged in similar group writing projects—Bernstein continued in his efforts. The negotiations involved in gaining approval for the final draft of the brochure were considerable. Members of the board argued about the order in which various items should be presented, as well as the wording. Because the brochure described the organization's various committees, it had to be approved by each committee. "Each committee had to approve the brochure, and they each wanted to add more information about their committee. I wanted the shortest, most direct brochure possible. It was a battle."

We were interested in the reasons why Bernstein, clearly a disciplined, task-oriented person ("I am very organized. So far as I know I have never missed a deadline for written work in my life."), originally accepted this task and then persevered in developing the brochure. Much of his resolve, apparently, grew out of frustration over the failure of past efforts. "I knew that a group of people would be involved, and I was afraid they'd dither it to death. But I hoped I would be able to get the brochure through, because we had been trying to develop a brochure for four or five years, and nobody in the organization had been able to succeed in writing one people could agree on. . . . Not having a brochure seemed preposterous to me because there are a lot more controversial and difficult things to write than that." As Bernstein described it, the process of gaining acceptance of the brochure involved patience, persistance, and even what he called "manipulation": "I can stare people down . . . I usually don't operate like that, but it was necessary to get the brochure approved."

Given these difficulties, which Bernstein described at considerable length, we were surprised when he responded to the questions "What is your favorite way to write? What would be the ideal situation for you?" not by indicating that he most preferred to write alone, but that "the ideal setup would be working with one or two people and getting together and talking about what it is we want to say, what chapters we want to have, how we want to say it, how people will react to ideas. [Talking like this] helps you get fired up and also encourages you to ask each other hard questions."

We also asked Bernstein a question about the "pride of ownership" he felt when writing alone versus writing together. Again, his answer surprised us: "When I work with other people, one or two other people, I feel that I do a much better job than I would have done alone. I extend myself further and I think I have a clearer idea of what we are trying to do. *It brings more out of me so I think it is more mine.* I don't mind sharing the credit" (our emphasis). Bernstein elaborated on the advantages of writing with one or two coauthors (rather than with a large committee or group of people) in response to the question "Do you think that cognitive processes change when people work together in groups as opposed to writing by themselves?":

Absolutely. When I am writing alone I always visualize an audience, but I hear my own experiences. . . . It's kind of a closed loop—there's no input from anyone else. When I'm working with other people there are several things that I must keep in mind: not just what the audience might say but what the person I'm working with is going to think of this line. And how to get the job done, how to get around some of the difficulties. . . . When I write with someone else I am engaging not just in a dialogue with the reader but with that other person. And I think it makes the result much better—unless I'm writing with too big a group, with a room full of picky people. . . . Working with someone else gives you another point of view. There is an extra voice inside your head; that can make a lot of difference. Others can see things about what I am doing or what I am saying that I can't see. And if they are good and we work well together, we can do that for each other.

Finally, we asked Bernstein to describe the characteristics of the people he has worked well with in the past. "First of all, a broad base of knowledge. I have a hard time dealing with people who only know their field and don't know anything else. . . . With any luck at all they will know some things that I don't know and so make [our writing] richer. I also work best with people who are task oriented, somebody who can enjoy an interesting conversation but realize that what we're here for is to get this article written. . . . And a sense of humor—that's a definite plus."

Clearly, though Bernstein has experienced his share of problems in writing collaboratively with others, in certain situations at least, for him the advantages outweigh the disadvantages: "In the real world you just can't operate alone unless you are a poet, and even then. . . ." As we were preparing to leave, we asked Bernstein the question that closed most of our interviews: "What advice would you give teachers of writing who want to prepare their students for collaborative writing experiences?"

> What I wish is that somebody would have started out by teaching me what language is, why we are writing, what writing is, what writers are trying to do. I wish that somebody had told me that when I wrote I should think about my purpose and my reader. . . . I didn't really learn to write in school. I have a good friend—a poet and newspaper editor. He and I wrote things together; we worked together at the mental health center. He was trying to find out something about mental health, and I was essentially teaching him about therapy. He was more a consultation and education person, back in the days when mental health clinics could afford to have people like that. I taught him about mental health, and he taught me about writing. And that's where I got my most important training in writing.

Technical Writers in a Construction Equipment Firm

"Correct," said Allan Warrior, a member of the Society for Technical Communication, when we asked if we had interpreted a printout accurately. "Not *right*. *Correct*. We do not use *right*," explained Warrior, "unless it is the opposite of *left*. Everything else is *correct*."

Defined exclusively as the opposite of *left, right* is part of a carefully constructed 2000-word controlled vocabulary developed especially for the international construction equipment manufacturing firm that employs Warrior as a technical writer. This prescriptively rigid style guide acts as a primary constraint on the technical writers who use it at the same time that it allows them to establish an intricate international collaboration.

Having a style guide is, as Warrior notes, far from unique: "Every technical writing group has to come up with a certain style guide. . . . Some of them are more formal than others but [even] if you go to a newspaper, they inevitably have a style guide." But the specificity and the formality of this guide is unusual. As is most often the case, this particular style guide grew out of very practical concerns. Faced with the need to produce operating and service manuals that could be used by diverse employees to assemble and maintain equipment in many non-English speaking countries, the firm turned to machine translation and to the loose translation produced by the people in the target country. The result was "pretty sterile." And, occasionally, pretty funny as well. One such translation problem featured a "feeler gauge": "There is a gauge we use in checking clearances, a machine gauge. It is a feeler gauge. Every mechanic in the U.S. knows what a feeler gauge is. But then it came back translated into French. The only word [the translator could find] for feelers were the little things on the end of a butterfly's antenna. This came back as 'Go catch a butterfly. . . .' "

The use of a strictly controlled vocabulary helped solve such problems. "The key element" in the language, notes Warrior, is that "one word can only have one meaning. Take, for instance, *switch*":

> We had a lot of trouble with *switch*. It is quite common for us to say "turn on the switch" or "turn off the switch." But switches don't turn. You see, we used to have oil lamps: you turned the light up, you turned the light down. Then the first electrical switches were rotary. But if you are in a country now where you have only had a wall switch that flips, try to tell them to turn the switch on. They wonder "What does that mean?" So we move the *switch* to the "on" position or . . . to the "off" position. . . . Another interesting point is that switch can be a noun or a verb in our language. We just throw it around and don't even pay attention to it. We are very careful about that. We just tell them it is a noun.

This vocabulary and "Max" (R Electronic Editor), the text editor program that checks the use of the vocabulary and several dozen other factors (such as no sentences longer than seventeen words; no more than two descriptors plus a noun; all negatives within four words of the verb; noun and verb close together; no inversion of word order; no use of *should, would,* or *could;* no passive verbs), are very much partners in the collaborative writing Warrior and his colleagues do. According to this team of writers, using the controlled vocabulary well "is kind of an art form. If we can write text so that the person reading it doesn't realize that it is in a controlled language, we think we have done our job."

The job cannot be done alone, however, as Warrior and his colleagues stressed again and again. Any piece of technical discourse they produce results from a complex and highly collaborative process, which typically begins when the company decides to come out with a new product. In such cases, Harold Scudder, head of the five-person writing division, assigns the project. "And then we go through and see what material has to be created. We make up a list. Then it is up to us to find out what engineering has done. A lot of times at that stage [the plans] are not complete yet, but we get involved as much as we can so we can learn about it. We start pulling out all the drawings and go through and interpret what there is, and we look for similarities to what else we have produced. . . ."

Eventually, the engineering division provides the writers with a "new product advance information guide," a set of preliminary drawings and a statement of aims, which the team studies for additional information. And as soon as a prototype and a rough draft of a manual to accompany it are developed, the writers "verify" or "try it out" by completely disassembling the product and checking to see if they can follow their own directions. In this stage of their work, they call not only on their own training (all have degrees in science and engineering as well as mechanical experience) but on the team engineers and team mechanics. "Afterwards," says Warrior, "we usually rewrite." The rewrite then travels back to the engineers: "We take what they give out and put it in our [language] and we feed it back through them. They mark it up again. And it is good because then we rewrite and it comes out better."

Throughout this process, the text editor program monitors the language and syntax of the manual, and the writers work with illustrators to create and label graphics. The draft copy is then "routed again to engineering, marketing, legal." The entire process, which takes "maybe six months," usually works smoothly: the team is small and comfortable with each other. Harold Scudder, the leader, "looks at the overall picture," "sets the priorities," and "does the choreography." In spite of the highly constrained nature of the writing that they do and the many levels of review to which their work is subjected, these writers find their collaborative experience "satisfying" and "challenging." Though each started out in some area of engineering, they moved into technical writing out of choice, not necessity. One team member said, "As an engineer, I always have to write . . . and all my life, words and language have been important. I enjoy words."

These writers also stressed the satisfaction that comes from the broadest form of collaboration their work calls for: establishing direct ties with one primary audience—those people around the world who operate and maintain their equipment. Ironically, they are able to establish this collaborative bond through the constraints imposed by their highly controlled language. Through it they create a text that readers in, say, Nepal, can use in constructing meaning. "We put things in our manuals that other people do not . . . but we do it because people need it, not only those people who will write the marketing information, but the people in the field who need to understand how it is supposed to work and how to fix it. We concentrate on writing for the end user." Thus in the work of this collaborative team, through reading and writing, readers and writers interanimate one another.

A Chemist Collaborating in Government-Funded Research

We asked George Irving, member of the American Institute of Chemists, retired research director of the United States Department of Agriculture, and a very active consultant/writer, if he could recall a particularly unsatisfying group-writing experience.

I would say one group-writing project I put a great deal of work into was an evaluation of the research program of the Department of Agriculture before I became administrator. We called it a committee on research evaluation and came out with a core report. It took us the better part of a year. We [all the bureau heads] spent an awful lot of time together discussing what the research program of the department was and what it should be, and we wrote a strong report saying all these things. It was largely ignored. The Secretary's office, for whom it was done, chose to ignore it completely. That was a major disappointment to everybody.

Irving's comments highlight two typical problems. The first, disappointment or dissatisfaction when the document fails to achieve goals or make an impact, applies to single-authored texts as well as to documents written collaboratively. The second problem, time ("It took us the better part of a year.") is mentioned frequently as a drawback to collaborative writing. Certainly Irving, whose long career has called for many different kinds of collaboration, is very much aware of this problem. Collaborative writing, he says, is "a slow way, a ponderous way," to get things done. In spite of this drawback, he says: "I don't know of a better way to tap the expertise in your organization. If you presume you know enough to answer all questions, then you don't need an organization at all. But if you have an organization you'd better use it, work through all the stages and all the people involved. I don't know of any other way to tap all the information you have available in preparing a statement."

Irving should know. While administrator of the Agriculture Research Service from 1963 to 1971, he supervised 16,000 people in 400 locations. This position demanded at least three different types of collaboration. Letters and other kinds of correspondence would be drafted by a wide variety of individuals, often after conversations with Irving. These letters would "sediment their way up and go through various rewrites until eventually I would sign it if I liked it." Another kind of collaboration involved preparing speeches, which he frequently had to give, and statements for the press or for various organizations. For these occasions, Irving and his group of assistants would "talk extensively about what I wanted to say; then they would prepare a draft, and I would go over it with them, and that would go through a couple of cycles until we got what we wanted." Even with such a carefully crafted document, Irving said, he had to remain flexible and responsive to particular audiences. "On some occasions when I got to the site of action and took a look at the audience and got the smell of the grease paint and all the rest of it, I threw the thing away and did something else entirely." On such occasions, Irving often relied on earlier conversations with his assistants to "invent" appropriate new material. A third kind of collaborative writing—"perhaps even more important"—involved preparing testimony for appearances before Congress. For these appearances, Irving typically worked with "fiscal types" and "legal reviewers" in addition to his assistants.

For most of his career, Irving has acted as the leader in collaborative situations.

And while he acknowledges the importance of leadership in effective group work, he likened the job to that of a "master of ceremonies," whose task "is like the person that stands beside the cement mixer; his job is to keep the stuff going down the chute. So . . . patience is probably the greatest virtue and then not necessarily wisdom but the ability to sit there long enough until the right answer comes up."

Patience is a virtue Irving had to call on in what he described to us as his longest collaborative effort. As consultant to the Federation of American Societies for Experimental Biology, Irving was asked to head up a team charged with evaluating the world's literature on all food additives—some 540 substances. The project took twelve years. In this effort, Irving assembled a group of fifteen—all experts "in practically all the fields needed for a thorough examination of additives—physiologists, biochemists, pharmacologists, allergists, nutritionists." When he identified "a few gaps," they added "a pediatrician and an oncologist and a food technologist." The large group seemed necessary to the task but went against the grain with Irving. As he said, "A group gets pretty big after you have more then three. After that you are working with a *gang*."

Nevertheless, Irving found this particular collaborative venture exciting and satisfying. Schedules presented a major problem since the group needed to meet "once a month for the first eight years" and "once every two months after that." Group members (usually two or three) carried out research and massive literature reviews and prepared drafts for the group. Initial drafts "were revised in the course of the sit-down meetings of the whole group." These were then "rewritten by our support staff [six professionals] and repolished and sent out for mail review. Quite a system, if you can imagine. We had 540 substances that were being reviewed and massive numbers of drafts in the air at all times, at all different stages."

When semifinal drafts were ready, the whole group went over them page by page, line by line. The work was very tedious and often controversial. If the group could not agree on precise wording, they talked the issue out until they all agreed "on the sense—what the group was willing to do." Then Irving "had the job of synthesizing it into language which again had to be approved by the whole group. It seems impossible, but we got there." After twelve years—twice as much time as Irving and the Federation had anticipated—all members became signatories to the report, which the FDA then used to make numerous decisions on additives, including such substances as MSG, sulphites, and caffeine. In retrospect, Irving says that he "and the whole group" enjoyed the effort. "I think we were surprised really that we could get that many people to stay together for twelve years on this rather rigorous business. We were all busy people—university professors and so forth—but once into this I think we were all just as immersed and enthusiastic as we could be."

In this brief glimpse of collaborative work among members of the chemistry profession, we were unable to speak with other team members whose perceptions—particularly of the enormous twelve-year project—might well have differed from Irving's. From his perspective as leader, however, Irving clearly felt the advantages of collaboration outweighed the disadvantages. He attributed his success at collaboration at least partially to "a natural extension of [my] writing efforts." Like most of the collaborative writers we interviewed, Irving reported a strong interest in language and communication, especially in writing. An assistant editor for an undergraduate publication, Irving went on to "write more newsletters for more different organizations than I can remember." The best way to become a writer—or a collaborative writer—is, in Irving's view, "to go at it and write. The more you write, the more you will find you are able to write and really communicate, work well, with people. If you don't write anything, then nobody can tell who you are. So—a lot of writing. No substitute for it."

A Manager of a Sanitary Authority

Several of Dick Miller's responses to our first two questionnaires intrigued us, so we were pleased when this member of the International City Management Association and manager of a sanitary authority (special district) in southern Oregon agreed to an interview. Miller's responses to our survey had been surprising in two respects. Unlike most respondents, even those who rated collaborative writing as productive and satisfying, Miller indicated that he could not list a single disadvantage to collaborative writing. Furthermore, again unlike most respondents, Miller noted that he had received substantial training that directly contributed to the effectiveness of his current on-the-job collaborative writing.

We began by asking Miller to describe the training he had received and to clarify how it had helped prepare him for collaborative writing tasks. As a preamble to his response, Miller detailed his long and successful career. This career began—and continued for twenty-seven years—in the air force. During this time Miller received extensive training in professional schools—"Squadron Officers' School of the air university, that sort of thing." He also continued his university studies, earning undergraduate degrees in chemistry from Boston University and in engineering from the University of Illinois and a master's degree in business administration from the University of Chicago. His formal education was sponsored by the United States Air Force.

Miller felt strongly that all of his educational experience had contributed to his current productivity and satisfaction with collaborative writing. He credited the air force with first enabling him to function well in groups: "In Squadron Officers' School you were organized as a group when you first arrived there . . . and you did everything as a group: group problem solving, group writing; everything was the group. . . . You wrote things—even reports—as a group." But Miller also cited his undergraduate report writing class at the University of Illinois and his engineering classes where, he said, "we had to work together and write up the experiments as a group, which was good." Finally, Miller commented on the helpfulness of his M.B.A. classes at the University of Chicago, where (in the mid-sixties) he studied organization and group theory. By that time Miller "had been in several command positions and organizations, fairly large ones." Unlike many who return to the university after substantial practical experience, Miller found his studies both relevant and stimulating: "My professors had damn good ideas."

Dick Miller retired from the air force in 1970, and he spent the next five years as the city manager of a small town in Oregon. Finally, he signed on as manager of one of Oregon's special districts, a form of local government. His special district, a sanitary authority, is responsible for developing and overseeing such potentially controversial projects as the construction of new sewer systems. "Every one of our projects," Miller notes, "vexes somebody. Constructing new sewers and sewer systems costs money."

Miller's staff is small. The total number of employees is eighteen (this includes construction and maintenance staff). Miller works most closely with four people: the heads of the engineering, maintenance, and financial services departments plus his executive secretary. In the course of their work Miller and his staff write a variety of documents: reports for their governing board, letters, memos, speeches— whatever is necessary to get the job done and to maintain good relations with the public.

Miller's approach to his job as manager is pragmatic: "We have a goal of putting out a project that will do the job at the least cost." And so is his approach to on-the-job writing. Miller and his colleagues collaborate when they need to—which turns out to be about once a week. As Bill Corrin, director of financial services, noted in a brief interview: "We don't have any formal procedure [for group writing]. We just get together those people involved. We discuss the issues, try to get input from each individual as to how we should respond to the problem. Then one of us takes on or is assigned the responsibility of actively formulating a response. It is that simple." Corrin, an accountant who had previously worked in a savings and loan institution, noted that when he first began working at the sanitary authority he felt somewhat uneasy about Miller's group-oriented management style: "If it were up to me, I'd probably not do it [work collaboratively with others] as often." He credited the group's productivity and good relations to Miller's effective leadership and especially to his ability to motivate his co-workers. "He has a natural ability to motivate people to do things. That is probably the biggest factor . . . Dick's approachable and gets people together, and I guess he just encourages you to participate. . . . [He also] makes you feel that you have contributed something . . . that is probably the prime motivator."

When we questioned Miller about his strategies for managing collaborative writing, his comments suggested that Corrin's assessment of his goals and methods was accurate. In talking about the collaborative writing that he and his colleagues do, Miller took a pragmatic, task-oriented approach. When we asked him if he had a different sense of ownership or satisfaction when he wrote alone, rather than with others, Miller responded: "I don't think about that much. [For me] the satisfaction comes when the chairman of our governing board says 'You have done a great job.' That is the satisfaction. I don't think about private authorship or anything like that; I just want to know if I did a good job."

Similarly, when we asked Miller if he approached a writing task that he would complete on his own differently from one requiring collaboration, Miller felt there was no distinction; indeed, he seemed surprised by the question. "I do the same thing whether I am working with a group or by myself. You still have to pull stuff together that you need to write from. And whether you get it from people or several publications—whatever you are working from—you have to do the same thing."

Like many executives, Miller relies heavily on his secretary, who in fact plays a significant role in the collaborative writing that occurs in his office. Glenna Johnston, Miller's executive secretary, does—as many secretaries do—much more than type, file, and handle office administration. Miller commented on the importance of her role, indicating that he relies on Johnston heavily not just for correction and editing but also for substantive comments. "Glenna got here a few months before I did, and we have worked closely together since then. If she thinks that something should be changed—I don't mean a misspelling but an idea—she is not bashful at all about mentioning it. I never get excited about that. And I always look at her comments. Ninety percent of the time I agree with her, and 10 percent I don't. And she accepts that: there's no problem there."

At times, in fact, Johnston coordinates the team's efforts or writes documents, such as environmental statements, that draw heavily upon research or boilerplate materials. "She puts [many documents] together except the engineering and the financial data; she gets this from Bill or Gary. . . . She also does a lot of resolution writing and things like this." In describing the review process that he uses even for single-authored documents, Miller carefully noted Johnston's contribution: "I pick their [his staff's] brains and then I do the writing myself. After I get it written I will . . . route it to the proper people to get feedback. Glenna [then] has a go at it, and she will come back with suggestions. Then we put it in final form. The process works very well."

(Johnston's role in the collaborative writing that occurred in this office intrigued us. Consequently, we regret that we were able to have only a brief conversation with Johnston, who indicated that in general she was very satisfied with her job. In fact, she enjoyed its variety and collaborative atmosphere a great deal. She did indicate, however, that she believed her current title did not accurately reflect her numerous reponsibilities.)

Unlike Bill Qualls and Albert Bernstein, who had obviously spent a great deal of time reflecting on the collaborative writing process and determining how better to manage that process, Dick Miller seemed to take collaborative writing for granted. Collaborating with others on reports, letters, memos: all this was simply an efficient way to get the job done. Miller was highly reflective about the larger questions of group dynamics and decision making, however. Two of his final comments to us reflect his approach to both collaborative writing and organizational management: "There is a time to speak and a time to listen. There is always time to do a job right."

A Research Associate at the Office of Educational Research and Information

Like Bill Qualls, the city planner with whom we began this series of snapshots of collaborative writers at work, Eleanor Chiogioji is not a typical member of her professional organization, the Modern Language Association. Chiogioji received a Ph.D. in English Literature and Language from the University of Maryland in 1981—academic training that would most obviously prepare her for a career in teaching. And Chiogioji had, in fact, taught a variety of writing and literature classes at the University of Maryland while completing her degree and during the years immediately following. But rather than pursue a job in a college or university, Chiogioji accepted a position at the Office of Educational Research and Improvement (OERI).

The OERI is a large federally funded program designed to improve the quality of education in the United States. The OERI comprises five major program areas: Information Services, Library Programs, the National Center for Education Statistics, Programs for the Improvement of Practice, and the Office of Research. Chiogioji is employed as a senior research associate in the latter program area, which is itself subdivided into four units. Chiogioji works in the Learning and Instruction Division of the Office of Research. This division operates with the following mandate:

> The Learning and Instruction Division supports basic and applied research for which learning and its relationship to the instructional process are the central focus. It addresses such issues as how children acquire information, values, and character, and develop their knowledge of content areas; how human thought processes develop; how children develop intellectually and become mature citizens; and what the implications of these findings might be for instruction. It also addresses the efficacy and efficiency of various instructional practices; examines interaction among teachers and students within classrooms; and studies the role of textbooks, workbooks, tests, and terminology in the instructional process.

The work of the Division is currently focused on four major areas: content, learning, instruction, and assessment.

As this brief review of the organization of the OERI indicates, Chiogioji's research division is part of a very large, complex bureaucracy. In fiscal year 1984, the OERI had a budget of $154.9 million to operate its ten federally authorized programs.

Unlike many of those we interviewed, Chiogioji was at the start of her career. In the summer of 1986, she was completing her second year at the OERI. Many of the colleagues with whom she worked most closely were also relatively new to their positions. Chiogiogi commented that she had felt particularly responsible for one collaborative project because "this was my third institutional grant competition, and my two colleagues had never been through one at all."

Chiogioji's position is clearly a demanding one. At the time of our interview she was acting as the monitor (or administrator) for one of her division's major programs, the Center for the Study of Writing, and she was also coordinating a major research grants competition in reading and literacy. When we asked her to describe a typical collaborative writing project, Chiogioji chose this grants competition, one still underway. She prefaced her remarks, however, by noting the important role that collaborative writing plays in all of her division's activities: "We could hardly get along here without any kind of collaborative writing. Everything we do here gets bounced back and forth—brainstorming, drafting, revisions. We're always working together." In fact, the process she described for us was collaborative from beginning to end, from the early conceptualization of the project, through the exploratory, drafting, and revision stages, and down to the final negotiations with superiors over the wording and the legality of the scope of work.

The research grants competition in reading and literacy, like many with which Chiogioji works, involved more than a year of effort. We spoke with Chiogioji during the summer of 1986, and she indicated that she and her colleagues had begun conceptualizing the project the previous January. After they had met a number of times independently, they invited a panel of national reading experts to meet in February in order to consider relevant research issues. Once this group had met, Chiogioji and three colleagues—her division director and two other research associates—met to "distill the panel's discussion." Together, this group of four individuals wrote an analysis of the panel's conclusions and drafted a memo with their own recommendations to the assistant secretary of education.

We came in and we worked ten to twelve hours a day, including Saturdays and Sundays—just constantly. . . . We fed each other ideas. Anne, who is a reading person, would do some sort of writing draft, xerox it, and we'd all discuss it. We'd take what the panel of reading experts said and our ideas and through that—just that constant going back and forth—we came out with a fairly good research agenda for the new reading center. We also came out with the research topics for the reading and literacy research grants competition.

In commenting on difficulties inherent in such a complex task, Chiogioji stressed the importance of the group developing a strong consensus, since they would bear joint responsibility for the recommendations they submitted to the assistant secretary of education.

After this task was completed and the memo accepted, the group faced another major task: drafting the scope of work. This part of the larger project took several months to complete. "We organized this project differently. We divided up tasks. We gave Conrad a lot of the boilerplate parts to put together because he was the only nonreading person, and he's got a wonderful legal mind. So he did that. Ann and I worked on the research areas, as well as the introduction and rationale. Our director came from his end, which was instruction and teacher education."

At the time of our interview, Chiogioji still had many months of work before this particular project would be completed. In describing the most recent work and what lay ahead, she again stressed the important role collaboration plays in this complex enterprise. After applications are received, for example, a review panel meets to evaluate them; the OERI team sits in on their discussions and later must synthesize them. "We have to be sure," Chiogioji says, that all team members "heard the same thing and that all of our notes meshed so that we could get a coherent evaluation for the secretary to read." In summing up, Chiogioji remarked that "the entire process of the competition is collaborative—the decisions and everything. But primarily the writing, because no one person can do this." Indeed, the pragmatic necessity of working collaboratively with members of her team was very clear to us, both from Chiogioji's comments and from the sample documents she shared with us. Chiogioji is herself a strong writer with an extensive knowledge of language and a highly refined sense of style. And yet she needs the full efforts of all team members. As she said, "It's impossible for any one person to complete this writing task alone."

Because of Chiogioji's advanced literary training, we were curious to know how she felt about the collaborative writing she did. Clearly, such a large and complex project could only be completed by a group of people working closely together. But did Chiogioji feel differently—experience less of a sense of ownership—about collaborative writing versus writing she completed alone? Her answer surprised us. "I hadn't even thought about it. No, I can't honestly say that I do feel differently about work I write alone or with others. I'm just as proud of what we produce together here. A lot of time that's a lot richer because we have multiple perspectives." In exploring this question further, Chiogioji speculated that her satisfaction and sense of ownership of collaboratively written documents may derive in part from the control that her group retains over the final form of the documents they produce. The writing that her group completes is reviewed by others, but because Chiogioji and her colleagues are recognized as experts in their fields, the documents come back to them for negotiation and final approval. Thus far in her career, Chiogioji indicated, she had been satisfied with the result of negotiations over substantive and stylistic issues.

When we asked Chiogioji to cite the main advantages of collaborative writing, she emphasized the conceptual fruitfulness of working with others: "One advantage of working with others is that you get multiple perspectives and more feedback. You throw out something or somebody throws out something, but you agree or disagree—and this is where the value comes up. It opens up another line for you to pursue." Such interaction, though valuable, can exact its own price however— the reduction of time for individual reflection and analysis. "When I'm engaged in that kind of give-and-take in a group setting, I don't have the leisure to follow my own line of reasoning as far as I want to. And that can disturb me. I like to see where my thoughts would lead." Chiogioji also cited another problem that can occur with group writing: stylistic difficulties resulting from varying styles and levels of writing ability. Finally, Chiogioji noted that occasionally group members can lose the big picture and get bogged down worrying about minor points.

Chiogioji had clearly thought a great deal about the next question we raised: "What traits characterize an effective collaborative writer?" "One of the challenges of collaborative writing is being able to listen so you can synthesize different viewpoints. You don't always come to an agreement, but you have to be able to cooperate enough in that collaborative arrangement to be able to trust each other's opinions and to be able to compromise. It's not always easy to compromise, especially in front of other people. . . . You also must be fair but tactful, and you've got to be flexible." Compromising can be especially difficult, she noted, given our society's traditional emphasis on individualism: "We're such a competitive society. Even if we get together to play bridge, we're at each other's throats." Chiogioji suggested that training in listening and in group dynamics might enable individuals to collaborate more effectively. And what advice would she give to other writers? Her answer summarized themes touched on in almost all our interviews: "Learn to listen. If you don't listen, you can't succeed. Good collaboration rests on a very tenuous relationship. In any kind of group work, there's got to be a lot of give-and-take, and sometimes a lot of giving. And here's the rub: it should have nothing to do with egos."

As with our other interviewees, listening to Eleanor Chiogioji left us with much to ponder and with growing appreciation for the complex tasks in which these writers and their colleagues are engaged.

SCENES OF COLLABORATION: REFLECTIONS

In the opening paragraphs of this chapter, we noted that we wanted to contrast the conventional image of writers at work—an image that privileges the solitary writer working in isolation—with a different picture, that of writers planning, gathering information, drafting, and revising collaboratively. The scenes of writing that we have described thus far clearly and powerfully challenge that conventional image of the writer working alone in a garret, a well-appointed study, or a library. The writers we interviewed may have private offices (they may even, as Albert Bernstein does, work at home), but their scenes of writing are peopled, busy—full of the give-and-take of conversation and debate.

The scenes of writing depicted in this chapter can help us re-situate both the writer and the writing process, but these scenes have their own limitations. They are, first of all, little more than snapshots of writers at work. Because of both time and methodological limitations—we conducted interviews, not case studies—our descriptions provide neither the depth nor the critical perspective characteristic of case studies and ethnographies. Furthermore, photographs, even the most casual snapshots, are composed, not found. A photographer looks through the camera's viewfinder and in so doing creates the scene that will later emerge. Photographers know that what they exclude from an image is at least as important as what they include. The photograph's frame emphasizes, but it isolates as well.

As researchers, the lens through which we looked at collaborative writing in action was, of course, our research design. This design specified that we limit our observations to members of seven professional associations, representing the humanities, social sciences, sciences, business, government, and industry. Our research design enabled us to gain much useful information about the writing done by individuals in these professional associations—information we will highlight in the latter part of this chapter. And it also enabled us to identify individuals who found collaborative writing both productive and satisfying, and who were willing to share their experiences with us.

But our research design also excluded other realities. Readers will undoubtedly have noted, for instance, that there are very few women in the scenes we have presented, and there are also no minorities. With the exception of the Modern Language Association and the Society for Technical Communication, members of the seven professional associations we studied were, perhaps not surprisingly, predominantly male (75 percent male; 25 percent female). Furthermore, respondents typically were well advanced in their careers. Their perspective is that of leaders, those who set the tone and establish the explicit and implicit protocol for collaborative endeavors.

Almost completely absent from the scenes of writing depicted in this chapter, then, are those who play supportive, not leadership, roles in collaboration. These individuals—persons such as Glenna Johnston and the professional staff who worked with Irving and his colleagues—have their own stories to tell about collaborative writing—stories that do not appear in these pages. This absence disturbs us. Yet we are aware that it is our research lens itself that has enabled us to see so clearly that which is absent from the scenes of writing portrayed here. Future research on collaborative writing will, we hope, endeavor to bring these submerged elements more clearly into view.

We do not present these portraits of collaborative writers at work as models for imitation. Our own reading of the interviews presented here most strongly emphasizes the need to problematize descriptions that could, if read naively, seem "neutral" or "objective." We agree with Richard Ohmann, who notes in *Politics of Letters* that the process of interviewing emphasizes with particular clarity the fact that "the writer cannot dissolve into neutrality." As anyone who has worked with transcripts of interviews knows, transcripts may indeed present "the raw moment of the interview itself," but they inevitably "make the event appear inchoate . . . any attempt to rearrange and highlight the material, to delete what seems trivial or irrelevant, to paraphrase and organize . . . any such attempt at a deeper fidelity brings the writer into the act as interpreter and judge, as sure as if he or she comments explicitly on the interview and its subject." Any discussion of interviewing inevitably, Ohmann notes, "problematize[s] any naive standard of objectivity" (255).

The scenes of collaboration we present in this chapter are crafted visions, not slices of life, or raw moments of reality. These snapshots of collaborative writers at work have, we believe, great value. Articulate, experienced, productive writers like Chiogioji, Bernstein, Miller, and Qualls can help us better understand how collaborative writing works and how to make it work more effectively. But in considering these interviews, we hope that readers will listen not only to what these individuals say but to what they do not say.

Someone reading these interviews uncritically might, for example, pass over many of our interviewees' strong emphasis on efficiency—on collaborative writing as a means to an end—as a simple point of fact. Our interviewees' pragmatic approach to language in general and to collaborative writing in particular was so prevalent and so deep-seated that it came to represent for us another purloined letter: an assumption so deeply ingrained as to appear commonsensical and thus hidden from view. This goal-driven pragmatism tends to view language primarily as a tool, a means of getting a job done, one that in turn suggests that language itself is neutral, a conduit through which a kind of "pure" information can be transferred from writer to readers. Collaborative writers aiming pragmatically at efficiency do not have the occasion to consider the way language constructs varying economic or political agendas, which are in turn ideologically freighted. And yet this highly pragmatic view of language, to our surprise, coincided in almost every case with a marked appreciation, and at times even reverence, for language and its power. The potential contradiction between these two views of language represented for us an illuminating, through complex and largely hidden, site of struggle. In Bakhtinian terms, these interviews contain multiple and competing "voices" of language, the heteroglossic nature of which seemed not to concern our interviewees. (It perhaps goes without saying that the highly pragmatic view of language held by those we interviewed is also at odds with the view widely held in our profession—of writing as a means of discovery, of getting in touch with the self, of coming to know rather than to report.)

The pragmatism reflected in our interviewees' dominant view of language also no doubt accounts for their tendency to accept constraints, which raises for us a number of questions. Because they help to achieve the goal, a controlled language of only 2,000 words or a tightly controlled CQM chart received almost universal praise from their users. As the interviews reveal, such constraints are viewed as exceedingly efficient tools whose careful guidelines in a sense free their users to attend to other important matters. But they also constrain and regiment in ways that the users felt unnecessary to explore or interrogate. Nor did our interviewees criticize collaborative writing; as successful collaborators, they tended to accept the construct almost as a given. We are aware, however, that some collaborative writing situations are far from productive or satisfying and that, indeed, collaborative settings can reify traditional patterns of power and authority and can isolate rather than bring people together.

Finally, because of our own constraints of time and funding, we were unable to learn from these interviewees much about the institutional context in which they wrote. For the most part they seemed to take their contexts for granted. We and our readers, however, cannot afford to do the same. By presenting these snapshots, we are not implying that we can fruitfully study collaborative writers in isolation or that we can bracket questions of purpose and politics. I. A. Richards once defined "meaning" as that which is missing from any statement, picture, or context. We offer these vignettes, then, not simply for what they record but, more importantly, for what they suggest about that which is missing.

SCENES OF COLLABORATION: BACKGROUNDINGS

When we first began our FIPSE-funded study of the collaborative writing practices of members of seven professional associations, we had no idea what conclusions our data would reveal. We did not know what the pieces of our particular puzzle looked like; we did not, in fact, even have a picture on a box to go by. Since that time, research on collaborative writing has increased substantially. In 1984, for example, only one presentation at the Conference on College Composition and Communication—our own—focused on collaborative writing. In 1989 an entire strand of sessions investigated this topic.

As a consequence of this growing interest in collaborative writing, the context for this report on our two surveys has shifted considerably. When we developed these surveys, we were concerned primarily with providing evidence that collaborative writing is a fact of life for members of these seven professional associations. Most teachers and researchers in composition now recognize that individuals in a wide variety of professions regularly write collaboratively. But many other questions remain unanswered and in some cases unrecognized.

The results of our two surveys enable us to provide useful information about the collaborative writing practices of the members of the seven associations we studied. The results of these surveys, however, have been more generative than conclusive. Rather than providing definitive answers, the surveys have enabled us to articulate the probing questions that guided not only our interviews but our continuing theoretical and pedagogical explorations as well.

Research Methods

The three-tiered research project this chapter reports on began with our desire to survey a random sample of members of professional organizations representing the sciences, applied sciences, social sciences, information sciences, humanities, business, and government. We chose the seven organizations (six during the early stages of research; a seventh, the Modern Language Association, was added when we secured additional funds) on the basis of these criteria:

1. the organization was a major one for the field
2. membership was national and included both academic and nonacademic professionals
3. membership lists were public or could be made available to us
4. the president or other official representative of the organization agreed to cooperate with our plan of research

Using these criteria as guides, we chose the following groups:

The American Consulting Engineers Counsel
The American Institute of Chemists
The American Psychological Association
The International City Management Association
The Modern Language Association
The Professional Services Management Association
The Society for Technical Communication

Survey 1. We then developed a cover letter (see Appendix A) and a survey questionnaire to be sent to a random sample of 200 members of each organization. The questionnaire went through several pilot studies, one with members of the Oregon State University Survey Research Department, one with a group from the Environmental Protection Agency, and another with writers at CH2M Hill, an engineering consulting firm. After sending the initial survey, we followed up with a postcard reminder and later with a second copy of our letter and questionnaire. Our goals in this initial survey were relatively simple: to determine the frequency, types, and occasions of collaborative writing among members of these groups. The response rate for this first survey was just under 50 percent.

Survey 2. For the second, more in-depth survey, we chose a purposeful rather than random sample of twelve members of each organization that had responded to our first survey. In choosing the twelve individuals, we looked for the following characteristics:

1. experience and satisfaction with collaborative writing
2. variety of collaborative writing experience
3. willingness to participate in the research
4. diversity in age, years on the job, geographic location, and sex

This second, much longer and more open-ended survey also went through several pilot stages of development and benefited from the criticisms of many writers. The eventual response rate for this survey was 99 percent.

Copies of the cover letters appear in Appendixes A and B along with the mean responses of each of the seven groups to each questionnaire. With the help of statisticians at Oregon State and the University of British Columbia, we subjected these data to a number of statistical analyses, including F- and T-tests, chi-square analysis, and multivariate analysis.

Results. The mean responses of all seven groups combined, for both Survey 1 and Survey 2, appear on the following pages.

SURVEY OF WRITING IN THE PROFESSIONS

This survey is intended to identify and define the nature, types, and frequency of writing done in your profession. For the purposes of this survey, writing includes any of the activities that lead to a completed written product. These activities include written or spoken brainstorming, outlining or note-taking, organizational planning, drafting, revising, and editing. Written products include any piece of writing, from notes, directions, or forms to reports and published materials.

1. In general, what percentage of your professional time is spent in some kind of writing activity?
    44   percent

2. What percentage of the time you spend in writing activities is devoted to each of the following? (Your figures should total 100 percent.)

		PERCENT
a.	Brainstorming and similar idea-generating activities	14 %
b.	Note-taking	13 %
c.	Organizational planning	13 %
d.	Drafting (including dictating) . . .	32 %
e.	Revising	15 %
f.	Editing (including proofreading) . .	13 %
	TOTAL	100 %

3. Technology is changing the way many people write. Please indicate the percentage of the time spent in writing activities that you use a word processor.
    28   percent

4. The situations in which people in the professions write may vary considerably. Please indicate the percentage of the time you spend in writing activities that is spent writing alone or as part of a team or group. (Your figures should total 100 percent.)

		PERCENT
a.	Writing alone	82 %
b.	Writing with one other person . . .	9 %
c.	Writing with a small group (2-5 persons)	7 %
d.	Writing with a large group (6 or more persons)	2 %
	TOTAL	100 %

5. How important do you think effective writing is to the
    successful execution of your job? (Circle one number.)
    (86%) 1   VERY IMPORTANT
    (12%) 2   IMPORTANT
    (2%) 3   NOT TOO IMPORTANT
    (0%) 4   NOT AT ALL IMPORTANT

6. Please indicate how frequently, in general, you work on
    the following types of writing, distinguishing between
    writing done alone and with one or more persons.
    (Circle one number for each.)

		VERY OFTEN	OFTEN	OCCASION-ALLY	NEVER
A.	LETTERS				
a.	Alone	1 (53%)	2 (23%)	3 21%)	4 (3%)
b.	With 1 or more persons	1 (1%)	2 (5%)	3 (43%)	4 (51%)
B.	MEMOS				
a.	Alone	1 (49%)	2 (24%)	3 (23%)	4 (4%)
b.	With one or more persons	1 (1%)	2 (7%)	3 (40%)	4 (52%)
C.	SHORT REPORTS				
a.	Alone	1 (38%)	2 (29%)	3 (28%)	4 (5%)
b.	With one or more persons	1 (2%)	2 (16%)	3 (43%)	4 (39%)
D.	LONG REPORTS				
a.	Alone	1 (5%)	2 (21%)	3 (40%)	4 (14%)
b.	With one or more persons	1 (4%)	2 (16%)	3 (43%)	4 (37%)
E.	PROFESSIONAL ARTICLES AND ESSAYS				
a.	Alone	1 (21%)	2 (13%)	3 (37%)	4 (29%)
b.	With one or more persons	1 (2%)	2 (8%)	3 (29%)	4 (61%)
F.	POPULAR ARTICLES AND ESSAYS				
a.	Alone	1 (8%)	2 (4%)	3 (23%)	4 (65%)
b.	With one or more persons	1 (1%)	2 (1%)	3 (12%)	4 (86%)
G.	USER MANUALS OR OTHER DETAILED INSTRUCTIONS				
a.	Alone	1 (14%)	2 (12%)	3 (35%)	4 (39%)
b.	With one or more persons	1 (5%)	2 (11%)	3 (30%)	4 (54%)
H.	NEWSLETTERS, BULLETINS, OR IN-HOUSE PUBLICATIONS				
a.	Alone	1 (10%)	2 (15%)	3 (36%)	4 (39%)
b.	With one or more persons	1 (5%)	2 (9%)	3 (29%)	4 (57%)
I.	CASE STUDIES				
a.	Alone	1 (8%)	2 (9%)	3 (20%)	4 (63%)
b.	With one or more persons	1 (1%)	2 (5%)	3 (18%)	4 (76%)
J.	PROPOSALS FOR CONTRACTS AND GRANTS				
a.	Alone 1	(14%)	2 (23%)	3 (32%)	4 (31%)
b.	With one or more persons	1 (9%)	2 (21%)	3 (29%)	4 (41%)
K.	LECTURE/ORAL PRESENTATION NOTES				
a.	Alone	1 (33%)	2 (20%)	3 (35%)	4 (12%)
b.	With one or more persons	1 (1%)	2 (5%)	3 (33%)	4 (61%)
L.	INSTRUCTIONAL OR COURSE-RELATED MATERIALS				
a.	Alone	1 (23%)	2 (15%)	3 (31%)	4 (31%)
b.	With one or more persons	1 (2%)	2 (7%)	3 (32%)	4 (59%)

M. BOOKS AND MONOGRAPHS
a. Alone 1 (9%) 2 (8%) 3 (17%) 4 (66%)
b. With one or more persons 1 (1%) 2 (3%) 3 (16%) 4 (80%)
N. OTHER
a. Alone (Please specify
   _____) 1 (31%) 2 (26%) 3 (14%) 4 (29%)
b. With one or more persons
   (Please specify _____)   1 (9%) 2 (20%) 3 (30%) 4 (41%)

7.   Collaboration in writing can, of course, take many
      forms. If you have written with a co-author or as part
      of a group, please indicate how frequently you use each
      of the following organizational patterns for that
      writing. (Circle one number for each.) IF YOU NEVER
      WRITE WITH ONE OR MORE PERSONS, PLEASE SKIP TO QUESTION
      11.

	VERY OFTEN	OFTEN	OCCASION-ALLY	NEVER

ORGANIZATIONAL PATTERNS
A. Team or group plans and
outlines. Each member drafts
a part. Team or group
compiles the parts and
revises the whole 1 (7%) 2 (15%) 3 (45%) 4 (33%)
B. Team or group plans
and outlines. One member
writes the entire draft.
Team or group revises . . . 1 (5%) 2 (21%) 3 (40%) 4 (34%)
C. One member plans and
writes draft. Group or
team revises 1 (8%) 2 (23%) 3 (40%) 4 (29%)
D. One person plans and
writes draft. This draft
is submitted to one or more
persons who revise the draft
without consulting the writer
of the first draft 1 (3%) 2 (7%) 3 (20%) 4 (70%)
E. Team or group plans and
writes draft. This draft is
submitted to one or more
persons who revise the draft
without consulting the writers
of the first draft 1 (1%) 2 (2%) 3 (16%) 4 (81%)
F. One member assigns writing
tasks. Each member carries out
individual tasks. One member
compiles the parts and revises
the whole 1 (6%) 2 (15%) 3 (40%) 4 (39%)
G. One person dictates.
Another person transcribes
and revises 1 (2%) 2 (6%) 3 (17%) 4 (75%)

8. The list of organizational patterns described in question 7 is not exhaustive. If you use another organizational pattern, please describe it in the following space.

9. In general, how productive do you find writing as part of a team or group as compared to writing alone? (Circle one number.)
   (13%) 1 VERY PRODUCTIVE
   (45%) 2 PRODUCTIVE
   (38%) 3 NOT TOO PRODUCTIVE
   (4%) 4 NOT AT ALL PRODUCTIVE

10. If you write with one or more persons, who most often assumes final responsibility for the written product? (Circle one number.)
    (13%) 1 EACH MEMBER OF THE GROUP OR TEAM SHARES EQUAL RESPONSIBILITY.
    (40%) 2 ONE MEMBER OF THE GROUP OR TEAM TAKES RESPONSIBILITY.
    (37%) 3 THE HEAD OF THE GROUP TAKES RESPONSIBILITY.
    (6%) 4 A SUPERIOR OR GROUP OF SUPERIORS OUTSIDE THE GROUP TAKES RESPONSIBILITY.
    (4%) 5 OTHER (Please specify _____)

11. Which one of the following best describes the type of employer for whom you work? (Circle one number.)
    (38%) 1 BUSINESS AND INDUSTRY
    (24%) 2 COLLEGE OR UNIVERSITY
    (17%) 3 LOCAL, STATE, OR FEDERAL GOVERNMENT
    (15%) 4 SELF-EMPLOYED
    (6%) 5 OTHER (Please specify _____)

12. About how many people are employed by your institution or company?
    ___4373___ NUMBER

13. And how many are employed at your branch, division, or department of that institution or company?
    ___177___ NUMBER

14. How many years have you been doing the type of work characteristic of your present job?
    ___15___ YEARS

15. Please state your title and briefly describe your major job responsibilities.
    _____ TITLE
    _____RESPONSIBILITIES

16. Please give the year of your birth.
    _____1937_____ YEAR

17. Are you: (Circle one.)
    (75%) 1 MALE
    (25%) 2 FEMALE

18. Is there anything else you can tell us about the
    writing you do in your profession that will help us
    better understand the nature, types, or frequency of
    that writing?

    (THANK YOU VERY MUCH FOR YOUR COOPERATION)

SURVEY OF WRITING IN THE PROFESSIONS
STAGE II: GROUP WRITING

This survey explores the dynamics and demands of group
writing in your profession. For the purposes of this
survey, <u>writing</u> includes any of the activities that lead to
a completed written product. These activities include
written and spoken brainstorming, outlining, note-taking,
organizational planning, drafting, revising, and editing.
<u>Written</u> products include any piece of writing, from notes,
directions, and forms to reports and published materials.
<u>Group</u> <u>writing</u> includes any writing done in collaboration
with one or more persons.

1. In general, do you work with the same person or persons
    in producing a written document? (Circle one number.)

1   YES ---->   (Please indicate the number of persons
                     in this group.)
    (35%)   __6__ NUMBER OF PERSONS IN GROUP
2   NO   ---->   (Please indicate the number of persons
                     in the three groups with which you most
                     regularly work.)
    (65%)   __3__ NUMBER OF PERSONS IN FIRST GROUP
                     __4__ NUMBER OF PERSONS IN SECOND
                           GROUP
                     __5__ NUMBER OF PERSONS IN THIRD GROUP

2. Please add any additional comments about the groups
    with which you work.

3. From the following list, please indicate the four kinds
    of documents that you most typically work on as part of
    a group, rank ordering them in terms of frequency
    written. (Place one letter in each of the appropriate
    boxes.)

__J__	MOST FREQUENTLY WRITTEN	A. Memos
		B. Short reports
		C. Long reports
__A__	SECOND MOST FREQUENTLY WRITTEN	D. Professional articles and essays
		E. Popular articles and essays
		F. User manuals or other detailed instructions
		G. Newsletters, bulletins, or other in-house publications
__B__	THIRD MOST FREQUENTLY WRITTEN	H. Letters
		I. Case Studies
		J. Proposals for contracts or grants

<table>
<tr><td>____C____</td><td>FOURTH MOST
FREQUENTLY
WRITTEN</td><td>K.</td><td>Lecture/oral presentation
notes</td></tr>
<tr><td></td><td></td><td>L.</td><td>Instructional or other
course-related materials</td></tr>
<tr><td></td><td></td><td>M.</td><td>Books and monographs</td></tr>
<tr><td></td><td></td><td>N.</td><td>Other (Please specify__)</td></tr>
</table>

4. In general, which of the documents cited in question 3 do you find <u>most</u> <u>productive</u> to work on as part of a group, and why? Please refer to all of these documents, not just the four documents you most frequently write.

5. In general, which of the documents cited in question 3 do you find <u>least</u> <u>productive</u> to work on as part of a group, and why? Please refer to all of these documents, not just the four documents you most frequently write.

6. When you participate in a group writing project, do you generally carry out each of the following activities alone, with other group members, or partly alone and partly with the group? If you are generally not involved in one or more of these activities, please circle 4 for not applicable. (Circle one number for each.)

	GENERALLY ALONE	GENERALLY AS PART OF GROUP	PARTLY ALONE AND PARTLY WITH GROUP	NOT APPLIC- ABLE
a. Brainstorming and similar idea-generating activities	1 (5%)	2 (44%)	3 (50%)	4 (1%)
b. Information gathering	1 (33%)	2 (14%)	3 (53%)	4 (0%)
c. Organizational planning	1 (15%)	2 (35%)	3 (46%)	4 (4%)
d. Drafting (including dictating)	1 (63%)	2 (6%)	3 (29%)	4 (2%)
e. Revising . . .	1 (32%)	2 (29%)	3 (39%)	4 (0%)
f. Editing (including proofreading . . .	1 (56%)	2 (4%)	3 (36%)	4 (4%)

7. Which of these activities (brainstorming, information-gathering, organizational planning, drafting, revising, editing) do you find <u>most</u> <u>productive</u> to perform as part of a group, and why?

8. Which of these activities (brainstorming, information-gathering, organizational planning, drafting, revising, editing) do you find <u>least</u> <u>productive</u> to perform as part of a group, and why?

9. Please indicate the frequency of use of prepared in-house or other "boilerplate" materials used in documents your group or groups produce. Such materials might include standard descriptions of equipment, facilities, staff, processes, or methods that are regularly included in various documents. (Circle one number.)

```
  1 NEVER    (PLEASE SKIP TO QUESTION #10)    (19%)
--2 SELDOM USED                               (42%)
--3 OFTEN USED                                (30%)
--4 VERY OFTEN USED                           ( 9%)

------>  9a.  Approximately how many "boilerplate"
              materials" do you use in a typical document?
              (Circle one number.)
```

(5%)   1   "BOILERPLATE MATERIALS" COMPRISE 75-100% OF A TYPICAL DOCUMENT

(14%)   2   "BOILERPLATE MATERIALS" COMPRISE 50%-74% OF A TYPICAL DOCUMENT

(18%)   3   "BOILERPLATE MATERIALS" COMPRISE 25%-49% OF A TYPICAL DOCUMENT

(63%)   4   "BOILERPLATE MATERIALS" COMPRISE 0%-24% OF A TYPICAL DOCUMENT

        9b. How productive do you find the use of such in-house or "boilerplate" materials? (Circle one number.)

(26%)   1   VERY PRODUCTIVE
(45%)   2   PRODUCTIVE
(28%)   3   NOT TOO PRODUCTIVE
(1%)   4   NOT AT ALL PRODUCTIVE

        9c. Do you have any additional comments about the use or productivity of in-house or "boilerplate" materials in group writing?

10. How often do the group or groups with which you work assign duties for completing a project according to a set plan? (The set plan might specify, for instance, that the group will plan and outline a proposed document together, then divide writing tasks so that each member drafts a part, and then reconvene so that the group can compile and revise the entire document.) (Circle one number.)

	1	NEVER	(PLEASE SKIP TO QUESTION #11)	(10%)
--	2	SELDOM		(16%)
--	3	OFTEN		(51%)
--	4	VERY OFTEN		(19%)
--	5	ALWAYS		(4%)

-------> 10a. When your group or groups follow a set plan to divide duties, who typically assigns the tasks each member of the group will accomplish? (Circle one number.)

(73%)	1	GROUP LEADER
(1%)	2	SUPERIOR OUTSIDE THE GROUP
(1%)	3	GROUP MEMBER OTHER THAN LEADER
(22%)	4	THE ENTIRE GROUP
(3%)	5	OTHER (Please specify_____)

10b. When your group or groups follow a set plan, how productive do you find its use? (Circle one number.)

(31%)	1	VERY PRODUCTIVE
(65%)	2	PRODUCTIVE
(4%)	3	NOT TOO PRODUCTIVE
(0%)	4	NOT AT ALL PRODUCTIVE

10C. Please briefly describe the set plan your group or groups most often use in assigning duties, or attach a copy of the plan with this questionnaire. (After describing this set plan, please skip to question #12.)

11. If the group or groups you write with do not follow a set plan to assign duties, how do you decide how those duties will be divided?

12. When you write as part of a group, how is authorship or credit most often assigned? (Circle one number.)

(40%)   1   TO ALL THOSE WHO PARTICIPATED IN THE PROJECT
(13%)   2   TO THE MAIN WRITER(S)
(6%)   3   TO THE GROUP LEADER
(3%)   4   TO THE WRITERS OF EACH SECTION OF THE DOCUMENT
(1%)   5   TO A SUPERIOR OUTSIDE THE GROUP
(30%)   6   TO THE COMPANY ONLY (NO PERSON IS CITED AS THE AUTHOR)
(7%)   7   OTHER (Please specify_____)

13. Are you satisfied or dissatisfied with the way authorship or credit is typically assigned in group writing projects in which you participate?

    -- 1   SATISFIED   (95%)
    -- 2   DISSATISFIED   (5%)

    ----> 13a. Please explain why you are satisfied or dissatisfied with the way authorship or credit is typically assigned in group writing projects in which you participate.

14. In your experience, to what extent are members of the group or groups with which you work likely to agree about each of the following areas? If you are generally not involved with one or more of these areas, please circle 5 for not applicable. (Circle one number for each.)

	VERY LIKELY TO AGREE	LIKELY TO AGREE	LIKELY TO DISAGREE	VERY LIKELY TO DISAGREE	NOT APPLIC-ABLE
a. Division of duties . .	1 (34%)	2 (60%)	3 (1%)	4 (0%)	5 (5%)
b. Research methodology . .	1 (15%)	2 (64%)	3 (11%)	4 (0%)	5 (10%)
c. Content or substance . .	1 (11%)	2 (67%)	3 (14%)	4 (8%)	5 (0%)
d. Format or organization of document . . .	1 (18%)	2 (65%)	3 (16%)	4 (0%)	5 (1%)
e. Style . .	1 (10%)	2 (56%)	3 (29%)	4 (3%)	5 (2%)
f. Grammar, punctuation or usage . . .	1 (26%)	2 (51%)	3 (14%)	4 (5%)	5 (4%)

g. credit or
responsibility
for document   1 (40%) 2 (41%) 3 (7%) 4 (1%) 5 (11%)
h. other
Please specify 1 (0%) 2 (4%) 3 (4%) 4 (9%) 5 (83%)

---

15.   When the group or groups with which you work come to
      the revision stage of a project, who most often does
      the actual revision? (Circle one number.)

      (33%)   1   GROUP LEADER
      (9%)   2   GROUP MEMBER OTHER THAN LEADER
      (13%)   3   ENTIRE GROUP
      (23%)   4   SEVERAL MEMBERS OF THE GROUP
      (14%)   5   TECHNICAL WRITER OR EDITOR
                      WITHIN THE GROUP
      (1%)   6   TECHNICAL WRITER OR EDITOR
                      OUTSIDE THE GROUP
      (7%)   7   OTHER (Please specify _____)

16.   Please briefly describe the stages of review a group-
      written document typically goes through from the time
      the initial draft is complete to the time it is
      delivered to the intended receiver. (Please include
      all levels of review--legal, editorial, scientific,
      technical, etc.)

17.   When you are working on a group writing project, how
      often do you use the following technologies? (Circle
      one number for each.)

	VERY OFTEN	OFTEN	OCCASION- ALLY	NEVER
a. Photocopying . . .	1 (77%)	2 (22%)	3 (0%)	4 (1%)
b. Conference phone calls	1 (9%)	2 (14%)	3 (46%)	4 (31%)
c. Teleconferencing . .	1 (0%)	2 (3%)	3 (15%)	4 (82%)
d. Electronic mail . .	1 (3%)	2 (9%)	3 (20%)	4 (68%)
e. Computer links . . .	1 (6%)	2 (14%)	3 (31%)	4 (49%)
f. Word processing . . .	1 (80%)	2 (10%)	3 (5%)	4 (5%)
g. Dictaphones	1 (14%)	2 (17%)	3 (26%)	4 (43%)
h. Other (Please specify _____)	1 (17%)	2 (6%)	3 (12%)	4 (65%)

18. Have any of the technologies listed in the preceding question affected the writing you typically do as part of a group? (Circle one number.)

```
      1   NO        (25%)
| --  2   YES       (75%)
|
| ------> 18a.  Please describe how any of these
               technologies have affected your writing.
```

19. In your experience, what are the three greatest advantages of group writing in your profession?

20. In your experience, what are the three greatest disadvantages   of group writing in your profession?

21. Please comment on how your participation in group writing contributes or does not contribute to your overall job satisfaction.

22. What advice would you give to someone in your field about how to write effectively as part of a group?

23. Were you given any on-the-job training to prepare you for the group writing you do? (Circle one number.)

```
      1   NO   (81%)
| --  2   YES  (19%)
|
| ------>  23a.  Please describe this training and comment on
                its effectiveness.
```

24. Do you feel that your high school and college English classes adequately prepared you for the group writing you do in your profession? (Circle one number.)

    1   YES   (39%)
-- 2   NO   (61%)

------> 24a. Please comment on how your high school or college English classes might have better prepared you for professional group writing tasks.

25. What degrees, if any, do you hold? Please list the degree (BA, MA, etc.), the major, the year awarded, and the awarding institution.

DEGREE	MAJOR	YEAR	INSTITUTION
_____	_____	_____	_____
_____	_____	_____	_____
_____	_____	_____	_____

26. Please add any additional comments that will help us better understand group writing in your profession.

(THANK YOU FOR YOUR COOPERATION)

Discussion

To establish reliable baseline data, we began by asking some fairly simple questions. To those questions we received unequivocal and straightforward answers. We wanted to know, first of all, how much writing members of these professional organizations did and what importance they attached to writing. Even given the broad definition of writing we posited, their answers surprised us: professionals told us they spent about half their time (44 percent) in some writing-related activity, and 98 percent of them rated writing as important or very important to the successful execution of their jobs. In short, writing counts for these people, and they are doing a lot of it.

Beyond such general information lay our more specific goals. How much of this writing was conducted collaboratively, and how productive did respondents find such collaboration? Answering the first of these questions proved a problem, partly because of a weakness in our first questionnaire and partly because of deep-seated definitions of writing. An early question (4) asked what percentage of time these professionals spent writing alone and what percentage writing as a team or with a group: they reported writing alone 82 percent of the time. The wording of the question and the commonsense view of writing as the physical act of putting pen or typewriter key to paper probably contributed to this anomalous response, for later answers contradicted this one. Further analysis of following questions, particularly those asking how frequently respondents wrote particular types of documents with others, revealed that collaborative writing is a widespread and well established phenomenon among members of these professional organizations, with 87 percent reporting that they sometimes write as members of a team or a group. A member of the American Institute of Chemists epitomized this contradictory response for us: after saying that he wrote alone 100 percent of the time, he later answered an open-ended question by reporting that every one of his numerous publications was co- or group authored. And is such co- and group authorship a productive activity, compared to writing alone? Fifty-eight percent felt that it is productive or very productive; only 4 percent felt it is "not at all productive."

We attempted to explore responses to the question of productivity in open-ended questions in Survey 2 which called for a description of the advantages and disadvantages of collaborative writing. Of the disadvantages cited, perhaps that most often mentioned involved what one engineer called "the tough task of making a common single style from numerous styles." According to our respondents, disagreements about style occur frequently in collaborative writing projects. At times, these conflicts seem to represent major difficulties, particularly, according to another engineer, "when several members of the group have distinct and well-developed individual styles." In other instances, respondents described these disagreements as frustrating but not major problems. One member of the Professional Services Management Association noted that "differing writing styles make editing more tedious," while a psychologist commented that "disagreements on style . . . may slow down the [writing] process." Whatever the situation, negotiating a common style among individuals who often, in the words of one engineer, have "their own writing style which they are not willing to give up," seems to be a recurrent problem in collaborative writing.

Another difficulty, one cited almost as often as that of achieving stylistic consistency, is the additional time many respondents felt group writing requires. (One city manager's response to our request for three disadvantages of group writing was an emphatic "Time. Time. Time.") Since time was also cited as an advantage by a number of respondents, who felt group writing helped them "spread the workload" and thus meet crucial deadlines, this emphasis on time as a disadvantage first seemed anomalous to us. We are still exploring the reasons why so many respondents believe that collaborative writing takes significantly longer than individual writing, but we suspect that its emphasis by respondents may indicate a sense of a loss of control over their personal work time occasioned by the numerous meetings that many group-writing projects require. It may also reflect the fact that many group-writing projects are simply larger, more time-consuming endeavors than those undertaken by individuals in these professions.

Or it may express the frustration of individuals who have participated in inefficient, poorly run collaborative writing projects. As might be expected, interpersonal skills and group dynamics play an important role in influencing both the effectiveness of the product and the satisfaction with the process of those involved. A chemist spoke for a number of other respondents when he asserted that "responsibilities really do need to be defined in order to get maximum efficiency." Not all people feel comfortable participating in such tightly controlled efforts, even when they recognize their importance, as the following comment by a psychologist suggests: "In large groups, a careful management plan is absolutely necessary—which doesn't work with people like myself."

A related problem frequently cited involves the equitable division of tasks. All too often, according to one member of the Society for Technical Communication, "unless all the workers are extremely conscientious, one person may end up doing the greatest amount of the work." According to one member of the Professional Services Management Association, such a failure to share responsibilities may reflect the fact that "many group members shirk writing duties." (One city manager listed the tendency of group-writing projects to "reveal [the] writing deficiencies of participants" as one of its three major disadvantages.) Or it may result, in the words of another Professional Services Management Association member, from the team members' failure to make a "total commitment" to a project. In negotiating these tasks and responsibilities, often under the pressure of tight deadlines and a schedule that may require some persons to participate in several collaborative projects at the same time, personal disagreements can occur, especially when some participants are "prima donnas" (the first disadvantage of group writing cited by one engineer). One member of the Society for Technical Communication observed, "As in anything, a group is only as good as its weakest member."

Finally, a number of respondents noted that group writing can result in what one psychologist called the "diffusion of responsibility" and a loss of personal satisfaction and sense of creativity. "[It's] never exactly as *I* want it," observed another psychologist, while a member of the Society for Technical Communication commented that "sense of ownership of the project is lessened and therefore the taking of credit must be shared. If you happen to be the one who did most of the work, there may be a sense of feeling 'ripped off.'" Another technical writer simply wrote, "Loss of ownership to group. (Ennui)."

These disadvantages, though perceived as serious, were balanced for the great majority of respondents by a number of important advantages. One of the most frequently cited advantages stressed the usefulness of having varying viewpoints, of "checks and balances," of "maximum input." Respondents also noted the following "advantages": joint knowledge, experience, and writing expertise; a variety of approaches and ideas; the strengths of all the members; different perspectives that generate better ideas for a better product. As this last comment indicates, a number of respondents believed that the increased participation of diverse group members resulted in a better, more accurate text. One person noted that group writing "enhances [the] completeness [of] the product [and] minimizes the inclusion of erroneous or potentially offensive material." Others cited the following related advantages: "reduces error"; "[the] brainpower of several professionals always results in better reports than that achieved alone"; "multiple input provides a richer document." Interestingly, a number of respondents also commented on the way in which the group-writing process can increase sensitivity to audience. Collaborative writing can encourage "clearer, more understandable documents," one chemist noted, "by involving group members of disciplines typical of the intended readers." A psychologist cited the way in which it helps participants develop a "better idea of [the] general impact [of a document] on [the] target audience." These comments suggest to us that collaborative writing is highly context based. What is productive in one situation may not be so in another. Nevertheless, our data support the conclusions that most professionals find collaborative writing a generally productive means of achieving their goals.

At this stage of our analysis, then, we had accomplished one early and largely unproblematized goal: to demonstrate the degree to which professionals engaged in collaborative writing and to get some sense of how useful they found such activi-

Singular Texts/Plural Authors

ties. But our two surveys provided at least rough answers to a number of other questions.

What Kinds of Documents Do Writers Collaborate On? The answer to this question seems clear: Some writers work collaboratively on almost every document relevant to their jobs. We asked specifically about the following documents:

letters
memos
short reports
long reports
professional articles
user manuals/instructions
newsletters, bulletins, etc.
case studies
proposals
lecture/oral presentation notes
instructional or course-related materials
books and monographs

Although frequency of response varied from document to document, members of each professional group reported working collaboratively, at least occasionally, on each type of document. Forty-two percent said they occasionally write short reports collaboratively, while 29 percent occasionally write professional articles or essays as part of a team or a group. We had anticipated that on-the-job writers would collaborate on such documents as reports and proposals. We were surprised, however, to discover that these professionals were as likely "often or occasionally" to write books or monographs collaboratively as they were to do so alone. The same held true for contracts and grants, case studies, user manuals, and long reports. Results of the second survey gave us further information as respondents listed the four kinds of documents they most often write collaboratively: proposals, memos, short reports, and long reports. While these four documents are most often produced in collaboration, all the other types received some "votes." Our data suggest, then, that collaboration is not specific to a limited number of documents, but rather that it is a frequently used strategy in producing documents of all kinds.

How Are Collaborative Writing Groups Organized? We had difficulty eliciting this information, primarily because we lack a vocabulary to discuss what people do when they write collaboratively. After extensive pilot testing and revising, we described the following seven organizational patterns and asked how often our respondents used them.

1. Team or group plans and outlines. Each member drafts a part. Team or group compiles the parts and revises the whole.

2. Team or group plans and outlines. One member writes the entire draft. Team or group revises.
3. One member plans and writes draft. Group or team revises.
4. One person plans and writes draft. This draft is submitted to one or more persons who revise the draft without consulting the writer of the first draft.
5. Team or group plans and writes draft. This draft is submitted to one or more persons who revise the draft without consulting the writers of the first draft.
6. One member assigns writing tasks. Each member carries out individual tasks. One member compiles the parts and revises the whole.
7. One person dictates. Another person transcribes and revises.

Our survey results suggest that writing groups use such patterns frequently, though hardly anyone had a name for them. In fact, some told us they realized that they were following set or preestablished organizational patterns only after completing our survey, vividly demonstrating the principle that what lacks a name, we often simply do not recognize. Others (particularly in the technical writers' group) said having such a pattern was indispensable to success and that following an "ineffective" organizational pattern could produce "disastrous results." Our second survey results confirmed these responses: 72 percent of these writers said their group writing followed a set organizational plan. More importantly, they perceived the plan as necessary and helpful: 95 percent found its use productive or very productive. We conclude, then, that collaborative efforts need to be carefully organized or orchestrated—a conclusion that our interviews bring dramatically to life.

Is Collaborative Writing Related to Overall Job Satisfaction? Our answers to this question must be tentative, for we gathered most information from open-ended questions and can report no hard figures or percentages in support of our conclusions. We became interested in the question, in fact, only when responses to the first survey elicited, almost incidentally, information about the pleasures and frustrations some group writers felt. As a result, in the second survey we attempted to gather more information about affective concerns by asking questions like: "Which writing activities do you find most productive (or least productive) to work on as part of a group?"; or "Please comment on how your participation in group writing contributes or does not contribute to your job satisfaction." In response to such questions, our participants cited a number of social and organizational "pluses," including the positive impact of "team building" and "a sense of group accomplishment." Because in most collaborative writing projects those involved in some sense "share in the final product," such group efforts can contribute both to effective group dynamics—"promoting collegiality," in one psychologist's words—and to an overall sense of shared mission or purpose.

Several respondents also observed that collaborative writing offers an effective and satisfying way of initiating recent graduates into the demands of their profession and to the demands of a new position. One city manager noted that collaborative writing can "train participants in organizational policy and in the expectations and thought processes of the chief administrator," while an engineer cited the way in which it "provides leadership for younger workers." A number of respondents noted that collaborative writing has personal, as well as social or organizational benefits. "It helps me stay fresh by discussing writing and seeing how other writers work," one technical writer noted, while an engineer commented that group writing "contributes to my job satisfaction in that it allows me to gain exposure and knowledge of different aspects of our profession in an actual work environment." Respondents commented on "the intellectual stimulation provided by group writing," and a number noted the importance of emotional support, which added to their job satisfaction. One member of the International City Management Association, who reported that she had been "writing grants with the same people for three years," observed that her "group is as much a support group as a professional team."

Put most briefly, these discursive responses suggest that a complex set of largely unidentified (perhaps even unrecognized) variables creates general satisfaction or dissatisfaction with both the processes and products of group writing. From these responses, we can tentatively identify a number of factors related to the degree of satisfaction experienced by those who typically write collaboratively:

1. the degree to which goals are clearly articulated and shared
2. the degree of openness and mutual respect characteristic of group members
3. the degree of control the writers have over the text
4. the degree to which writers can respond to others who may modify the text
5. the way credit (either direct or indirect) is realized
6. an agreed upon procedure for resolving disputes among group members
7. the number and kind of bureaucratic constraints (deadlines, technical or legal requirements, etc.) imposed on the writers
8. the status of the project within the organization

These are the elements that appeared (in answers to these open-ended questions) most closely related to job satisfaction. They are, of course, not quantifiable or generalizable. Nevertheless, they provide a basis for further study of the affective dimensions of collaborative writing.

What Characterizes Effective Collaborative Writers? The last open-ended question on our second survey (22) asked respondents to give advice to "someone in your field about how to write effectively as part of a group." The qualities most often recommended included listening well, flexibility, patience, and not being overly sensitive about one's writing. As one engineer noted: "Forget everything you learned in writing courses. Listen ultra intensely; don't let your feelings get hurt by criticism; don't hesitate to ask questions or change styles; and be verbose. It's always easier to erase than to go back and reconstruct original thought processes." Similarly, a chemist exhorted colleagues to "resist being vain or sensitive; . . . be responsive but not submissive to suggestions for change in what you have written; learn to recognize and accept reasonable alternatives; avoid nit-picking beyond the point of diminishing returns; practice writing at every opportunity, even though in this era of telephones and recorders there is a great temptation to avoid it." After recommending flexibility and adaptability, a city manager added a thoughtful postscript regarding the importance of being able to vary perspectives on any given problem: "Think about your audience before writing and while writing, as if they were listening to your thoughts as you put them down."

A number of respondents also pointed to mentoring ability and leadership as characteristics of effective collaborative writers. Younger employees particularly stressed the cooperation, openness, and support a strong mentor can provide and noted the assurance gained by having a mentor as a collaborator. But those at the upper end of the hierarchy also stressed the importance of effective mentoring. A senior engineer, for example, spoke of helping the group's new members to "blossom as fast as they can" by "spending time after hours talking through problems and projects." One key to effective leadership in collaborative writing efforts seems to be flexibility. A number of professionals pointed out that leadership roles are rarely constant; group members must be able to lead on one project and follow on another. This flexibility, they also noted, is most often learned in what amounts to a kind of collaborative apprenticeship.

As with our question about job satisfaction, this question about the traits of effective collaborative writers yields no easy answers and certainly no quantifiable conclusions. Yet the many long answers we received to this open-ended question suggest an emerging profile of effective collaborative writers. They are flexible; respectful of others; attentive and analytical listeners; able to speak and write clearly and articulately; dependable and able to meet deadlines; able to designate and share responsibility, to lead and to follow; open to criticism but confident in their own abilities; ready to engage in creative conflict.

We were struck, as we tried to see the shape of this profile in our mass of data, by the number of people who listed "ability to work well with others" as the most important factor in success in their fields, often adding the "ability to write well" as a secondary—though not unimportant—criterion. As one technical writer vividly put it: "No one here loses a job because of incompetence; they lose jobs if they can't work with others." We do not take this comment as a justification for incompetence—far from it. Rather it suggests to us that competence is a necessary but not a sufficient condition for success. Today and in the twenty-first century, our data suggest, writers must be "able to work together." They must, in short, be able to collaborate.

Does Collaborative Writing Occur in Various Modes? But what form(s) will the collaboration that future workers need to do take? As we studied responses to our survey, pushing hard to see profiles and patterns and guidelines, we noted a dominant language in descriptions of collaborative settings, organizational frameworks, and roles. This dominant language emerged as highly structured and hierarchical, with power and authority distributed vertically within the hierarchy. This hierarchical mode of collaboration was apparent in the responses to our surveys and to our interviews. But as we probed our data, sifting back through our transcripts of interviews and responses to our questionnaires, we found traces of descriptions that did not fit this hierarchical mode. These traces suggested a more loose, fluid mode of collaborative writing, one that focused more often on the processes of collaboration rather than on the end products, one that emphasized dialogue and exploration rather than efficiency and closure.

We will return to a discussion of these two modes, the hierarchical and the dialogic, in chapter 5. Our recognition of these varying modes, suggestive as they are of competing epistemologies and theories of language, had the effect of further problematizing our view of collaborative writing, forcing us once again to interrogate our original goals and assumptions and to ask what competing political and economic agendas may be inscribed in collaborative acts, how ideology may construct varying views of and purposes for collaboration. If writers have traditionally been written as solitary individual units, does collaboration necessarily write them in a different or differing way? Our seemingly simple, straightforward research project thus refused to be neatly packaged and reported but instead brought us into an ever widening current of historical and theoretical issues, all focusing on what it means, in any particular time and place, to be "a writer." To these historical and theoretical issues we now turn.

INTERTEXTS

The theatre, of course, is the most collaborative of all the arts. Though Shakespeare was an adaptor rather than a collaborator in almost all of his work, he obviously [in the words of playwright George Abbott] "took parasitical advantage of other people's ideas." The collaborator and the adaptor are close kin, and either title has won great literary distinction and success in the theatre.
—J. W. Miller, Modern Playwrights at Work

* * * * *

The electronic medium now threatens to reverse the attitudes fostered by the press by breaking down the barrier between author and reader. When the reader becomes the author's collaborator, authorship loses its privileged status. Anyone can become an author and send his merest thoughts over one of the networks to hundreds of unwilling readers.—J. David Bolter, "Information and Knowledge: The Computer as a Medium of Humanistic Communication"

* * * * *

The legal status of the author will always be derived from the culture's prevailing views on individual freedom and private property. . . . Because it is clear from the outset that Racter's work [a computer program; Racter is short for raconteur] has no author, readers are forced to confront the processes by which they derive meaning. It is the ultimate deconstructive text. . . . All meaning is provided by the reader.

[One of Racter's poems]—"From water and from time / A visage bounds and tumbles / I seek sleep and need repose / But miss the quiet movement / Of my dreams."—James Ledbetter, "Racter, the Poetic Computer: The Case of the Disappearing Author"

*   *   *   *   *

"And it is to be remembered that during all those years the writer [Ford] wrote every word that he wrote with the idea of reading aloud to Conrad, and that during all those years Conrad wrote what he wrote with the idea of reading it aloud to this writer."

Ford left Joseph Conrad: A Personal Remembrance as his monument to Conrad. I cannot help reading "The Secret Sharer" as Conrad's tribute to Ford in rendering so uncannily the psychological experience of close collaboration.—Sondra J. Stang, The Ford Madox Ford Reader

*   *   *   *   *

Collaborating in art is like a ping-pong of ideas in which the subtlest mixture of agreement and challenge weaves itself into the participants' concentration.—Lucio Pozzi, quoted in announcement for Artistic Collaboration in the Twentieth Century. Hirshhorn Museum Exhibit, Smithsonian Institute.

*   *   *   *   *

Novelist Margaret Atwood is critical of the emphasis often placed on the writer as an enclosed self. "Readers and critics both are addicted to the concept of self-expression," Atwood says, "the writer as a kind of spider, spinning out his entire work from within. This view depends on a solipsism, the idea that we are all self-enclosed monads, with an inside and an outside, and that nothing from the outside ever gets in."—Margaret Atwood, Second Words: Selected Critical Prose

*   *   *   *   *

An established Firm does not change its style and title when, for any reason, one of its partners may be compelled to leave it.

The partner who shared all things with me has left me, but the firm has not yet put up the shutters, and I feel I am justified in permitting myself the pleasure of still linking the name of Martin Ross with that of E. OE. Somerville.—Author's note, The Big House of Inver (Prefatory note by Somerville, who jointly wrote novels with Ross; The Big House of Inver was published after Ross' death.)

*   *   *   *   *

His name is Greek, his nationality is French and his history is curious. He is one of the most influential mathematicians of the 20th century. The legends about him are many, and they are growing every day. Almost every mathematician knows a few stories about him and is likely to have made up a couple more. His works are read and extensively quoted all over the world. There are young men in Rio de Janeiro almost all of whose mathematical education was obtained from his works, and there are famous mathematicians in Berkeley and in Göttingen who think that his influence is pernicious. He has emotional partisans and vociferous detractors wherever groups of mathematicians congregate. The strangest fact about him, however, is that he does not exist.

This nonexistent Frenchman with the Greek name is Nicolas Bourbaki (rhymes with Pooh-Bah-Key). The fact is that Nicolas Bourbaki is a collective pseudonym used by an informal corporation of mathematicians.—Paul R. Halmos, "Nicolas Bourbaki"

*   *   *   *   *

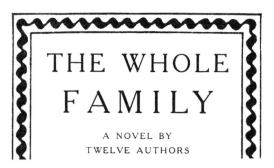

THE WHOLE FAMILY

A NOVEL BY TWELVE AUTHORS

William Dean Howells, Mary E. Wilkins Freeman, Mary Heaton Vorse, Mary Stewart Cutting, Elizabeth Jordan, John Kendrick Bangs, Henry James, Elizabeth Stuart Phelps, Edith Wyatt, Mary R. Shipman Andrews, Alice Brown, Henry Van Dyke. Copyright 1907, 1908 by Harper & Brothers. All rights reserved. Published October 1908.

According to their editor, Elizabeth Jordan, this project "was a mess!" and the writing became as much of a contest as a collaboration, "with each author trying to impose his vision on the entire work."—Alfred Bendixen, "It Was a Mess! How Henry James and Others Actually Wrote a Novel"

*   *   *   *   *

The reader may ask: What harm is done by honorary authorship? Indeed some of our colleagues have argued that the custom of routinely placing the name of a senior scientist, usually the head of the laboratory, on a paper—regardless of his contribution—is widely followed and does no harm. We disagree . . . : honorary authorships falsify the assignment of responsibility for published research and increase the likelihood that inaccurate data will be published.— Walter W. Stewart and Ned Feder, "The Integrity of the Scientific Literature"

*   *   *   *   *

When I write interactive fiction for the computer, I'm "just a writer," or so my programmer says. He's written "the authoring system" that puts my words to work, that allows the reader to interact with my story on the screen. Although I'm writing the text, it's the authoring system that allows my characters to interact, the settings to change, the moon to rise and sink during the course of the story. Without the authoring system, my story would just be paper.—Sarah Sloane, Interactive fiction writer, letter to author, Andrea Lunsford

All kinds of approaches are needed to throw full
light upon the objects of our study.—Kenneth Burke
(*Language* 36)

3 / The Concept of Authorship:
Explorations and (Dis)Closures

In chapter 2 we established that, at least in the seven professional associations we studied, collaborative writing is a fact of life. Though some individuals within these associations may not become involved in collaborative writing projects, the responses to our surveys, as well as our interviews, indicate that collaboration and collaborative writing are regular activities in these professions. Our research, then, and that of others, such as Faigley and Miller, indicates that writing teachers err if, in envisioning students' professional lives upon graduation, they imagine them seated alone, writing in isolation, misplaced Romantic spirits still struggling in a professional garrett to express themselves. Although some of our students will commit themselves to professions, such as creative writing, where solitary writing is the norm, most will work in situations where they are at least as likely to participate in a group brainstorming session for a proposal or edit a collaboratively written report on-line as they are to sit alone in their office, pen (or computer keyboard) in hand.

Although our surveys and interviews provide useful information about the collaborative writing practices of individuals involved in a range of professions, they do not—and cannot—address a number of important theoretical questions. What do we mean when we say that someone—a nationally known writer, like John McPhee or Joan Didion, or a student in our freshman composition class—is the author of an essay? Why in our culture is authorship regularly attributed to some documents (essays, poems, letters) but not to others (advertisements, contracts, instructions)? What is at stake when we argue about the authorship of a text, whether an anonymous Jacobean play or a student's research paper, parts of which we suspect may have been plagiarized? What kind of relationship between authors and texts does the term *authorship* imply?

Until recently few critics would have thought to ask questions such as these. Because the concept of authorship as an inherently individual activity is so central to our Western cultural tradition, it appears at first sight transparent, obvious, in Geertz's terms, commonsensical—especially, perhaps, to writing teachers. An author, such a teacher might say, is one who struggles with and through language to create something new, a text that embodies the writer's meaning. And the word *authorship,* like *ownership* or *professorship,* simply reflects an appropriate and necessary connection between authors and their texts.

In this chapter we question this commonsensical view of the nature of authorship—a view that is directly related to the Western philosophical tradition defining the autonomous individual as the source or foundation of all knowledge. By examining the history of this concept, we hope both to demonstrate how "constructed" our concept of authorship is—not commonsensical or inevitable at all but a complex reflection of our culture—and to explore the reasons why our culture has systematically (if unconsciously) emphasized those aspects of the writing process that involve individual, rather than group, effort. A number of influential literary theorists have recently become concerned with the nature and status of the author: we discuss these varying critical perspectives on the problem of the author and consider their implications for a postmodern conception of authorship. Finally, we examine a number of contemporary practices, such as corporate and honorary authorship, that implicitly—and sometimes explicitly—challenge the traditional concept of the author. As this summary suggests, the approaches taken in these pages is one motivated by the notion of perspectives by incongruity. By juxtaposing radically different and in many ways incommensurate discourses—from empirical investigation in scientific citation studies to the abstruse theorizing of literary studies—we hope to bring our own subject, collaborative writing, into a more richly situated context.

THE MYTH OF THE SOLITARY AUTHOR: AN EXAMPLE FROM THE SCIENCES

Just how deeply entrenched in our culture is the assumption that authorship is inherently an individual enterprise? The absence of discussions of collaborative writing in our freshman composition texts and the well-established image of the writer as an isolated, often alienated, hero provide just two examples of this phenomenon, which we will discuss at greater length later in this chapter. In our research on collaborative writing, research that has been—given the absence of a unified body of studies on the subject—necessarily diffuse and wide-ranging, we unexpectedly came across another telling example, and from a surprising source. Researchers in the sociology of science have argued that an increase in collaborative practices is one of the most salient characteristics distinguishing premodern and modern science. Despite this fact, sociologists engaged in citation index studies—studies which rely upon a full and objective counting of the number of times one or more scientists' research is cited by others—have until recently only used the first author's name in compiling data for analysis.

Since writing teachers may not be conversant with research in the sociology of science, much less with the particular type of research known as citation index analysis, some explanation of this apparent anomaly may be helpful. In general, as Charles Bazerman notes in "Scientific Writing as a Social Act: A Review of the Literature of the Sociology of Science," researchers in this field since the 1960s have attempted to explore the structure of science by examining "the values of science and their enforcement; the rise, structure, and interaction of specialities; rewards and competition; and the relationship between cognitive structure and social structure in scientific fields" (157). Although some scholars, such as Ziman, Popper, Lakatos, and Toulmin, attempt to explore these issues by developing general theories of the way in which scientific knowledge is created and disseminated, others have attempted to use empirical methods of analysis, particularly citation index studies, to understand the same phenomena.

Citation index studies capitalize on what Robert Merton, one of the founders of the sociology of science, calls "the seemingly paradoxical character of property in the scientific enterprise: the circumstance that the more widely scientists make their intellectual property available to others, the more securely it becomes identified as their property" (vi–vii). Scientists cannot claim a discovery as their own, then, unless they publish their work. (From this perspective, as Price argues in *Little Science, Big Science,* the scientific paper might best be viewed as "a social device rather than a technique for accumulating quanta of information" [65].) And, once published, the impact of the work—the degree to which it is recognized by knowledgeable peers as a contribution to research in their field—can best be gauged by its continued influence—an influence that can most accurately be measured, according to sociologists of science, by counting the number of times other scholars cite a work.

Using such tools as the *Science Citation Index,* a multidisciplinary index to scientific literature developed by Eugene Garfield in the 1960s and described in his *Citation Indexing: Its Theory and Application in Science, Technology, and Humanities,* sociologists have employed citation data for three related purposes. "Some studies," G. Nigel Gilbert notes in "Referencing as Persuasion," "have used the number of citations received by a paper as an indication of its scientific quality, significance, or worth. Likewise, the number of citations obtained by an author has been used to measure the impact of his or her work on the scientific community. In other studies, citation patterns have been employed to derive maps of the structure of scientific specialties and disciplines" (114).

Whether one agrees with the purposes for which citation studies have been employed—and to a humanist, toting up citations may seem like a bizarre way of assessing an individual's contribution to a field—a great deal is potentially at stake in these studies. Citation index studies have been used to determine the productiveness of both individual scholars and departments; they have also enabled researchers to "diagram the intellectual structure of an historical line of research" (Garfield 98), such as the major advances in genetics in a certain period. Only recently, however, have scholars begun to question one very important feature of this method: most sociologists of science follow the *Science Citation Index* and *Social Science Citation Index* in disregarding all but the first author of a paper.

Why might the failure to cite all authors of a paper represent a potentially significant methodological problem? To answer this question, one must consider the highly collaborative research and writing practices of modern scientists. In *Little Science, Big Science,* Price indicates that the trend toward increasing collaboration best distinguishes premodern from modern science. Price argues, in fact, that the dramatic increase of collaboration in the sciences (a trend evidenced by an equivalent increase in coauthored articles) represents "one of the most violent transitions that can be measured in recent trends of scientific manpower and literature" (88–89). In many of the sciences, a number of forces, including the technological complexity of research, the nature of funding (which encourages large research teams), and the increase in interdisciplinary research together simply mandate collaboration. The two articles in the physical sciences that attracted the most citations in 1976 and 1977 had 40 and 41 coauthors (Garfield 1979). Both articles, written by scientists at the SLAC-Laurence Berkeley Laboratory, reported on research confirming the existence of the meson, a new subatomic particle. Researchers in some fields, such as high energy physics, publish articles listing extremely high numbers of coauthors. In "Traditional Interpretations of 'Authorship' and 'Responsibility' in the Description of Scientific and Technical Documents," Anne B. Piternick notes that *Physical Letters* and *Physical Review Letters* "frequently publish papers with 70 or 80 authors; a recent example had 139" (22). Clearly, as Zuckerman and others have argued, "Collaborative research is, in varying degrees, a functional requirement of contemporary scientific investigation" (277).

Given the collaborative nature of modern science, why were those engaged in citation studies content to count only first authors of multiauthored papers? Why did they not realize that ignoring all but the first author compromised their efforts to determine the nature of scientific productivity and chart the structure of modern science? We suspect that, despite the evidence all around them, these researchers clung tenaciously, if unconsciously, to the conventional assumption that authorship is inherently an individual activity. Consequently, it seemed perfectly natural to cite the first author for the work represented by a paper, even when it was collaboratively researched and written.

Those engaged in citation studies have begun to acknowledge the methodological flaws in past research. Eugene Garfield, who founded citation indexing, has recognized the problems posed by the *Science Citation Index's* omission of citations for all authors of an essay. In his 1979 analysis, Garfield observes that:

> Preliminary stratification studies at ISI [the Institute for Scientific Information] have shown that failure to include secondary author papers in citation counts introduces a substantial error at the very highest stratum of cited scientists. A list of the 250 most cited scientists, taken from a compilation of only primary-author counts, had only 28% of its names in common with a similar one from a compilation of all-author counts. Further studies are being conducted to determine the degree of error throughout the entire range of scientists.
>
> As long as this uncertainty persists, the only fair way of developing relative citation counts is to compile the performance of all published material that is listed on a comprehensive bibliography [by repeating the citation with the name of each author and thus assuring what sociologists call a "complete" versus a "straight" count]. At ISI, where studies are conducted on a scale that requires computer compilation, this is standard practice, and in 1978 the same procedure was put into effect for all stratification studies. (242–43)

Sociologists, such as Porter, Lindsey, Long, McGinnis, and Allison, have also begun to consider the consequences of using straight citation counts in studies in the sociology of science. Lindsey argues that, "One of the most serious errors in empirical judgment made in the sociology of science has been to count both publications and citations with procedures that take no account of multiple authorship. Measurement thus introduces increasing errors as multiple authorship increases. Since scientific publication is now characterized by extensive multiple authorship, this error has become critical" (145–46).

SHIFTING CONCEPTIONS IN THE HISTORY OF AUTHORSHIP

This example of the treatment of collaboratively written essays in citation index studies suggests how deeply held is our assumption that authorship is necessarily an individual activity. How did this assumption become so firmly entrenched in our culture? Although we can hardly present a full history of the concept of authorship here, we can point to certain critical features of such a discussion. Throughout, our concern will be to emphasize that the concept of individual authorship, which strikes most people as not only commonsensical but also somehow inevitable, is actually a cultural construct, and a recent one at that.

To understand how "constructed" our concept of authorship is, we might look to the Middle Ages, with the reverence for authority, the reliance on scriptoria for copies of manuscripts, and the development of such rhetorical arts as the *ars dictaminis,* manuals for letter writing that, at their most elaborate, provided countless formulas and models for imitation. (The *Practica sive usus dictaminis,* described by James J. Murphy in *Rhetoric in the Middle Ages* as the "final stage in an automatizing tendency which had been an undercurrent in the *ars dictaminis* from its earliest days," almost succeeded in making "letter-writing a skill . . . possible to any person capable of copying individual letters of the alphabet" [259].) In *The Friar as Critic: Literary Attitudes in the Later Middle Ages,* Judson Boyce Allen attempts to help scholars understand what it meant to be an author or reader in this period. Aware of the difficulty of his task, Allen comments that:

> When we are faced with medieval authors and readers alike, we are faced with a *foreign, non-empirical sensibility.* We are confronted by authors who are for the most part content to repeat inherited materials, making their own primary contribution . . . in the area of decoration, and often content to remain anonymous: if they name themselves, it is only in the later Middle Ages that they are not primarily doing so in order to solicit prayers. At the same time we are confronted by readers, or more properly hearers, who already know what the story means, who have probably heard it before, and who, in a sense, are attending the ornamented celebration of a received truth. (59, our emphasis)

Where Allen describes medieval writers and readers in terms of their "foreign, non-empirical sensibility," Hans Robert Jauss prefers to emphasize the alterity, or "surprising otherness" of medieval literature (182). In his 1979 essay "The Alterity and Modernity of Medieval Literature," which he characterizes as an effort to "legitimate the contemporary interest in medieval literature" (181), Jauss describes what he calls the "humanist model" of texts—a model that privileges "the written character of tradition, the singularity of authorship, and the autonomy of the text understood as a work" (188). Medieval literature, Jauss argues, shares none of these characteristics. In fact, he asserts, in Germany at least, "medieval literature is even more alien that that of the antiquity which is further away in time, for . . . the reception of Aristotelian poetics and of the aesthetic canon of antiquity (which henceforth became *classical*) by Renaissance humanism cut almost all connections with medieval literature and art" (187).

Jauss' characterization of medieval authors and readers confirms and extends Allen's analysis. In part because the majority of those for whom these texts were written heard rather than read them, these "addressees" (188) viewed individual texts "neither as a one-time, self-enclosed, and final form, nor as an individual production of its author, to be shared with no one else" (191). Similarly, those who composed texts in this period did not see themselves as creating anything original or new. In fact, according to Jauss, the cosmology of the period insured that "the object of art had an always already 'built-in' significance for the medieval author; he did not have to search for it first, let alone confer it himself upon a reality without significance" (192). Furthermore, in contrast to humanist and modern authors, the medieval writer wrote "in order to praise and to extend his object, not to express himself or to enhance his personal reputation" (192).

During the Middle Ages, scholars like Allen and Jauss argue, authors (in the modern sense of the term) did not exist: there was no distinction made between the person who wrote a text and the person who copied it. Nor, as Victor Bonham-Carter observes in *Authors by Profession,* was there any distinction "between a literary work and the material on which it was written. The underlying Common Law principle that a man should be allowed undisturbed enjoyment of his property applied equally to both" (11). Some medieval writers did demonstrate an interest in protecting their work from unauthorized repetition or alteration by others. In *From Script to Print: An Introduction to Medieval Vernacular Literature,* for example, H. J. Chaytor describes how troubadours in medieval France "complicated their rhyme schemes to prevent interpolations by the unscrupulous" (119). Finally, however, our contemporary concept of plagiarism did not exist because the concept of "literary property," according to Spitzer and others, had not come into being.

The views articulated by Allen and Jauss are shared by a number of other scholars who have studied medieval discursive practices. In *The Discourse of Modernism,* Timothy J. Reiss argues that medieval "views of 'person' and 'self,' of 'will' and 'intention,' are utterly different from what will be found by the time of the Renaissance." As a consequence, Reiss observes, it is misguided to attempt to trace discursive "continuity between the Middle Ages and our modernity" (72). Whereas modern discourse exemplifies what Reiss characterizes as "the analytico-referential discourse of assertion and possession, of permanent and universal human reason, and of absolute objective truth" (37), the Middle Ages adhered to a different model. This model "is a collective one in which the sign as a 'unit' of meaning or the human as an 'individual' in society has no significance at all save as it can be referred to the corporate community or social discourse on the one hand and guaranteed by the Divine on the other" (94).

Despite the predominance of this model during the Middle Ages, scholars have nevertheless located traces of the modern concepts of the self and the author during this period. In "Assertion of the Self in the Works of Chaucer," John Hurt Fisher connects the beginning of the modern concept of the author to the narrative "I" of Chaucer within the *Tales.* Fisher's argument builds on the substantial body of work tracing the creation and the rise of the individual and individualism in Western society (see Colin Morris, *The Discovery of the Individual 1050–1200,* and Walter

Ullman, *The Individual and Society in the Middle Ages*). As Morris notes, "Several art forms and fields of study, which are particularly concerned with the individual, began at this time: autobiography, the personal portrait, and satire among them" (158).

The story of the emergence of the concept of the individual self is too complex and multifaceted to be examined in detail here. Scholars agree, however, that an important chapter in this story is heralded by Renaissance philosopher Rene Descartes' celebrated dictum "*cogito ergo sum.*" Indeed, most scholars studying the rise of the individual in Western culture agree with Jean A. Perkins that "without Descartes the whole development of individualism would have been unthinkable; it was he who placed the individual human being at the very center of the universe and at the same time radically divorced this same figure from the rest of the world" (13). This separation between subject and object, knower and known, is intricately bound up in an epistemology that situates knowledge within the self, one that provides a necessary condition for the development of the concept of "originary authorship."

But in the Middle Ages such conditions were not yet in place. The Middle Ages was, of course, hardly an unchanging or simple monolith. As Jacqueline T. Miller notes in *Poetic License: Authority and Authorship in Medieval and Renaissance Contexts,* there undoubtedly were manifestations in the Middle Ages of a "tension between the desire for creative autonomy and the pressure of inherited or conventionally accepted authoritative systems or voices" (6). But the Middle Ages' immersion in a hierarchical and corporate or communal worldview precluded the development of individualism as it later appeared in the West. Similarly foreign are Descartes' "solitary thinker" and our modern concept of "originary authorship."

The conditions necessary to the development of these and other modern concepts did not arise suddenly in the Renaissance. Rather, the Renaissance represents a critical period of transition that witnessed the development of printing, a crucial precondition of modern authorship, and the gradual transformation of the patronage system. During the Renaissance, too, writers as well as other artists developed a growing artistic self-consciousness, albeit one not yet professionalized and protected by copyright laws. Nevertheless, as Martha Woodmansee notes in "The Genius and the Copyright: Economic and Legal Conditions of the Emergence of the 'Author,'" in the Renaissance (and on up to the eighteenth century) writers continued to view themselves as "vehicles or instruments" (427). Most typically, the Renaissance writer considered himself a craftsman, "the master of a body of rules, preserved and handed down to him in rhetoric and poetics, for manipulating traditional materials in order to achieve the effects prescribed by the cultivated audience of the court to which he owed both his livelihood and social status" (426).

Uneasily coexisting with this view, however, was the recognition that sometimes writers did more than refashion traditional materials. In these rare instances, writers considered themselves, and were considered by others to be, inspired—either by God or by the muse. In either case, writers did not see themselves as personally reponsible for their creations: the concepts of artistic originality and of writing as intellectual property were as yet inchoate. (Even Milton, writing at a later time, concealed his identity as an author until the early 1640s, when his desire to be publicly identified as a supporter of Cromwell took precedence over his preference for anonymity. Milton continued to decline to profit financially from his work, however. Only the Restoration, which deprived him of his pension and other resources, caused him to consent to the now historic agreement with Samuel Smiles for the publication of *Paradise Lost*.)

The history of the concept of authorship cannot be separated from the evolution of authorship as a profession. During the Renaissance, the development of printing and the resulting increase in the demand for books helped establish publishing as a profit-making venture. The situation of writers was very different from that of publishers, however. Writers survived through patronage or supported themselves through alternative employment. As Bonham-Carter notes, during this period "writing was not yet regarded as a profession to which you devoted your life, hoping that it would yield you a livelihood. Rather, it was a form of civilized communication that, among educated people, was quickly replacing the oral traditions of the past" (12).

During the Elizabethan period in England, playwrights did write with profit—or at least the hope of a livelihood—in mind. Only those authors who were also actors and thus members of the company performing their work, however, could expect to receive any financial benefit other than a one-time payment. For, with a few exceptions, the actors, members of companies that functioned much like present-day cooperatives, owned the plays the company produced. In the introduction to *The Composition of Shakespeare's Plays,* Albert Feuillerat emphasizes that during this period both actors and authors "had a candid respect for the public taste which alone was responsible for lucrative returns" (4). Dramatists, Feuillerat notes, viewed playwriting as a profession, but they would have found the pretensions of modern playwrights decidedly foreign: "[Playwrights] offered without shame whatever the actors demanded. Furthermore, they considered their work so ephemeral it would lose its vitality as soon as it had attained the dozen performances which marked a reasonable success. It certainly never occurred to them that they might achieve any lasting reputation as writers of the spoken word" (4–5). Most plays, including Shakespeare's early plays, "appeared without an author's name on the title page" (6). Furthermore, once a company purchased a play, it felt free to make whatever alterations the actors wished: "A certain amount of reworking came naturally enough during the rehearsals, but far more important revisions of an author's text were frequent and often went so far as to change the very nature of the play" (7).

As Alvin Kernan indicates, the Elizabethan theatre was indeed "a business, one of the first to be organized in terms of venture capital" (178). But it was a business in which the playwrights were generally least likely to profit. Although it is by no means the only factor responsible for the development of the concept of authorship, the ability to profit from one's writing—an ability eventually guaranteed by copyright laws—did in fact play a crucial role in establishing not only the profession of letters but equally important notions of originality and the ownership of texts.

These assumptions about the relationship between authors and texts have become so firmly established in our legal codes and, even more importantly, in our cultural and social values, that it is hard to believe they have not always informed our thinking. As Martha Woodmansee points out, however, not only is "the 'author' in its modern sense . . . a relatively recent invention" ("Genius" 426), but the protection afforded by copyright laws that contemporary writers take for granted was once a hotly contested issue—one with no preordained or inevitable outcome. In the most general sense, the debate over copyright laws lasted from 1710, when an Act of Queen Anne attempted to regularize the procedure by which authors sold books to publishers, to the efforts of Dickens and other Victorian and early twentieth-century writers to establish international copyright agreements.

As Lucien Febvre and Henry-Jean Martin observe in *The Coming of the Book: The Impact of Printing, 1450–1800,* England took the lead in these efforts. Queen Anne's Act of 1710 for the first time legally recognized "the author and not the bookseller . . . as the proper holder of copyright" (164). Even in England, however, the establishment of laws approximating modern copyright conventions developed slowly and only after much debate. The 1710 Act of Queen Anne only gave authors control of the publication and sale of their works for fourteen years and for a second fourteen years if they were still alive at the end of the first period. Not until 1814 did a new act extend the first fourteen years to twenty-eight years or the life of the author. Subsequent years saw continued legislation. Bonham-Carter lists the following acts as representative of some of the legislation in England, Europe, and America that contributed to the development of modern copyright laws: the 1833 Dramatic Copyright Act, the 1938–55 International Copyright and Customs Acts, the 1842 Literary Copyright Act, the 1886 Berne Convention, the 1891 Chase Act, the 1896 Paris and 1908 Berlin Revisions of the Berne Convention, and the 1911 Copyright Act.

Those studying the history of copyright laws emphasize that it was not bureaucratic inertia or ineptitude that caused the slow, difficult development of copyright laws, though the wheels of bureaucratic and legal change ground at least as slowly then as now. It took almost 200 years for modern copyright laws to develop because the assumptions about the relationship between authors and texts that now seem self-evident, and even commonsensical, simply did not exist. At the start of her essay, Woodmansee reprints the following entry for "Book" in the *Allgemeines Oeconomisches Lexicon* of 1753—the depiction of which, in its depriveging of the author as just another member of a production team, strikes modern readers and writers as almost fantastic:

> *Book,* either numerous sheets of white paper that have been stitched together in such a way that they can be filled with writing; or a highly useful and convenient instrument constructed of printed sheets variously bound in cardboard, paper, vellum, leather, etc. for presenting the truth to another in such a way that it can be conveniently read and recognized. Many people work on this book before it is complete and becomes an actual book in this sense. The scholar and the writer, the papermaker, the type founder, the typesetter and the printer, the proofreader, the publisher, the book binder, sometimes even the gilder and the brass-worker, etc. Thus many mouths are fed by this branch of manufacture. (Zinck col. 442, cited in and translated by Woodmansee, "Genius" 425)

It is important to note here how "the truth," according to this definition, exists separately from those whose efforts help to bring about its embodiment in book form.

Before copyright laws could seem not only just but inevitable, society had to accept the idea that there is a crucial distinction between the production of literary texts and, say, the raising and selling of apples and that the writer's role in creating a book is somehow privileged—different from that of the printer or bookbinder. Central to the establishment of the concept of writing as intellectual property were the claims about the writer's unique role in the creation of texts originally articulated by Edward Young in his 1759 *Conjectures on Original Composition* and developed by numerous writers and theorists (including the Romantics) in England and Europe.

In "The Genius and the Copyright," Woodmansee analyzes how these aesthetic claims interacted with legal-economic arguments in the debate in eighteenth-century Germany over copyright laws. For a variety of reasons, there was more resistance to copyright laws in Germany than in England. For one thing, as Woodmansee observes, "The professional writer emerged considerably later in Germany than in England and France" (431). Germany in the eighteenth century was also still transforming itself from "the limited patronage of an aristocratic society . . . [to] the democratic patronage of the marketplace" (433). Publishers, though profiting more than writers, were themselves beset with problems of piracy. Their only legal protection, the privilege, differed from early English copyright laws in that it "was not really a law at all but, as the word itself suggests, a special concession or dispensation conditionally granted to printers or publishers who enjoyed the favor of the court" (438). And Germany in the eighteenth century was comprised of 300 independent states.

Martin Luther's view that knowledge, given freely to men and women by God, should be shared equally freely with others, also mitigated against writers' efforts to establish their work as intellectual property. In "Live and Let Live," Lessing's proposal for reorganizing the current methods of publishing and distributing books (written in 1772 but never completed and published only after his death), Lessing comments specifically on the impact of this German attitude toward knowledge:

> What? The writer is to be blamed for trying to make the offspring of his imagination as profitable as he can? Just because he works with his noblest faculties he isn't supposed to enjoy the satisfaction that the roughest handyman is able to procure—that of owing his livelihood to his own industry? . . .
>
> But wisdom, they say, for sale for cash! Shameful! Freely has thou received, freely thou must give! Thus thought the noble Luther in translating the Bible. Luther, I answer, is an exception in many things. Furthermore, it is for the most part not true that the writer received for nothing what he does not want to give away for nothing. Often an entire fortune may have been spent preparing to teach and please the world. (Lessing, *Werke* V 781, cited in and translated by Woodmansee, "Genius" 437)

Woodmansee is unequivocal about the primary catalyst of both our modern concepts of authorship and of copyright laws. These conceptions are

> the product of the rise in the eighteenth century of a new group of individuals: writers who sought their livelihood from the sale of their writings to the new and rapidly expanding reading public. In Germany this new group of individuals found itself without any of the safeguards for its labors that today are certified in copyright laws. In response to this problem, and in an effort to establish the economic viability of living by the pen, these writers set about redefining the nature of writing. Their reflections on this subject are what, by and large, gave the concept of authorship its modern form. ("Genius" 426)

In redefining the relationship between writers and texts, German theorists, such as Goethe and Fichte, drew upon Young's *Conjectures on Original Composition*. In fact, Young's work, according to Woodmansee, had a much stronger impact in Germany than in England precisely because the German writers' struggle to establish their intellectual property rights was more intense. Between 1773 and 1794, for instance, publishers, legal experts, poets, and philosophers wrote so many treatises on the appropriate way to regulate the book trade that Ernest Martin Graff published a *Forschungsbericht*, or survey, that reviewed "twenty-five of the separate publications and thirty-five of the essays written over the twenty-five year period leading up to its appearance in 1794" ("Genius" 440). Those opposed to the establishment of copyright laws did so on two main grounds: (1) a book, being a physical object, becomes the publisher's property (and then the buyer's) once it is purchased from the writer; and (2) ideas, once expressed, belong to all, not just to the person who first articulated them. This latter argument is forcefully presented in the following statement by Christian Sigmund Krause:

"But the ideas, the content! that which actually constitutes a book! which only the author can sell or communicate!"—Once expressed, it is impossible for it to remain the author's property. . . . It is precisely for the purpose of using the ideas that most people buy books— pepper dealers, fishwives, and the like, and literary pirates excepted. . . . Over and over again it comes back to the same question: I can read the contents of a book, learn, abridge, expand, teach, and translate it, write about it, laugh over it, find fault with it, use it poorly or well—in short, do with it whatever I will. But the one thing I should be prohibited from doing is copying or reprinting it. . . . A published book is a secret divulged. With what justification would a preacher forbid the printing of his homilies, since he cannot prevent his listeners from transcribing his sermon? Would it not be just as ludicrous for a professor to demand that his students refrain from using some new proposition he had taught them as for him to demand the same of book dealers with regard to a new book? *No, no, it is too obvious that the concept of intellectual property is useless. My property must be exclusively mine; I must be able to dispose of it and retrieve it unconditionally.* Let someone explain to me how that is possible in the present case. Just let someone try taking back the ideas he has originated once they have been communicated so that they are, as before, nowhere to be found. All the money in the world could not make that possible. (Krause, cited in and translated by Woodmansee, "Genius" 443–44; our emphasis)

We have quoted the accounts presented in Woodmansee's extensive review of primary sources to emphasize just how debatable—how *non*commonsensical and *non*obvious—the concepts of authorship and of intellectual property rights that we take for granted were during this period. More than a hundred years after Krause argued against the concept of intellectual property, Richard Rogers Bowker, author of an early twentieth-century American study of copyright laws, *Copyright: Its History and Its Law,* still felt the need to defend this concept.

It is sometimes said, as a bar to this idea of [intellectual] property, that no thought is new— that every thinker is dependent upon the gifts of nature and the thoughts of others thinking before him, as every tiller of the soil is dependent upon the land as given by nature and improved by the men who have toiled and tilled before him—a view of which Henry C. Carey has been the chief exponent in this country. But there is no real analogy—aside from the question whether the denial of individual property in land would not be setting back the hands of progress. If Farmer Jones does not raise potatoes from a piece of land, Farmer Smith can; but Shakespeare cannot write *Paradise Lost* nor Milton *Much Ado,* though before both Dante dreamed and Boccaccio told his tales. It was because of Milton and Shakespeare writing, not because of Dante and Boccaccio who had written, that these immortal works are treasures of the English tongue. It was the very self of each, *in propria persona,* that gave these form and worth, though they used words that had come down from generations as the common heritage of English-speaking men. Property in a stream of water, as has been pointed out, is not in the atoms of the water but in the flow of the stream. (3–4)

Bowker's defense actually echoes the eighteenth-century arguments that succeeded in establishing authors' claims of intellectual property rights—arguments perhaps most cogently expressed in Fichte's influential "Proof of the Illegality of Reprinting: A Rationale and a Parable." Following Young, Fichte asserted the existence of an organic relationship between a writer's ideas and the form in which they are expressed. This organic connection, Fichte argued, is so fundamental that to appropriate the form of a writer's ideas by reprinting a text is, in essence, to steal the writer's self, for "each individual has his own thought processes, his own way of forming concepts and connecting them. . . . All that we think we must think according to the analogy of our other habits of thought; and solely through reworking new thoughts after the analogy of our habitual thought processes do we make them our own" (Fichte, 227–28; cited in and translated by Woodmansee, "Genius" 445). Rather than locating ideas in God or in previous texts, Fichte identifies the source of ideas in writers themselves. Through their own thought processes, writers transform ideas so that they reflect their own individual genius.

A short step leads us from Fichte to the Romantics, whose assertions of originality, all the more striking because of their contrast with the increasing alienation and loss of independence catalyzed by the Industrial Revolution, helped further establish this new view of the writer as author. No longer would the writer be one of a number of craftspersons participating in the creation of a book. Wordsworth's and others' descriptions of the author's responsibility and achievement guaranteed a privileged place for both authors and their creations: "Genius is the introduction of a new element into the intellectual universe: or, if that be not allowed, it is the application of powers to objects on which they had not before been exercised, or the employment of them in such a manner as to produce effects hitherto unknown" (Wordsworth 184).

It is important to recognize that arguments like Young's, Fichte's, and Wordsworth's inherently and inevitably limit authorship to individuals writing alone. For if texts express an author's individual genius, how can a single text manifest the essential being of more than one person? The organic connection between writer and text—a connection so strong that the text in some sense represents or embodies the author—would be broken. Thus the same theoretical move that elevated certain kinds of poetry and prose to "literature" and guaranteed writers the ability to earn a living from their writing also inevitably defined the activity by which they did so as essentially isolating, even alienating. Terry Eagleton comments on some of the consequences of this move in his "Small History of Rhetoric":

> [During the Romantic Period] "Literature"—a privileged, "creative" use of language—was
> . . . brought to birth, with all the resonance and panoply attendant upon traditional rhetoric,
> but without either its "authoritarianism" or its audience. The former was countered by the
> "aesthetic": the latter compensated for by The Author. . . . In the absence of that known
> audience that was in a strict sense a material condition of rhetoric, the creative authorial
> subject was duly enthroned, source or medium of a transcendental discourse that spurned
> rather than wooed "the public." (107)

The question of how the work of literary authors came to be privileged by this growing and diverse body of readers and by English teachers over that of "ordinary" writers—journalists, scholars, scientists, and students—has yet to be fully explored. But as Eagleton notes, the Romantic period and later the Victorian period seem to be crucial times of transition, at least for England and for America. The Romantic poets self-consciously and defiantly asserted their separateness from the rest of British society. But that society assimilated them nevertheless, using their poetry as an escape from the general dreariness and competitiveness of life during the Industrial Revolution. The Romantic poets, they believed, expressed the best part of themselves—a part repressed in the Darwinian economic struggle that characterized that period. In their poetry, the Romantics achieved an independence, self-understanding, and organic wholeness that most Victorians found impossible to establish in their daily lives.

The Victorians' near adulation of authors such as Dickens, Scott, and Thackeray undoubtedly helped to establish what has come to be called the man-and-his-work tradition of literary criticism—a critical program that depends in essential ways on the identification of author and text. This identification is so complete, in fact, that the distinction between author and text almost collapses. Consider the following discussion of the difficulties inherent in literary criticism as presented by J. W. Saunders in *The Profession of English Letters*. Saunders has just been attempting to distinguish individuals whom he calls true men of letters from, say, hack journalists in terms of the differing products these writers produce:

> Another difficulty in discriminating between one book and another is that in the words we are always aware of the writer himself, of his uniqueness as a person, and of the life he sees about him, and these presences stand in the way of an objective opinion about an artifact, unconnected now that it is complete with its creator. If the writer is a little man, little in humanity, and if his insight into other men is limited, his book will be a mean book, no matter how good his technique or gift of the gab. If he is a big man, big in humanity, and his insight into other men is profound, his book is apt to be an important book, sometimes in spite of itself. . . . [Finally] the great authors lie on our bookshelves, superbly different from each other, and superbly indifferent to the attempts of critics to make them conform with each other. (7–8)

Readers who find Saunders' equation of authors' moral stature and humane vision with the texts they compose naive may be surprised to discover that *The Profession of English Letters* was published in 1964. Clearly, Saunders was writing at the end of the strongest period of the man-and-his-work criticism; he had not yet learned the new dictum that critics must look to authors' texts, not to their lives, to support their judgments about a work. For a variety of reasons, including the subservient role it allotted to critics and its emphasis on the *man* in man-and-his-work, this critical approach no longer seems reasonable. As Woodmansee points out, however, critics representing a broad theoretical spectrum still "share the belief that criticism has essentially to do with the recovery of a writer's meaning" ("Genius" 448).

In "What is an Author?" Michel Foucault urges scholars to examine "how the author became individualized in a culture like ours, what status he has been given, at what moment studies of authenticity and attribution began, in what kind of system of valorization the author was involved, at what point we began to recount the lives of authors rather than of heroes, and how this fundamental category of 'the man-and-his-work criticism' began" (141). As our own brief review of the history of the modern concept of authorship indicates, not only philosophical and aesthetic but legal, social, and economic factors must be considered. And yet, as Woodmansee notes, the issue of how various "levels of discourse . . . interact is one that historians of criticism have barely explored. This omission is unfortunate because it is precisely in the interplay of [these] . . . levels that critical concepts and principles as fundamental as that of authorship achieve their modern form" ("Genius" 440).

CONTEMPORARY CRITICISM AND THE PROBLEM OF THE AUTHOR

Problems are created, not found—at least in the scholarly world of ideas. Twenty years ago, most American literary critics would not have recognized the status of the author as problematic. They would, of course, have been familiar with specific cases where literary attribution was questionable. (Arguments over the authorship of certain or all of Shakespeare's work comprise perhaps the best known example of this phenomenon.) But they could only have been puzzled by assertions that the status of the author itself was not commonsensical and obvious but problematic and subject to revision.

Those familiar with contemporary criticism recognize that the status of the author is no longer taken for granted. In fact, the concept has been problematized, deconstructed, and challenged to such an extent that discussions of the problem of the author are decidedly old hat in literary circles. But because such discussions may be less than familiar to many teachers of writing and because the literary theorists who have so destabilized the concept rarely if ever attend in any concrete way to the pedagogical implication of such a destabilization, we think it worthwhile to review some of the most important challenges mounted by literary theorists to the traditional concept of the "author." Such challenges are important for what they can suggest about the nature and practice of collaborative writing.

As early as 1968 in his essay "The Death of the Author," Roland Barthes called attention to the author as a peculiarly modern construct. "The author," Barthes asserts, "is a modern figure, a product of our society insofar as, emerging from the Middle Ages with English empiricism, French rationalism and the personal faith of the Reformation, it discovered the prestige of the individual, of, as it is more nobly put, the 'human person' " (142–43). After lamenting that "the image of literature to be found is ordinarily centered on the author, his person, his life, his taste, his passions" (143), Barthes calls for a reversal of criticism's privileging of the author and the related devaluing of the reader: "Classic criticism has never paid any attention to the reader; for it, the writer is the only person in literature. . . . To give writing its future, it is necessary to overthrow the myth: the birth of the reader must be at the cost of the death of the Author" (148). Although Barthes' call for the death of the author may seem to present a radical challenge to literature in general and the author in particular, other interpretations of its significance question this view. (Interested readers may wish to consult Peggy Kamuf's analysis of Barthes' essay in *Signature Pieces: On the Institution of Authorship,* where Kamuf considers whether Barthes has "perhaps done nothing else than exchange the 'tyranny' of the idea of the author for that of the reader" [10].)

Since Barthes' essay appeared, an increasing number of critics representing an increasingly diverse range of critical perspectives have identified the problem of the author as a crucial issue facing contemporary criticism. In "What Is an Author," Foucault emphasizes not just the constructed nature of the concept of authorship but also its overdetermined power. "The coming into being of the notion of 'author' constitutes the privileged moment of *individualization* in the history of ideas, knowledge, literature, philosophy, and the sciences. Even today, when we reconstruct the history of a concept, literary genre, or school of philosophy, such categories seem relatively weak, secondary, and superimposed scansions in comparison with the solid and fundamental unit of the author and the work" (141, our emphasis).

Rather than naively assuming an unproblematic identification of author and work, Foucault argues, critics must recognize that authorship is essentially a function, one that "serves to characterize a certain mode of being of discourse" (147). Only certain texts have authors, after all. Many others—such as computer programs or federal regulations—do not. These distinctions are hardly accidental. Instead, they reflect "operations that we force texts to undergo, the connections that we make, the traits we recognize as pertinent, the continuities that we recognize, or the exclusions that we practice" (150).

Unlike Barthes, who in "The Death of the Author" calls for the reader to supplant the writer, Foucault argues for a more radical shift, one that would view texts as contested sites in a complex, situated world of political, cultural, economic, ideological, and other forces. Such a shift, Foucault observes, would inevitably change the kinds of questions literary critics ask of texts.

We would no longer hear the questions that have been rehashed for so long: "Who really spoke? Is it really he and not someone else? With what authenticity or originality? And what part of his deepest self did he express in his discourse?" Instead, there would be other questions like these: "What are the modes of existence of this discourse? Where has it been used, how can it circulate, and who can appropriate it for himself? What are the places in it where there is room for possible subjects? Who can assume these various subject-functions?" And behind all these questions we would hear hardly anything but the stirring of an indifference: "What difference does it make who is speaking?" (160)

It is not surprising that theoreticians such as Barthes and Foucault should highlight the consequences of any effort to redefine the author for literary criticism as a scholarly and professional activity. As Josué V. Harari comments in "Critical Factions/Critical Fictions," "It is a well-documented fact that 'author' and 'criticism' have developed together along institutionalized lines from the sixteenth century until the present day" (69). It may not be accidental, then, that current efforts to question or devalorize the author have coincided with a redrawing—or collapsing—of the boundaries between criticism and literature. When the author of a literary work was viewed as uniquely empowered and self-expressive, criticism and the critic could be no more than a handmaid to literature. In a poststructuralist literary world, however, poem and commentary share the same status: they are text. And, as Harari notes, "The text offers a new economy in which no one language is privileged over any other. It is the utopian meeting place of subject and language, a *working* space . . . where meaning is in permanent flux and where the author is either an effect or a 'guest' of the text and not its originator" (40).

Although those who find poststructuralist theory unsatisfying have at times charged critics such as Derrida and others with attempting (consciously or unconsciously) merely to dethrone the author so the critic can reign, there are more deepseated reasons why the author has, for many modern critics, become a problem. Perhaps the most important of these involves a much broader questioning of the nature of the subject. Since Descartes, the notion of the self or subject as the individual cogito—the source of knowledge and hence of broader social and cultural meaning—has been accepted in the Western tradition. Within this existing ideology, Catherine Belsey notes, "It appears 'obvious' that people are autonomous individuals, possessed of subjectivity or consciousness which is the source of their beliefs and actions" (58). Scholars in a range of disciplines, such as Richard Rorty, Clifford Geertz, Thomas Kuhn, and Stephen Toulmin, have begun to question this assumption.

A recent collection, *Reconstructing Individualism: Autonomy, Individuality, and the Self in Western Thought*, presents essays originally delivered at a conference entitled "Reconstructing Individualism" held at Stanford University, 18–20 February 1984. The editors of this collection, Thomas C. Heller, Morton Sosna, and David Wellbery, cite the following as one of the general assumptions that informed this multidisciplinary conference: "Some form of individualism—broadly perceived as the view that the individual human subject is the maker of the world we inhabit—has been a key factor in the life of the West for the last five hundred years. Modern definitions of the self and psychology, of ethical responsibility and civic identity, and of artistic representation and economic behavior all rest on the notion of an individual whose will and values, whose expressions and preferences are essential constituents of that reality" (1). Those contributing essays to this volume include sociologists, historians, philosophers, educators, and critics of English, German, and Italian literature. Although these scholars' approaches and methods are diverse, all recognize the need to critique the concept of the individual, to rethink the subject and subjectivity.

Within literary studies, quite naturally, this concern with rethinking the subject has focused on textual issues and on the status of the author as the individual-who-produces-text. Structuralism, of course, shifted the emphasis from the full subject to the text as systemed structure. But by directly addressing epistemological and metaphysical questions, poststructuralists, including Derrida, question the status of the subject, and thus of the author, even more strongly.

There are other reasons why some literary critics have become engaged with the problem of the author. Marxists, for instance, question the traditional author's purported independence (an independence often achieved by voluntary or imposed isolation). Rather than privileging the author as inspired creator, critics such as Raymond Williams prefer to view the author as

> a characteristic form of bourgeois thought. No man is author of himself in the absolute sense which these [traditional] descriptions imply. As a physical individual he is of course specific, though within a determining genetic inheritance. As a social individual he is also specific, but within the social forms of his time and place. The crucial argument then turns on the nature of this specificity and these forms, and on the relations between them. In the case of the writer one of these social forms is central: his language. To be a writer in English is to be already socially specified. But the argument moves beyond this: at one level to an emphasis on socially inherited forms, in the generic sense; at another level to an emphasis on socially inherited and still active notations and conventions; at a final level to an emphasis on a continuing process in which not only the focus but the contents of consciousness are socially produced. (192)

Writing not as a Marxist but as a critic committed to the belief that texts cannot fruitfully be studied in isolation from their cultural, legal, political, and economic contexts, Edward Said also questions the traditional connection of author and text: "To what extent is a text itself not something passively attributable, as effect is to cause, to a person? To what extent is a text so discontinuous a series of subtexts or pretexts or paratexts or surtexts as to beggar the idea of the author as simple producer?" (58).

Feminists have, in diverse ways, also questioned the conventional concept of the author, recognizing that the problem of the author has been a particularly important one for women—until our own century often denied not only the possibility of authoring but of writing. As Elaine Showalter notes in her introduction to *The New Feminist Criticism: Essays on Women, Literature, and Theory*, early feminists generally focused on exploring "the misogyny of literary practice: the stereotyped images of women in literature as angels or monsters, the literary abuse or textual harassment of women in classic and popular male literature, and the exclusion of women from literary history" (5). Accordingly, feminist critics in England and America viewed the conventional concept of the author largely as a pragmatic problem. When they considered the status of the author in patriarchal Western culture, they asked questions like the following: How can feminists claim literary *author*ity for works by women conventionally excluded from the canon, such as Harriet Beecher Stowe's *Uncle Tom's Cabin*? How can they locate and convince others to publish (or publish themselves) such neglected masterpieces as Kate Chopin's *The Awakening*? How can they enable their female students to recognize that recounting the stories of their lives is as valid as more traditional academic and professional writing?

As Toril Moi indicates in *Sextual/Textual Politics: Feminist Literary Theory*, this pragmatic approach to feminist criticism dominated the early efforts of many Anglo-American feminists. In her study, which contrasts the projects of Anglo-American and French feminists, Moi criticizes Anglo-American feminists for failing to question "the notion of the unitary self, the central concept of Western male humanism" (7). This humanism, Moi charges, is "in effect part of patriarchal ideology. At its centre is the seamless unified self—either individual or collective—which is commonly called 'Man.'. . . In this humanist ideology the self is the *sole author* of history and of the literary text: the humanist creator is potent, phallic, and male— God in relation to his world, the author in relation to his text" (8).

Arguments like that of Toril Moi have raised new issues in contemporary feminist theory—issues which foreground the problematic status of the author and the theoretical and political consequences of a failure to critique this construct. Although many feminists remain committed to efforts to recover and promote writing by women, few can avoid addressing questions raised by such French feminists as Julia Kristeva, Helene Cixous, and Luce Irigaray. Though these theorists' projects are hardly identical, all raise as central two related questions: (1) What does it mean to be a woman? and (2) What does it mean to be a woman writing? The resultant probing, which Peggy Kamuf characterizes as "thinking-beyond-the-subject," challenges "the metaphysical construction of women's exclusion . . . [and] the 'phallocentrism' at the base of virtually all Western habits of thought" (vii).

It would be impossible to leave this review of literary critical challenges to the traditional concept of the author without mentioning the work of the Russian Marxist critic Mikhail Bakhtin. His dialogic theory of language foregrounds context rather than text, and the focus on context—a multiple set of conditions—makes any particular word or phrase in the language "heteroglossic"—a polyphonous collision of possibilities:

> Thus at any given moment of its historical existence, language is heteroglot from top to bottom: it represents the co-existence of socio-ideological contraditions between the present and the past, between differing epochs of the past, between different socio-ideological groups in the present, between tendencies, schools, circles, and so forth. . . . As a living, socio-ideological concrete thing, as heteroglot opinion, language, for the individual consciousness, lies on the border between oneself and the other. . . . The word does not exist in a neutral and impersonal language . . . but rather it exists in other people's mouths, in other people's contexts. (*Dialogic* 291–94)

Bakhtin's notion of heteroglossic language implies a polyphonic self, one that can never constitute the single "voice" traditionally ascribed to the author. Indeed, Bakhtin's dialogics denies the very possibility of anything approaching a unitary individual self. Gary Saul Morson notes, "For Bakhtin, the creation of a self is the selection of one innerly persuasive voice from among the many voices you have learned, and that voice keeps changing every time it says something" (232).

"There are," critical biographers Clark and Holquist quote Bakhtin as stating, "no pure texts, nor can there be" (169). Any text, in Bakhtin's view, is fundamentally not just shared but heteroglot, hybrid, competing. And the author of a novel—Dostoyevsky, for example—is similarly impure and multiple. "Dostoyevsky and his characters are all equally compounded of language. They are words, combinations of their own and others' words, all selves constructed out of other selves" (Clark and Holquist 246).

Given his belief in the profoundly polyphonic, contested nature of language, it is perhaps appropriate that Bakhtin's own authorship of a number of texts should also be disputed. The question of the authorship of certain works sometimes attributed to Bakhtin can probably never be fully resolved. It is generally accepted, however, that Bakhtin chose to publish a number of major and minor studies under the names of others. *The Formal Method in Literary Scholarship* first appeared as the work of his friend Medvedev, while *Marxism and the Philosophy of Language* and *Freudianism: A Critical Sketch* were published as the work of his colleague Vološinov. Clark and Holquist, whose critical biography helped introduce Bakhtin to the West, have commented that "the problem of answering the apparently naive question of who wrote which of the disputed texts addresses the same set of complexities that Bakhtin placed at the heart of his theories. If, as he maintained early and late, the relation between self and other is the key to all human understanding, and if 'Quests for my own word are quests for a word that is not my own,' then how can we ever assign responsibility for the acts that words are?" (169).

As this brief review of literary theory has demonstrated, the concepts of the author and of authorship (the assignment of "responsibility for the acts that words are") have indeed become contested and radically unstable. Though it may at times seem tempting to dismiss inquiries such as those we have discussed here as merely speculative or theoretical, our study of shifting conceptions in the history of authorship indicates that material changes in the conditions of authorship are often accompanied by vigorous intellectual debate over the nature and definition of this concept, such as that occurring today. We believe, then, that these theoretical probings should inform and test both the theory and the practice of teaching writing.

CONTEMPORARY DISCURSIVE PRACTICES AND CHALLENGES TO THE TRADITIONAL CONCEPT OF AUTHORSHIP

The preceding brief discussion of literary studies has demonstrated that the concept of the author is at present radically destablized in theory. We should not be surprised to discover that this same instability appears also in contemporary discursive practices. In this closing section of chapter 3, we look at a number of practices, such as corporate authorship, the increasing attribution of honorary authorship in the sciences, and the electronic media—practices that implicitly, and sometimes explicitly, challenge the traditional concept of authorship. Because these activities are embedded in current practices, it can be difficult to assess their significance and to recognize the connections between apparently disparate phenomena. Future critics charting the development—and possible dissolution and reconstitution—of the concept of authorship may see consequences that we can only hint at here. Nevertheless, because these practices suggest that our teaching of writing is in many ways naive, and because they may be helpful in understanding the phenomenon of collaborative writing, we have chosen to include them here.

Although it is tempting to begin this discussion by presenting such extreme deviations from the traditional concept of authorship as ghostwriting and managed textbooks, we wish to begin by describing a less striking—but perhaps more unsettling—indication that the status of the author is destabilized and problematic. We refer here to the reports of those who, more than any other group, must confront the problem of the author on a daily basis—the librarians who must catalogue the increasing volume of printed and other material published each year. As Michael Carpenter indicates in *Corporate Authorship: Its Role in Library Cataloguing*, librarians have always found the traditional concept of authorship difficult to apply. Some of their difficulties, Carpenter notes, derive from ambiguities inherent in the concept of writing. As part of an effort to explain why the conventional concept of authorship, described by Carpenter as "authorship by origination," is inadequate, Carpenter in effect deconstructs the word *writing* into the following categories: "writing down," "writing up," "writing out," "writing in," and "writing over" (126).

By "writing down" Carpenter refers to "the kind of writing requiring the least intellectual involvement on the part of the writer because it is essentially mere transcription of what is dictated" (126–27). A businessperson dictating a standard letter of transmittal is in Carpenter's terms "writing down," and so is a student writing down a professor's lectures or a court reporter transcribing criminal proceedings. Generally, "writing down" does not, Carpenter believes, "appear to be a necessary condition for authorship," although notable exceptions (Boswell's life of Johnson, Robert Craft's reports of conversations with Stravinsky) certainly exist (127).

The activity that Carpenter describes as "writing up" most closely approximates the traditional concept of authorship. "Writing up," Carpenter observes, "involves the creation of the semantic content of a precise text" (127). "Writing up" challenges writers to produce both form and content: Carpenter cites as a paradigmatic example of "writing up" Yeats' practice of writing his poems from prose drafts. Because of the writer's "high degree of intellectual involvement" with the material (127), those engaged in the activity of "writing up" would naturally be considered authors. Carpenter cites a number of cases, however, in which such designation does not occur. One such example: "Experiments are done in a large library, and the experimenter asks an assistant to write up the results. It is conceivable that the assistant, in addition to doing the writing up, has also performed the actual experiments and participated in their design. Yet it frequently occurs that only the name of the chief experimenter appears on the title page, while the assistant receives no recognition in the publication" (129).

"Writing out," Carpenter observes, has two diverse meanings. Secretaries "write out" ideas when they fill out notes taken during a business meeting. Depending on how he or she completes the task, someone ghostwriting an autobiography may be "writing up" or "writing out." The activity that Carpenter refers to as "writing out" occurs when "the formulation of the ideas into language takes place just prior to or simultaneously with their expression in written form" (131). "Writing out" may or may not justify ascription of authorship, Caprenter notes, depending on whether the ideas expressed were conceived by the writer or by others.

Contracts, invoices, will forms, all are examples of Carpenter's fourth category, "writing in." This activity can involve something as simple as dating a lease or filling out an invoice, but it can also require the complex adaptation and interweaving of boilerplate materials as occurs, for instance, in large grant proposals. Although Carpenter does not discuss the appropriateness of basing claims for authorship in situations involving "writing in," current practices clearly vary. An educational researcher applying for an individual grant and for a team contract research grant might draw upon the same boilerplate materials in writing both grant proposals. In the first situation, the researcher would undoubtedly be cited as the author of the grant proposal, while in the second he or she would not.

Carpenter uses the term "writing over" to refer to a number of related phenomena, including revising, compiling, redacting, abridging, and expanding. In all of these activities, a number of factors can influence the likelihood that a person will be cited as an author. Carpenter notes that "the rewriter who adds new textual material or provides a supplement is usually considered the author" (132), while an editor who revises a text for style is not. When is updating considered so substantial as to, in effect, create a completely new text? The answer to this and other similar questions seems completely context dependent.

As the preceding summary of these intriguing categories demonstrates, Carpenter has subjected the traditional concept of authorship to rigorous examination—one that would not be necessary, he notes, if librarians were not faced with the demands of cataloguing group-written materials. "With the solitary writer it is not necessary to make the distinctions already made in this chapter, except for the intrinsic desire to bring out logical complications in what are apparently single phenomena" (134). These complications are indeed sufficiently unyielding that Carpenter is forced to conclude that cataloguers must abandon adherence to the origination theory of authorship: "One is not sure what constitutes authorship by origination, either as the facts actually are or as they are represented to be in connection with a publication. The difficulties posed by the presence of continua and boderline questions remain" (137).

Carpenter developed his meticulous study for the most pragmatic of reasons—to respond to a situation that he presents as a crisis for library cataloguers:

> A casual inspection of bibliographies of government documents reveals an increasing rate of [corporate] publications in recent years. The publications of learned societies, not only their transactions but even more their abstracting services, have increased in both numbers of titles and amounts of materials in the same span of time. The production of technical reports—almost all of which emanate from corporate bodies such as universities, government agencies, and foundations—and government-sponsored research institutes seems to have "exploded" even more recently. . . . Corporate entry is a fact in the world of library cataloguing. Its limits and extent are not settled and cannot be until a justification for treating corporate bodies as authors can be found. (4)

Carpenter's intriguing deconstruction of writing into "writing down," "writing up," "writing out," "writing in," and "writing over" might be viewed as a preliminary response to Foucault's call in "What Is an Author" for an analysis of "author functions." Yet Carpenter makes no reference to Foucault's work or to any other literary investigations of the problem of authorship. He is writing as one cataloguer faced with a problem to others in similar situations.

The studies of Carpenter and others emphasize the extent to which contemporary challenges to the concept of authorship reflect material changes in writing practices and in the ways in which written products are "counted" as intellectual property. In "Traditional Interpretations of 'Authorship' and 'Responsibility' in the Description of Scientific and Technical Documents," Piternick emphasizes the conditions that have caused discipline-oriented abstracting services to focus on the contribution of the individual, while other abstracting services "place more emphasis on the responsibility of the employer, as compared with the individual scientist, for a particular document" (25). These distinctions have pragmatic consequences for those using these services, as Piternick emphasizes with the series of questions that begin her essay: "Why do the bibliographic descriptions in *Government Reports Announcements* always list a corporate name first? Why do scientific and technical abstracting services of AACR and AACR2 list only a maximum of three authors? Why is it difficult to find conference proceedings volumes using *Chemical Abstracts*? Why do some abstracting services not index corporate names?" (17).

Why do all abstracting services not use the same decision-making procedures? The reason, Piternick believes, derives most strongly from the differing situations of those performing research. Some scientists work independently. In this situation the scientist, often a university professor, "'dreams up' a research project, obtains funding to carry it out, and then directs the work" (19). Resulting research is published in peer review journals, with the scientist, and possibly team members, accepting both responsibility and credit for their efforts.

Scientists completing contract research face a very different situation. These scientists do not "dream up" research projects; instead, they respond to highly limited requests for proposals. More importantly, the funding agency contracts not with the scientists who write the grant application but with their employers. The terms of the grant may or may not allow scientists to publish research findings, presented as required reports to the contractor, in conference papers or journal articles. Scientists may also conduct research for an employer, such as a drug company. Research conducted in this setting is "directed to solving problems or developing new products or processes which will make more money for . . . [the] employer" (20). Scientists conducting research in this setting may be free to publish their research, though often only after the process of applying for a patent has begun.

Various abstracting services, Piternick argues, inevitably respond to the differing situations of their primary users. Discipline-oriented abstracting services, such as *Chemical Abstracts,* have focused on "journal articles and conference proceedings. . . ; on the contribution of the individual; and largely on independent research." Not surprisingly, these abstracting services typically "list and index all whose names appear as 'authors' on a title page" (21). Other abstracting services, such as *Government Reports Announcements and Index* (GRA) and *Scientific and Technical Aerospace Reports* (STAR), proceed quite differently, emphasizing employer or corporate responsibility. Thus, in these services, "the corporate name, which would appear as an affiliation after the personal author name(s) in the discipline-oriented services, here takes precedence over the personal name(s)" (25).

Piternick provides examples that graphically demonstrate the problems that can result when a discipline-oriented abstracting service indexes:

> The nature of research in High Energy Physics is such that it involves the collaboration of many scientists, resulting in papers with large numbers of "authors." In 1962 a group of collaborators published a communication in *Physical Review Letters* under the names of the three laboratories where they worked instead of their own names (much to the indignation of the Editor of that journal). *Physics Abstracts* made no mention of the three institutions in the bibliographic description and they were not indexed; in other words, the paper was treated as anonymous.

> In 1970, papers on the analysis of lunar rocks retrieved in the July 1969 moon landing began to appear. One of these published in *Science* was attributed to "The Lunar Sample Preliminary Examination Team." The individual members of the team, 62 in number, were listed alphabetically by name in a footnote as "the people who contributed directly to obtaining the data and to preparation of this report." The reaction of *Chemical Abstracts* to the report was to ignore the team designation and to list as authors the first name appearing in the footnote, along with "et al." to represent the other 61 team members, in both the bibliographic description and the authors' index. (24)

In these two cases, individuals who desired to be identified as members of teams were denied this form of attribution. The first team was denied any role at all and consigned to anonymity, while the second team—or at least its first-named member—unwillingly had authorship thrust upon them.

Although in her article Piternick emphasizes the significance of recognizing "the importance of the context of research in influencing practices in description and indexing" (33), her focus, like that of Carpenter, is pragmatic. Current divergent practices in attributing authorship to scientific and technical documents make it difficult for users to access the information they need. At the close of her discussion, Piternick indicates the urgency of addressing the problems raised in her essay "before the online revolution sweeps over us" (31).

Piternick's concern is warranted, for electronic media have indeed already had an impact on the problems faced by librarians. In a brief article in *Science* titled "Copyrights Obsolete in an Electronic Age, OTA Finds," Eliot Marshall summarizes an April 1986 report by the Office of Technology Assessment. Arguing that both copyright and patent laws will need to be revised in response to electronic media, the report observes that, "It may be hard to establish who an author is, or what percentage of the product he or she may rightly claim, when many people contribute simultaneously to a data-base or computerized product. Many things, from newspaper articles to airplane designs, are created by joint efforts focused in a single computer's brain" (572).

It is no accident that scientific and technical documents present the most challenging problems for librarians. For, as we indicated in our discussion of citation index studies in chapter 1, modern science is a thoroughly collaborative enterprise. As such, current scientific practices present a number of challenges to the traditional concept of authorship.

Perhaps the most central of these challenges involves the practice of "honorary authorship," the naming of individuals as coauthors who have not been directly involved with the research reported in published papers. Honorary authorship extends well beyond the relatively common practice of including the name of a senior scientist—the head of a project or laboratory—on a paper, whether that scientist has contributed to the research (or even read the report) or not. In an article in *Science,* "The Publishing Game: Getting More for Less," William J. Broad notes that honorary authorship can include "the free and easy listing of those who had isolated a cell line, clone, or virus—a practice that can result in hundreds of 'papers' for the isolator" (1137).

The same article in *Science* reported that honorary authorship inevitably contributes to a new and unsettling phenomenon in scientific publishing: individuals who write journal editors insisting that their names be removed from articles accepted for publication. Evelyn S. Meyers, managing editor of the *American Journal of Psychiatry,* was interviewed by *Science* about this practice. These requests occur most often, according to Meyers, when a research group disbands or evolves "and the lead author of the splinter group will list all the original groups out of courtesy." If members of the original group "do not like the direction that the research took," they may request that their names be removed (1138).

The increasing incidence of coauthorship in the sciences also raises important questions about ethics and the responsibility for a text. The *Science* article describes a typical case, involving research published in the *New England Journal*:

> The lead article in the 12 January 1978 issue of the *New England Journal* was a report on paranoid schizophrenics, authored by four researchers. Soon after it came out, [Arnold] Relman [editor of the journal] noted that a similar article published in the January 1978 issue of the *American Journal of Society* reached conclusions that were the opposite. He also noted that the papers shared two authors in common. "Coauthorship," the *New England* editors wrote in a 18 May column on the incident, "like sole authorship, must surely imply responsibility for a paper and not merely endorsement of parts of it. If it does not, who if anyone is responsible?" (1137)

The authors of an article in *Nature* about the case of Dr. John Darsee, a scientist who forged data that played a role in more than 100 publications over a three-year period, also question the ethics of honorary authorship. Walter W. Stewart and Ned Feder studied 109 publications by Darsee and forty-seven other scientists. Their objective "was to discover whether [their examination of the published scientific reports] would throw light on the vigilance of referees, of editors of journals and of Darsee's coauthors in meeting the standards conventionally accepted as necessary in the scientific literature" (207). Their results, they believe, cast some doubt on the integrity of scientific literature.

Their analysis of the errors in Darsee's published papers, supplemented by reports from committees investigating the fraud, led Stewart and Feder to question the role of honorary authors. "Honorary authorships falsify the assignment of responsibility for published research and increase the likelihood that inaccurate data will be published. The honorary author is in a poor position to judge the validity of the work, yet he often lends a prestige that may lull other coauthors, the reviewers and the readers into uncritical and inappropriate acceptance" (213). Several articles responding to Stewart and Feder's study continued the discussion of this complex issue, one which will hardly disappear. An editorial on "Fraud, Libel, and the Literature" in this same issue noted: "Coauthorship as such is a necessary consequence of the way that science is now practiced, enabling people with different skills to work together on a project; it is also capable of being abused" (182).

The questions raised by honorary authorship only highlight ethical problems inherent in scientific collaboration and attribution. Researchers in sociology and psychology have devoted considerable attention to the ethical and pragmatic consequences of attribution. Articles by Zuckerman; Patel; Clemente; Mitchell; Spiegel and Keith-Spiegel; Over; Bridgwater, Bornstein, and Wallenback; and Over and Smallman all explore collaborative practices in their own or other fields. Spiegel and Keith-Spiegel's research is of particular interest because it explores a number of possible collaborative research situations in the field of psychology. Spiegel and Keith-Spiegel sent a questionnaire describing these situations—the continuing research team, the highly qualified subdoctoral assistant, professor and student collaborative research—to three groups of psychologists, who were asked to determine which of several provided options for attribution they believed to be appropriate. One of Spiegel and Keith-Spiegel's hypothetical situations follows, along with the survey results:

Professor and Student Collaborative Research

A professor and one of his students collaborated on a research idea for the student's assigned class project. They designed the experiment together, the student collected all of the data, analyzed them statistically, and wrote up a report. The professor rechecked the data analysis and found that no errors were made: the professor also revised the paper in a form that would be acceptable for publication.

Survey Results

(a) The student should have senior authorship, and the professor, junior authorship. (58%)

(b) The professor should have senior authorship, and the student, junior authorship. (32%)

(c) The professor and student should flip a coin to determine authorship. (4%)

(d) The professor should only receive footnote credit because he assisted primarily in his function as a teacher. (50%)

(e) The student should only have footnote credit because the writing and eventual publication were made possible by the professor's skill, experience, and status. (0%) (741)

In response to the need to make judgments about authorship in situations such as these, some professional associations, such as the American Psychological Association, have developed guidelines designed to resolve these issues. Nevertheless, given the changing nature of scientific research and the institution-specific nature of scientific practices, much concern remains. In an article on "Authorship Recognition of Subordinates in Collaborative Research," Alan G. Heffner found that "quantitative and qualitative data from the social and natural sciences suggest that publication credit is not always accorded on the basis of universalist principles. It was also found that females may have fewer opportunities in collaborative research to contribute to the same extent as males and that when they do, they are frequently excluded from authorship" (377).

The complexity and ethical sensitivity of this situation—not to mention its very real consequences—has prompted some individuals to call for revisions in methods of attributing authorship. Simon, for instance, suggests the creation of a coding scheme that would clarify an author's role in a project. "Perhaps a several-dimensional code scheme could resolve the dilemma. For example, it might be possible to indicate with a single integer or letter whether a coauthor was responsible for all, most, an equal share, a small part, or none of the initiation of the project. Another integer or letter could express what part of the field work a coauthor did. Still another integer or letter could tell who drafted the article" (266). Given the difficulty of developing and enforcing such a coding system, readers may not be surprised to discover that scientists and others concerned with the status of authorship in their field so far have vented their frustration through humor, rather than attempting to revise the current system of scholarly attribution.

In his "Modest Proposal," Ralph E. Weston proposed in 1962 that physicists "apply the concept of 'team research' logically, consistently, and enthusiastically." Individual scientists in such groups must "forego the pleasure of seeing their names emblazoned in 8-point Baskerville and accept authorship designated by a group name" (78), such as the Harvard-MIT "Yankees." Weston goes on to propose the formation of subgroups of teams and the careful recording of "writing averages" (79). Weston signed his article "Ralph Emerson Weston, R. Emerson Weston, R. E. Weston, Ralph E. Weston, and several others" (80).

University teachers in the humanities might be tempted to dismiss as unfortunate but irrelevant to their own situation the scientific collaborative practices described here. And, certainly, collaborative research is less common in the humanities than in the sciences and social sciences. Whether or not they are writing collaboratively, however, all professionals today must respond to the consequences of the electronic media in an age increasingly dependent on the generation and exchange of information. In "Information and Knowledge: The Computer as a Medium of Humanistic Communication," J. David Bolter emphasizes the need for humanists to focus on the ways in which electronic technologies are altering the nature of literacy. Bolter notes that the interactive nature of electronic text has important consequences for the reader-writer relationship and for the concept of authorship.

> This interactive partnership redefines the very nature of authorship. . . . Collective authorship has a long tradition. In the age of manuscripts, notes were added and altered by generations of anonymous scholars, and words and phrases originally meant as glosses were sometimes copied directly into the text. A very different view of authorship grew up in an age of printing. A printed book was by nature monumental. . . . The electronic medium now threatens to reverse the attitudes fostered by the press by breaking down the barrier between author and reader. When the reader becomes the author's collaborator, authorship loses its privileged status. Anyone can become an author and send his merest thoughts over one of the networks to hundreds of unwilling readers. His act of "publication" is neither an economic nor a social event. And he can hardly claim to own the copyright to words that he sends so casually over phone lines and cables and satellite links to destinations he cannot even name. (7)

It has become commonplace in composition studies to emphasize that writing and reading are inherently and inextricably embedded in a culture's technological, social, political, economic, legal, and ideological practices. This chapter's multiperspectival investigation of the concept of authorship confirms and deepens the implications of this assertion, as it reminds us that terms like *author* and *authorship,* which can seem commonsensical, natural, and inevitable, are instead—as Bakhtin would have us understand—contested sites that, if interrogated, can reveal much about our culture. In "Terministic Screens," Kenneth Burke notes that "any given terminology is a *reflection* of reality; by its very nature as a terminology it must be a *selection* of reality; and to this extent it must function also as a *deflection* of reality" (45). Our discussion in this chapter indicates the extent to which our concept of authorship is itself a construct. Rather than representing an inherent and natural connection between the "man (sic) and his work," authorship functions in multiple, complex, and often conflicting ways. This constructed nature of authorship—and challenges to the traditional concept—appear in many contemporary sources in the sciences and the humanities, in corporations and in libraries. These challenges have great suggestive power for writing teachers, who deal every day with student authors producing texts. A central question raised by the perspectives presented in this chapter is to what extent our teaching practice is challenged by the historical and theoretical explorations and discursive practices reviewed in this chapter.

INTERTEXTS

Today the climate for learning in most colleges and schools is one of competition. Students compete for grades, withhold information from one another to "get ahead," to maintain their competitive advantage, and on many campuses there is widespread cheating.

But our most consequential human problems will be resolved not through competition, but collaboration. And what we need in education is a learning climate in which students work together. In such an atmosphere, truth emerges, as authentic insights are conscientiously exchanged.—Ernest L. Boyer, "Cooperation, Not Competition"

*   *   *   *   *

It's a sunny Saturday afternoon, yet all over America students saddled with group projects are stuck indoors, munching on chocolate chip cookies, guzzling beer, and arguing about what Nietzsche meant when he said, "In individuals, insanity is rare, but in groups, parties, nations, and epochs, it is the rule."

"Look, guys, forget Nietzsche," says the Pragmatist. "We're going to be here all night if we don't finish tabulating these surveys."

"Well, I think Chris should be here to help us," chimes in the Whiner. "Why should we do all the work? Wheeeeeeeere's Chriisssss?"

"I called him an hour ago. He said he'd be over in 10 minutes. Let's get started on these. . . ."

"I think we should take a vote," says the Defender of Democracy. "Now, everybody in favor. . . . "

"In favor of what?"

"Taking a vote."

"Look, as soon as I finish typing this up, I'll let you guys know what conclusions we've reached," announces the Workhorse, who's over in the corner flailing away at her Smith-Corona.

"Why do professors always assign these pain-in-the-ass projects?"

"It teaches us to work together. . . ."

"It fosters a sense of academic community. . . ."

"It gives us some new and different perspectives. . . ."

"It means fewer papers to grade."

AH, THE DREADED GROUP PROJECT.—Robin DeRieux, "Brewing Up a Great Group Project"

*　　*　　*　　*　　*

We have argued in this book that educators can help women develop their own authentic voices if they emphasize connection over separation, understanding and acceptance over assessment, and collaboration over debate; if they accord respect to and allow time for the knowledge that emerges from firsthand experience; if instead of imposing their own expectations and arbitrary requirements, they encourage students to evolve their own patterns of work based on the problems they are pursuing. These are the lessons we have learned in listening to women's voices.—Belenky, Clinchy, Goldberger, and Tarule, Women's Ways of Knowing

*　　*　　*　　*　　*

Institutionally at least, collaboration to some extent suggests cheating and sneakiness. So we're not doing "real work"; we're not slaving alone in our little cold garrets suffering to write poetry in isolation. Collaboration for us is a revolutionary act; we are directly subverting the romanticized notion of what a poet is, and by extension, what a poem is.—Miriam May and Jamie Shepherd, "Collaboration as Subversion"

*　　*　　*　　*　　*

Regardless of their specific model and method, most writing courses are based on the notion of the subject as a rational, coherent and unitary individual who, at all times, is present to himself.—Mas'ud Zavarzadeh and Donald Morton, "Theory Pedagogy Politics: The Crisis of 'The Subject' in the Humanities"

*　　*　　*　　*　　*

Better college teaching will occur classroom by classroom, with close attention to how students learn as well as to what they learn, said speakers at the American Association for Higher Education's annual meeting here last week.

Learning through collaboration was widely hailed as an effective approach to "taking teaching seriously," the conference's theme.

Yet speakers pointed out that American higher education by nature promotes competition, not cooperation, and may fail in its own ambitions as a result.

"The 'implicit curriculum' at colleges and universities is one of turf battles, intellectual compromises, competitive grading, and a peer-review process that threatens rather than supports faculty members," Mr. Astin said.

"Students learn those lessons all too well," he added.—Scott Heller, "Collaboration in the Classroom Is Crucial if Teaching Is to Improve, Educators Say"

*　　*　　*　　*　　*

The fact that the College [of Basic Studies at Boston University] has chosen to retain a group research and writing project for twenty-four years underscores the faculty judgment, supported by student feedback, that this experience is useful and educationally desirable for the students.—William E. Davis, Jr., and George F. Estey, "Research and Writing by Student Groups: Difficult But Rewarding"

*　　*　　*　　*　　*

Teachers often do not practice what they teach. That's a sentiment no one would deny, but I have recently been especially struck by the gap between theory and practice when it comes to collaboration. Many teachers, especially writing teachers, encourage students to work and learn together, but most of us rarely collaborate in our own professional writing.—Eugene Garver, "Collaborating Philosophically"

*   *   *   *   *

The collaborative process, when applied to the curriculum, may also reveal new approaches to the challenges that face American higher education in the next decades. New populations of students need to become collaborators in shaping programs and courses that address their needs; collaborators who can bring together the perspectives of non-Western cultures with those of the West will be essential to creating an education that is more globally enlightened; and collaborators who understand the practical world of our social institutions beyond the walls of learning need to engage with those within it.—Karen T. Romer, "Collaboration: New Forms of Learning, New Ways of Thinking"

*   *   *   *   *

Recognizing that the happiest students are actively involved in their own education, more and more colleges are encouraging their undergraduates to collaborate with professors. In laboratories and libraries, faculty members and students are working elbow-to-elbow on research projects ranging from the study of warped galaxies to the causes of winter depression.—Katherine S. Mangan, "Undergraduates, Professors Collaborate on Research at More and More Colleges"

The "symbol-using animal," yes, obviously. But can
we bring ourselves to realize just what that formula
implies, just how much of what we mean by
"reality" has been built up for us through nothing
but our symbol systems? Take away our books, and
what little do we know about history, biography,
even something so "down to earth" as the relative
position of seas and continents? . . . In school, as
they go from class to class, students turn from one
idiom to another. The various courses in the
curriculum are in effect but so many different
terminologies. And however important to us is the
tiny sliver of reality each of us has experienced
firsthand, the whole overall "picture" is but a
construct of our symbol systems. To meditate on
this fact until one sees its full implications is much
like peering over the edge of things into an ultimate
abyss.—Kenneth Burke (*Language* 5)

4 / The Pedagogy of Collaboration

The concepts of author and authorship, so radically destabilized in contemporary literary theory and current discursive practice, have not surprisingly been problematized in the field of rhetoric and composition, where scholars have challenged the
traditional exclusion of student writing from claims to "real writing" and "authorship" and explored the ways in which *author*ity can be established and experienced
by students, in spite of the distinction ordinarily drawn—albeit implicitly—between
literary "authors" and student "writers." In both areas of study, the move to examine
processes—either constitutive theories of reading or constitutive theories of writing—reflects shifting epistemological assumptions that foreground the relationship
between individuals and social groups. Using the work of Stanley Fish and David
Bartholomae as the locus for a discussion of "parallel tracks" in literary and composition studies, Patricia Sullivan notes that both theorists "move from an earlier view
of knowledge as an individual construction to the view that knowledge is a function
of the linguistic norms of a discourse community." Both fields, she continues, have
shifted attention from "extracting truth from autonomous texts" to understanding

the "ways that discursive practices constitute knowledge of texts" (in literature) and with the "ways knowledge is constructed by the writing practices of . . . various discourse communities" (in composition) (19–20).

In composition studies, interest in discourse communities has gone hand in hand with a growing interest in social construction theories of knowledge—theories which attempt to situate the known in communal contexts. "Writing as a social process" has, in fact, become something of a buzz or catchphrase as articles on small group collaborative efforts, peer response techniques, and the social nature of writing and reading appear in growing numbers. We shall examine this movement, generally referred to as collaborative learning, at a later point in this chapter and will suggest ways in which it still holds an implicit view of solitary, originary authorship.

HISTORICAL PERSPECTIVES ON COLLABORATIVE LEARNING

Before doing so, however, we should attempt to situate this discussion of collaborative learning in a historical context that represents a playing out of a persistent tension in American culture—the tension between the individual, the isolated Cartesian self, and the community. This tension is vividly captured by Alexis de Toqueville in his analysis of the American character. To describe this character, he uses a newly coined word *individualism* (which he differentiates from *egoism*): "Individualism is a calm and considered feeling which disposes each citizen to isolate himself from the main of his fellows and withdraw into the circle of family and friend; with this little society formed to his taste, he gladly leaves the greater society to look after itself." As such individualism increases, Toqueville notes:

> More and more people who though neither rich nor powerful enough to have much hold over others, have gained or kept enough wealth and enough understanding to look after their own needs. Such folks owe no man anything and hardly expect anything from anybody. They form the habit of thinking of themselves in isolation and imagine that their whole destiny is in their hands. . . . Each man is forever thrown back on himself alone, and there is danger that he may be shut up in the solitude of his own heart. (506–8)

Toqueville feared the results of unmediated growth of "individualism" and argued that it could be best countered by a strong tradition of community and of public discourse: "Citizens who are bound to take part in public affairs must turn from private interests and occasionally take a look at something other than themselves" (510). This strong civic involvement with public discourse was, in Toqueville's view, the balancing factor that would keep America from developing into a society of naturally exclusive, autonomous individuals, a society which would not, he feared, easily be able to resist totalitarianism or despotism.

In part, the founding document of America, the Declaration of Independence, reflects both the profound drive toward individualism and the commitment to community and public discourse that Toqueville found in the American character—dual ideals that have been inscribed in our history and that have often been in tension with one another. (These ideals are examined and related to tensions in contemporary America by Bellah and his colleagues in *Habits of the Heart: Individualism and Commitment in American Life*.) So we might expect to find evidence of this tension in American education and, more particularly for our purposes, in the teaching of rhetoric and writing. And indeed we do. As Michael Halloran has demonstrated, the earliest rhetorical instruction in America was influenced by Cicero and Quintilian, and the Roman concept of the "ideal orator" as the public-spirited person speaking well animated such instruction. But this essentially rhetorical emphasis on the Greek and Roman "commune," on communal values and shared meanings, diminished in the nineteenth century as oral discourse was displaced by writing, as new objective methods of testing arose, and as the academy emphasized competition over cooperation, autonomous electives over the classical core curriculum, and the autonomous individual over the social. By the end of the nineteenth century, traditional rhetorical instruction had been largely displaced by emerging English departments heavily imbued with Romantic theories of genius and of originality, with a concept of writing as an individual, solitary act, and with philological and exegetical traditions that emphasized the autonomous writer and text. (See Gerald Graff's recounting of this history in *Professing Literature*, which treats English departments but not rhetorical instruction or theory.)

Nevertheless, some educators resisted the trend toward individualism and isolation in English instruction. Anne Gere's recent monograph on the history of writing groups in America reveals that peer response techniques and small group collaboration have been advocated and enjoyed by some citizens and teachers since the colonial period—in mutual improvement groups such as Benjamin Franklin's Junto, in the Lyceum- and Chautauqua-generated societies, and in the women's clubs and literary societies (see *Writing* 32-54). Fred Newton Scott and his student Gertrude Buck both advocated more natural social conditions for composition instruction and evaluation in schools, while Alexander Bain's *On Teaching English* praised the practice of writing with an eye toward reading draft versions to a society of peers and revising on the basis of discussion. And in the colleges and universities, the great popularity of literary societies and other speaking societies offered an opportunity for cooperation and extensive collaboration.

As Mara Holt has demonstrated, collaborative pedagogy—while never dominant—has a rich history and tradition. Basing her study on an examination of academic journals from 1911 to 1986, Holt traces this collaborative thread, arguing that "the rationales and practices of collaborative pedagogy consistently reflect social and intellectual and economic trends of the sociohistorical movement in which they are located" ("Learning" 235).

As the twentieth century proceeded, the dominant emphasis on individualism, on writing as an individually creative act, and on "objective" testing as a means of evaluating the intellectual property of solitary writers, continued to be questioned by a marginal collaborative pedagogy. Most influential was the work of educational philosopher John Dewey, who argued tirelessly for seeing the education of each individual in a social and communal "context." He notes in *The Public and Its Problems:* "Individuals still do the thinking, desiring, purposing, but *what* they think of is the consequence of their behavior upon that of others and that of others upon themselves" (24). Dewey's calls for "new" or "progressive" education began early in this century; and throughout his career, he insisted that learning occurs in *interaction*, that social context is of utmost importance in the classroom, and that we should reform our traditional model (which privileges the individual) by enhancing "the moving spirit of the whole group . . . held together by participation in common activities" (*Public* 54–55).

Dewey influenced generations of teachers and scholars, among them Sterling Andrus Leonard, who argued as early as 1916 in "The Correction and Criticism of Composition Work" that "oral and written composition are developed in a socially organized class to carry out real projects . . . in a spirit of hearty cooperation" (598). In his 1917 *English Composition as a Social Problem,* Leonard goes on to say that:

> We must not make the mistake of assuming that training in composition is purely an individual matter. Most self expression is for the purpose of social communication. . . . Our whole use of language has a social setting. The futility of much of our past teaching has been due to our mental blinders to the social function of language. One has only to compare the situation of ordinary conversation with that of a class exercise in oral composition to realize how far we have forgotten the social genesis of speech. Worthy social conversation cannot be made at command of any person in authority. Ordinary human beings would not endure hearing the same item of discussion repeated by each person present. Nor would one care to say what everyone else had already said. Yet these are some of the striking characteristics of a composition exercise. If we are to make our training real, we must naturalize it, which is to say we must socialize our teaching of composition. (viii–ix)

Dewey's interactionist or constructivist approach to learning and knowledge gained increasing support in the 1930s from the work of George Herbert Mead, who argued that meaning is not individually wrought but is instead constructed through social interaction. In *Invention as a Social Act,* Karen Burke LeFevre cites Mead's work as providing a theoretical foundation for a view of invention as collaborative, noting that "other social thinkers, such as Martin Buber and Ludwig Wittgenstein, [move from] what have traditionally been regarded as private psychological entities out into the realm of social interaction and contextualization of knowledge" (73). In addition, Jean Piaget's work with children took a social constructivist approach to knowledge and learning as he demonstrated that children learn through *interaction* with others and with things in their environmental contexts.

Dewey devotees (whose reductivist rendering of Dewey's work seems to have been uncritically accepted by E. D. Hirsch, who uses Dewey as a whipping boy in his cultural literacy argument) did much to rigidify and trivialize his original arguments; his influence faded during the exigencies of the war years. The critique of traditional education, with its teacher-centered classrooms and its emphasis on "working alone" and on "originality" continued, however, primarily in Britain. M. L. J. Abercrombie's *Anatomy of Judgment: An Investigation into the Processes of Perception and Reasoning* (1960) and her later *Aims and Techniques of Group Teaching* (1970), for instance, evolved from her work with groups of medical students. Abercrombie was convinced that small group discussion provided the most effective way to help those students become more sophisticated and accurate at diagnosis and, hence, better physicians. Reacting to a report of a Committee of the Royal College of Physicians that argued: "The average medical graduate . . . tends to lack curiosity and initiative; his powers of observation are relatively undeveloped; his ability to arrange and interpret facts is poor; he lacks precision in the use of words" (*Anatomy* 15–16), Abercrombie devised an experimental teaching course that would help students, through collaboration, learn to recognize diverse points of view, diverse interpretations of the results of an experiment, and thus to form more useful and accurate judgments.

> My hypothesis is that we may learn to make better judgments if we can become aware of some of the factors that influence their formation. We may then be in a position to consider alternative judgments and to choose from among many instead of blindly and automatically accepting the first that comes; in other words, we may become more receptive or mentally more flexible. The results of testing the effects of the course of [collaborative group] discussions support this hypothesis. (*Anatomy* 17)

Abercrombie's emphasis on contextualizing knowledge and her realization that communally derived diagnoses are generally accurate and effective served as a direct challenge to the traditional individualism and isolated competitiveness endemic to most medical school curricula and higher education in general.

At roughly the same time, Edwin Mason presented a strikingly similar challenge to British secondary schools and, along the way, coined the phrase *collaborative learning*. Charging that "to work in a school day after day and feel that we are doing more harm than good, and that with the best will in the world, is too much to bear" (7), Mason set out to reform the school system, which he believed was "meeting neither the needs of the young nor the demands of the world" (8). As a result, Mason proposed a radical restructuring of this system, one which would replace the current competitive, authoritarian, overly specialized or departmentalized, and hence "alienated" program with one emphasizing interdisciplinary study, small group work, collaboration, and dialogue—largely in the spirit of John Dewey. The remainder of his remarkable book describes such a curriculum and advises teachers on how best to implement it.

As Abercrombie's and Mason's work began to have at least a small impact on pedagogical thinking, so too did that of the Brazilian teacher Paolo Freire, whose *Pedagogy of the Oppressed* appeared in 1968. Arguing that literacy is best taught in the social contexts of people's own lives, Freire faulted traditional education with promoting not genuine public literacy but passivity, alienation, and conformity instead. In his work, Freire aims to empower his student-colleagues to reclaim, reinterpret, and hence reenact their own lives and to gain growing awareness of how social forces work in dialogic relationship with individual experience to enslave—or to liberate—and to create the realities they inhabit "communally." Friere's work has most recently been presented as a challenge to the traditional teaching of writing in Ira Shor's *Freire for the Classroom: A Sourcebook for Liberatory Teaching*, which calls for a commitment to social and political contextualizing of all learning and on a renegotiation of power and authority in all classrooms.

These examples demonstrate that the drive toward individual autonomy, competitiveness, and isolated selfhood has always been countered, often only in a whisper but at other times in a louder, clearer voice, by a call for community, for shared public discourse, for working together for some common good. And, as Gere has shown, we could write part of the history of writing instruction in the twentieth century in just such terms.

CONTEMPORARY COMPOSITION STUDIES AND THE QUESTION OF COLLABORATION

The last twenty years are generally regarded as having witnessed a large shift in writing pedagogy, sometimes as a growing awareness of process and context, sometimes (following the work of pioneers like Moffett, Emig, and Britton) as a move from teacher-centered to student-centered learning models. We wish to acknowledge the effects of these largely positive shifts, most of which in our view run counter to the traditional valorization of autonomous individualism, competition, and hierarchy. But in spite of these pedagogical efforts, most day-to-day writing instruction in American colleges and universities still reflects traditional assumptions about the nature of the self (autonomous), the concept of authorship (as ownership of singly held property rights), and the classroom environment (hierarchical, teacher-centered).

We may look to contemporary composition studies as an illustration in point.

Over the past few years, a number of scholars have attempted to understand this emerging field of study by proposing a naming of parts, a taxonomy. Richard Young identifies the two major "groups" in the field as the "new Romanticists" and the "new Classicists," the former stressing the interiority and essential mystery of composing, the latter stressing exteriority and structured procedures for composing. Patricia Bizzell modifies and amplifies this distinction, grouping composition studies into two camps—those who view composing primarily as "inner-directed" and "prior to social influence" and those who view composing as "outer-directed" and based on "social processes whereby language-learning and thinking capacities are used and shaped in . . . communities" ("Cognition" 215). In several essays and a monograph on twentieth-century writing instruction, James Berlin offers a taxonomy of his own, contrasting what he calls "objective" and "subjective" rhetorics with a tripartite division of "transactional" rhetoric.

Similar taxonomic arguments are advanced from differing perspectives by several others, including Lester Faigley and Stephen North, but are probably put most strongly by LeFevre. In *Invention as a Social Act*, LeFevre contrasts what she calls the Platonic view of inventing and composing ("the act of finding or creating that which is . . . written as individual introspection; ideas begin in the mind of the individual writer and then are expressed to the rest of the world" [1]) with a social view of inventing and composing. This social view takes a constructivist approach to knowledge and posits that the "self" (in some ways similar to what Wayne Booth calls the "range of selves" or Foucault calls "subject positions") is socially constituted; hence, composing is essentially a social collaborative act.

These taxonomies of composition studies overlap and differ in a number of ways, and as all taxonomies inevitably do, they limit—indeed they often distort—what we perceive about our own field of study. So we mention them here not to endorse any particular taxonomy of rhetoric and composition studies, but to make one point that strikes us as particularly telling: the composition theorists and teachers most often identified with collaborative learning and peer response techniques—James Moffett, Donald Murray, Peter Elbow, Ken Macrorie—are also usually identified with Bizzell's "inner-directed" group or Berlin's "expressionist" group, which posit the uniqueness of individual imagination and see writing as a means of expressing an autonomous self. Ironically, then, the very writers most often associated with collaborative learning hold implicitly to traditional concepts of autonomous individualism, authorship, and authority for texts.

The work of Peter Elbow provides perhaps the best example of the tension and potential contradictions we have been describing. For years, Elbow has encouraged writers to work in groups, reading their work aloud for oral responses, out of which revisions grow. "Elbow grouping" is, in fact, a widespread phenomenon; we have encountered such groups of writers from Hawaii to New York, all expressing the efficacy of group work. Yet in spite of its emphasis on the importance of audience response to revision, Elbow's work rests on assumptions about individualism and individual creativity that fail to problematize traditional conceptions of the author and that deny the social nature of writing. For Elbow, expressing personal authenticity requires not social interaction but mining the depths of the self, searching inside the self for a unique voice. As he says in *Writing Without Teachers*, "The mind's magic. It can cook things instantaneously and perfectly when it gets going. You should expect yourself at times to write straight onto the paper words and thoughts far better than you knew were in you" (69).

In his recent books, *Writing with Power: Techniques for Mastering the Writing Process* and *Embracing Contraries: Explorations in Learning and Teaching,* Elbow continues to posit the individual self as the essentially mysterious source of creation, frequently calling on the "magical" ways writers discover their unified voices. *Writing with Power,* in fact, ends with a chapter on "Writing and Magic." As Greg Myers notes in a critique of Elbow, "Magic is the only possible source for such [individual] ineffable energies. . . . [Such] metaphors prevent any analysis of the social conditions of our writing" (165). Such a stance is reflected in Elbow's recent essays, in which he argues that writers often must ignore audience (or any "others") in order to get to the heart and soul of what they want to say (1987, 1988).

The composition theorist most closely associated with social construction and collaborative learning theories in general and peer group response in particular is Kenneth Bruffee. Bruffee became interested in peer tutoring as a means of helping students "practice judgment collaboratively, through a progressive set of analytical and evaluative tasks applied to each other's academic writing in a context which fosters self-esteem" ("Brooklyn" 450). Yet in his early work on peer tutoring and in his text, *A Short Course in Writing,* Bruffee also holds to the concept of single authorship and individual creativity (students write alone and then revise after getting peer response, much as in the Elbow method) even while acknowledging the degree to which "knowledge is a social phenomenon, and the social context in which we learn permeates what we know and how we know it" (116). In his more recent work, however, Bruffee has moved to resolve the potential contradiction, arguing that our ability to read and write has its roots deep in our "acquired ability to carry on the social symbolic exchanges we call conversation" ("Conversation" 642).

As Bruffee readily notes, only recently has he come to contemplate the full theoretical significance of such an epistemology for the teaching of writing and reading. Drawing on the work of scholars in a number of disciplines—Stanley Fish in literary studies, Lev Vygotsky and Irving Goffman in psychology and sociology, Thomas Kuhn and Richard Rorty in philosophy, and Clifford Geertz in anthropology—Bruffee argues that what and who we are and what we write and know are in large part functions of interaction and of community. Thus writing and reading are, essentially and naturally, collaborative, social acts, ways in which we understand and in which "knowledge is established and maintained in the normal discourse of communities of knowledgeable peers" ("Conversation" 640).

As Berlin points out, Bruffee's later works were "from the start based on a conception of knowledge as a social construction—a dialectical interplay of investigator, discourse community, and material world, with language as the agent of mediation. The rhetorical act is thus implicated in the very discovery of knowledge—a way not merely of recording knowledge for transmissions but of arriving at it mutually for mutual consideration" (*Rhetoric* 175–76). But Bruffee's emphasis on collaboration and consensus, or social context, has been criticized, most recently by Mas'ud Zavarzadeh and Donald Morton, who say that:

> There is in Bruffee no sense of the politics of cognition that organizes this socially constructed knowledge. Society and the social for him (as for Rorty) are cognitive domains—areas in which knowledge somehow appears by means of such apparatuses as agreement and convention and so forth. As a result of such a conservative (cognitive) theory of knowledge, . . . the subject is presented as an uncontested category. . . . Bruffee's collaborative learning/teaching is, in other words, the latest reproduction of the "management" of the subject and the latest effort to save it through collaborative learning and the *Conversation of Mankind*. The teacher in this model is the manager of the classroom—an agent of social coalescence. (14–15)

Bruffee has also been criticized by Myers, who charges that "while Bruffee shows that reality can be seen as a social construct, he does not give us any way to criticize this construct. Having discovered the role of consensus in the production of knowledge, he takes this consensus as something that just is, rather than as something that might be good or bad" (166).

Myers is insisting that those interested in collaborative learning step back and ask what such learning will be used for, what aims and purposes and motives are served, who will and will not "count" as a collaborator (and why), where power and authority are located. Others in the composition community echo this concern. Richard Ohmann has long criticized composition textbooks for treating student writers as though they were isolated, cut off from any cultural, political, or social contexts. Ohmann's latest work, *Politics of Letters*, extends this critique to most contemporary teaching. Similar critiques of the asocial nature of composition instruction appear in the work of Charles Yarnoff, David Bartholomae, Charles Bazerman, Patricia Bizzell, and James Berlin (see "Rhetoric").

Other work has recently focused on context and communal aspects of learning. In particular, Shirley Brice Heath's ethnographic studies demonstrate how writing and reading must be seen as developing within a social context in which talk plays a major role. David Bleich's *The Double Perspective: Language, Literacy, and Social Relations* examines the ways in which learning is situated in and beyond our classrooms; his chapter on "Collaboration Among Students" offers particularly useful (and concrete) advice. At the Center for the Study of Writing, Linda Flower and her colleagues are working to relate the cognitive factors in composing to their social contexts. Still others, focusing on professional and work-related writing, stress the importance of social and political contexts in such writing (e.g., Lee Odell and Dixie Goswami's collection of essays *Writing in Nonacademic Settings* or Janis Forman and Patricia Katsky's "The Group Report").

The early work of Elbow and Bruffee has been augmented in this decade by a large and growing body of work on collaborative learning, much of it linked to the National Writing Project and to writing across the curriculum movements. (See Trimbur for a review of work on collaborative learning.) In addition to the work of LeFevre and Gere, we now have studies by Colette Diaute and Bridget Dalton on collaboration in young school children, by Anthony Paré on collaboration in the high school setting, and by the authors represented in Bouton and Garth's *Learning in Groups,* to name only a few. This interest in and growing commitment to the principles of collaborative learning grow out of and are informed by the philosophical tradition on which Bruffee's work builds.

COOPERATIVE VERSUS COLLABORATIVE LEARNING

Paralleling this movement in composition and English studies is one in psychology and education, though its epistemological bases are considerably different. The cooperative learning movement has amassed large amounts of empirical data to support the claim that the strategies and principles they espouse really do enhance learning. The literature in this area is voluminous and grows out of the tradition of research in group dynamics. Robert Slavin says in "An Introduction to Cooperative Learning Research," "cooperative learning methods are based on social psychological research and theory, some of it dating back to the early 1900s. . . ." In the remainder of this overview article, Slavin describes an "extensively researched and widely used set of cooperative learning methods," structured, systematic instructional strategies capable of being used at any grade level and in most school subjects. All of the methods involve having the teacher assign the students to four- to six-member learning groups composed of high-, average-, and low-achieving students—"boys and girls, black, Anglo, and Hispanic students, and mainstreamed academically handicapped students as well as their non-handicapped classmates" (6–7).

One such method Slavin has developed is Jigsaw II, in which "students are assigned to four- to five-member teams. They read narrative materials, such as social studies chapters, short stories, or biographies, and each team member is given a special topic on which to become an expert. The students discuss their topics in 'expert groups,' then return to teach their teammates what they have learned. Finally, the students take a quiz on the material, and the quiz scores are used . . . to form individual and team scores" (7–8).

The methods Slavin describes have been tested in numerous projects, including a series of studies conducted by Slavin and others at Johns Hopkins University and by Sharan in Tel Aviv on the effect of cooperative learning on race relations (see DeVries and Edwards, "Student Teams and Learning Games: Their Effect on Cross-Race and Cross-Sex Interaction"; Slavin, "Effects of Biracial Learning Teams on Cross-Racial Friendship Interaction"; and Sharan, "Cooperative Learning in Small Groups: Recent Methods and Effects on Achievement, Attitudes, and Ethnic Relations"). More recently, researchers have focused on analyzing interaction patterns in cooperative groups (Webb, "Student Interaction and Learning in Small Groups") and, particularly, on how to design a classroom conducive to cooperative learning (Graves and Graves, "Creating a Cooperative Learning Environment: An Ecological Approach").

Discrepancies and inconsistencies across these studies certainly exist, and some, such as Michaels, have challenged the claim that cooperative methods improve achievement. On the whole, however, the evidence produced by proponents is impressive. On the basis of a long series of studies, in fact, Johnson and Johnson, of the University of Minnesota Cooperative Learning Center, claim the following "outcomes" for cooperative learning:

1. higher achievement and increased retention
2. greater use of higher level reasoning strategies and increased critical reasoning competencies
3. greater ability to view situations from others' perspectives
4. more positive relations with peers regardless of ethnic, sex, ability, social class, or handicapping differences
5. more positive attitudes toward school, learning, and teachers
6. higher self esteem
7. greater collaborative skills and attitudes necessary for working effectively with others (*Learning* 9)

In addition to these advantages, research in cooperative learning poses a strong challenge to the efficacy of tracking, demonstrating that children of differing abilities learn better in mixed groups than they do in "tracks."

Growing as it does out of positivist, empiricist, and behaviorist assumptions, the research on cooperative learning has a different epistemological basis from that of collaborative learning in the Bruffee tradition, one that posits an externally verifiable "reality" which serves as stimulus for various responses. Furthermore, its research agenda demands hypotheses that are confirmed or refuted, problems that are solved, questions that are answered. And the tasks the students collaborate on are rigidly structured and controlled. In spite of these shortcomings, however, this research has important implications, and indeed the methods developed by Slavin, Johnson and Johnson, and others may come close to what George Hillocks, Jr., is calling for as "environmental" tasks in his book *Research on Written Composition: New Directions for Teaching*. Such work deserves to be better known by teachers and researchers in composition if only in order to mount a systematic interrogation of its assumptions.

THE CHALLENGE OF COLLABORATIVE WRITING

The work on both cooperative and collaborative learning surveyed here all moves toward contextualizing instruction; the work on collaboration, in particular, emphasizes the ways in which knowledge is constructed among members of communities. The recent attention given to collaborative writing might thus seem a natural extension or a subset of collaborative learning theory. Yet collaborative learning theory has from its inception failed to challenge traditional concepts of individualism and ownership of ideas and has operated primarily in traditional ways. Students may work together on revising or on problem solving, but when they write, they typically write alone in settings structured and governed by a teacher/authority in whom power is vested. Studies of collaborative writing, on the other hand, make such silent accommodations less easy to maintain and as a result offer the potential to challenge and hence re-situate collaborative learning theories.

Much of the work on collaborative writing has focused on the world of work. Studies by Mary Beth Debs, Janis Forman, Stephen Doheny-Farina, Faigley and Miller, and Geoffrey Cross, as well as by the authors of this book, examine collaborative writing in a number of job-related settings. Others, such as Deborah Bosley, Sharon Hamilton-Wieler, Karen Spear, and Charles Cooper, have attempted to build collaborative writing into classroom contexts. In a 1986 survey, Hallie Lemon found that the composition faculty at Western Illinois University use collaboration at every stage of the writing process, including drafting. Extensive research on this kind of "shared document" collaboration is being carried out by a Purdue University research team in an effort to define kinds of collaborative writing and to describe the processes involved in such group writing tasks. Their research includes a case study of collaborative writing groups (see Meg Morgan, et al.). Also at the college level, O'Donnell and colleagues have conducted experiments that support the claim that group-produced documents are perceived as better than those individually produced.

In a study of writers in seven contexts (including junior high, high school, upper division undergraduate and doctoral students, a chemist, a general manager, and a civil engineer), Stephen P. Witte has identified four forms of collaborative writing and concludes that across these seven contexts "writing became increasingly more collaborative and collaborative in different ways" (2–3). Thomas L. Hilgers and Daiute have explored the uses of collaborative writing with younger children. Nevertheless, as Nancy Allen and her colleagues point out, because "very little detail is known about collaborative writing processes in general . . . there is a need for in-depth study of the features of collaborative writing [defined as] a situation in which decisions are made by consensus" ("Shared-Document" 1–2). We would add that much more careful attention needs to be given to just what is meant by consensus and to the ways consensus is or is not achieved.

John Trimbur has begun such exploration in "Consensus and Difference in Collaborative Learning," in which he builds on the work of Habermas to argue that we must "distinguish between consensus as an acculturative practice that reproduces business as usual and consensus as an oppositional one that challenges the prevailing conditions of production" by providing a "critical instrument to open gaps in the conversation through which differences may emerge" (27). Joseph Harris extends this critique of consensus and offers an argument for "community without consensus" in his "Idea of Community in the Study of Writing."

While we clearly need more and better studies on the processes and varieties of collaborative writing, some directions already seem clear. Just as collaborative writing potentially challenges the hegemony of single, originary authorship, so do a mix of historical, social, theoretical, and pedagogical forces all centered on a destabilized author/writer and on context, community, and the social nature of knowledge and learning present a series of challenges to higher education in general and to the teaching of composition in particular. We turn now to examine the pedagogical implications of these challenges.

Closest to home is the challenge to traditional classroom format and to the teacher's role. Our classrooms after all posit power and authority in the teacher. At best, students are in apprenticeship to authority; they do not help constitute it. Ohmann acknowledges this challenge when he probes the issue of student "powerlessness" in our classes: "The writer's situation is heavy with contradictions. She is . . . invited both to assume responsibility for her education and to trust the college's plan for it; to build her competence and to follow a myriad of rules and instructions; to see herself as an autonomous individual and to be incessantly judged" (252). As one concrete way of contesting such alienating tensions, Ohmann uses collaborative group interviews, including one of himself. This interview, Ohmann notes, can help establish student "ownership of the writing task in two ways. First, it demystifies my role in the class, opening up my goods and values as a subject for inquiry on the students' terms, taking them off the secret agenda. Second, it changes the relationship of their writing to what I have said in class, turning the latter into material for analysis and criticism rather than the graven words of authority" (256).

But even in the most collaborative of our classrooms, the authority to organize and evaluate rests with the teacher. As Trimbur notes, "Even when I'm not in the room, my authority remains behind, embedded in the very tasks I've asked students to work on. . . . If anything, I have never felt more powerful than in the collaborative classroom precisely because I know much more about what's going on, how students are thinking about the issues of the course, what language they are generating to talk about these issues and so on" (Letter). As Foucault's work suggests, collaborative writing itself constitutes a technology of power, one we are only beginning to explore. As we carry out such exploration, as we investigate the ways in which collaborative writing challenges traditional power relationships, we need to bring students into these discussions, asking them to work with us to examine how authority is negotiated, shared, distributed. At least potentially, we would argue, collaborative writing holds out the promise for a plurality of power and of authority among teacher and students, what Ohmann calls an "opening up" of the classroom.

The hierarchical bases of power in our classrooms reflect the larger stucture of our educational institutions. Most university calendars, divided neatly into semesters or quarters, reflect a positivistic approach to learning: knowledge is "packaged" into discrete segments and dispensed to passive recipients, fast-food style, through four years. Such a system posits students as isolated units, all of whom learn in similar ways and at similar speeds. The time necessary for group cohesion to occur, for examination of group dynamics involving consensus and dissensus to take place, much less for a consideration of the issues at stake in a seemingly simple question such as "Who is the author of this essay?" is not easily found in such a system. The research and the scholarship reviewed here strongly suggest that just as we must rethink our roles as teachers in a collaborative writing classroom, so also must we rethink our use of time in the college curriculum. At the very least, we must become aware of how such matters as the use of time reflect assumptions and traditions that may no longer fit with our educational goals.

We could of course point out other institutional constraints that mitigate against a pedagogy of collaboration. Most notable is traditional classroom design. Large cavernous lecture halls in which students see only the backs of other students' heads, and classrooms whose bolted down desks face dutifully toward the slightly raised lectern in front present major stumbling blocks to collaborative learning and writing. But ingenious teachers can and will devise ways to change the settings that impede their efforts to undermine traditional teacher-centered pedagogies.

Other institutional practices, bound as they are in ideology, may prove more intractable to change than will classroom settings. Among these we see the examination system as particularly problematic. This system, barely a hundred years old, is rooted solidly in positivitic assumptions: knowledge is objectifiably knowable and can be measured and counted. Such a tradition goes hand in hand with the conception of a solitary, sovereign writer with individually owned property rights. This view of knowledge calls for a controlled testing situation and valorizes the hard data such situations yield as proof of success or failure. Testing as we know it is by definition acontextual, antisocial, anticommunal. And our dependence on testing at all levels of the educational system seems only to be growing. Yet the movements discussed in this book all question the very foundations on which these testing practices rest.

Our sense is that a thorough reexamination of the grounds of testing practices in higher education will have to follow rather than precede curricular reform. And in this area the research on collaborative learning and writing may have a more immediate impact. Our current curriculum is still based on a model of content coverage: classes must clip along, covering a certain number of units in a certain number of days. But this model is under increasing attack on a number of fronts and for a number of reasons. Most obviously, it is simply no longer possible for any one person to cover all the material in any field, even a fairly narrow one. Less obvious but equally important is the growing realization that what we teach in this inexorable drive to cover our content areas is not necessarily or even probably what is learned. Here the research in learning theory is clear and unequivocal: real learning occurs in interaction as students actively use concepts and ideas or strategies in order to assimilate them. The pedagogical implications here are equally clear: less may well yield more in terms of learning.

What follows from this line of reasoning is the need to reconsider course structure in terms of assignments that will engage students in interaction and active collaborative learning. One of the engineer respondents to our survey of collaborative writing remarked: "Perhaps it would be possible for English teachers to pay some attention to collaborative writing in their classrooms." What is much less clear is whether writing teachers are ready and willing to examine their own teaching practices to see in what ways they use collaborative writing (if they use it at all) in traditional, teacher-centered ways and in what ways they use a more liberatory mode of collaborative writing.

COLLABORATIVE WRITING IN THE CLASSROOM

As we have indicated already, our vision of this book changed in several important respects during the six years that we worked on it. No discussion has been so substantively reconceived as the following section on pedagogy. When we began our research on collaborative writing, we envisioned developing detailed, specific guidelines for teachers—guidelines that would address such issues as the characteristics of effective collaborative writing assignments and the most efficient ways to organize and evaluate group efforts. We will discuss issues such as these in the following pages, but rather than presenting complete definitive guidelines, our discussion will be much more exploratory.

Why? Our hesitation to proffer definitive guidelines and suggestions to teachers reflects the capacity of collaborative writing to "open out" or problematize both theory and practice. The more we reflected on the data we gathered through our surveys and questionnaires, the more we recognized how deeply embedded and contextualized actual collaborative writing practices are in the world of work. Our reflections on our interviews, in particular, emphasized to us the importance of addressing issues of gender, class, race, and power and of raising questions—hard questions—about collaborative writing in institutional settings: what are the consequences of our interviewees' highly pragmatic, goal-oriented view of collaboration for women and students of color in our classrooms? Can the same activities that might prepare students such as these to write effectively with others in the workplace also empower these students so they can function as full participating members of collaborative writing groups? At present, we have only the vaguest answers to these and similar questions.

Our historical and theoretical explorations of the concept of authorship raised similarly complex issues. If in a Bakhtinian sense all writing, whether drafted by an individual working alone or by a group of persons working together, is collaborative, how can we best help students recognize and build upon this heteroglossic understanding of language? Some carefully structured assignments that enable students efficiently and productively to complete group writing projects may risk—precisely because they are so carefully structured and sequenced—silencing or diminishing the polyphony of competing voices that many teachers want to encourage students to hear, and to speak. Which, then, is a better collaborative writing assignment—one that strives to enable students to confront language in all its heteroglossic richness or one that helps students learn how practically and efficiently to get the job of writing together done?

Our inability to resolve questions such as these frustrates us. In a recent essay in *The Chronicle of Higher Education*, Annette Kolodny worries about the tendency of feminist critics to focus less and less on concrete specifics of classroom power and pedagogy and more on esoteric theorizing. Her warning applies, we believe, to those in composition studies as well. In our field, pedagogy has traditionally been the strongest link in our chain; composition theorists could never easily ignore the exigencies of their everyday classrooms. We are concerned that our discussion here may seem to signal a retreat from a concern for pedagogy to the abstruse, but much less challenging, world of theory.

Nothing could be further from the case. Our reluctance here to detail specific, concrete guidelines reflects instead our growing appreciation of the complexity of our rhetorical situation as teachers and our awareness of the profound ways that explorations of collaborative writing challenge not only many traditional classroom practices in English studies but our entire curriculum. Rather than risk premature closure on issues of great significance, we prefer to emphasize the questions rather than the answers.

This is not to say, however, that we have been unable to draw any conclusions based on our research. Our own experiments with collaborative writing assignments, as well as many discussions with colleagues who have generously shared assignments with us, warrant a number of conclusions. Poor collaborative writing assignments are artificial in the sense that one person could really complete the assignment alone: such assignments lead only to busy work and frustration. Poor collaborative writing assignments also fail to provide guidance for students about the processes they might best use to complete the assignment effectively. Students are simply assigned a topic or a project and abandoned to negotiate the minefield of interpersonal and group processes alone.

Successful collaborative writing assignments may vary substantially in goals, methods, and desired outcomes. Most substantial collaborative writing assignments, however, share the following characteristics:

1. They allow time for group cohesion (but not necessarily consensus) to occur and for leadership to emerge.

2. They call for or invite collaboration; students need to work together in order to complete the assignment effectively. The Purdue researchers have tentatively identified three types of tasks which invite such collaboration: "labor-intensive" tasks that need to be divided into smaller subtasks in order to be accomplished effectively and efficiently; "specialization" tasks that call for multiple areas of expertise; and "synthesis" tasks that demand that divergent perspectives be brought together into a solution acceptable to the whole group or an outside group (see Allen et al. "Shared-Document").

3. They allow for the evolution of group norms and the negotiation of authority and responsibility. In a study of a writing group, Rance Conley identifies at least five "bases of authority": in the group itself, from the profession, from the role played in the group, from genre conventions, and from the strength of a member's writing.

4. They allow for and encourage creative conflict and protect minority views. Learning theorists refer to this principle as "inclusiveness," by which they mean recognizing, valuing, and incorporating individual diversity into the whole.

5. They allow for peer and self-evaluation during and after the assignment.

6. They call on students to monitor and evaluate individual and group perfor-

mance and to reflect on the processes that made for effective—or ineffective—collaboration.

As readers may already have realized, this list does not directly address the question of how teachers should structure collaborative writing assignments other than to indicate the crucial importance of building in opportunities for the evaluation and monitoring of individual and group performance. Should teachers carefully develop collaborative writing assignments so that students are given explicit directions (if not commands) at each stage of the task? Or should teachers rely upon a less hierarchical, teacher-centered approach? The latter may better facilitate empowered, student-directed collaboration. But what about the product that must result from this collaboration and the dissonance, frustration, and inefficiency that can occur when students must take a primary role in instigating and structuring all collaborative activities?

A similar disagreement exists about the best way to form collaborative groups. Some teachers feel strongly that they are best situated and qualified to establish such groups. They may group students on the basis of their students' interests, experiences, majors, and writing skills. Or they may ask students to complete an inventory of their backgrounds, interests, and competencies. Other teachers insist that such careful selection is not necessary—indeed, that it may interfere with the early development of effective group dynamics. Still others argue that no one method of grouping will suffice, that the decision must be made anew with every new class of students.

Groups themselves may vary in size; we ourselves have used groups ranging from two to nine members. The role that groups can play in a class may also vary. Some teachers structure several weeks—at times, an entire course—around one or more group projects; others use them as a means of carrying out more limited and brief activities. And some teachers use them mainly as a means of organizing discussions.

Teachers interested in developing collaborative writing activities for their own classes need to recognize the diverse range of assignments that can engage students. Collaborative writing can be as limited as a twenty-minute group revision of a single paragraph, or it can structure the goals and assignments for an entire term. (In the latter case, not all assignments would be co-written, but all would in some sense involve students in collaborative learning activities. Students might engage in individual research or drafting, for instance, but do so in the context of group-defined goals and projects.) In our travels, we have spoken with teachers who have developed ingenious and exciting collaborative writing projects: a small graduate agriculture class cooperatively producing a textbook for their own course; a group of undergraduates devising a policy statement to use in explaining and justifying

American timber and lumber duties to a group of Canadian students; and a group of honors physics students hammering out an "alternative to Armageddon," a proposal they would later present to an open town forum. Certainly one of the most carefully studied assignments we know of is one developed by the Purdue researchers and used in a business writing course. Allen, Morgan, and Atkinson have generously allowed us to reproduce this assignment, which appears in Appendix D, along with another carefully constructed group-authored assignment from Anthony Paré.

Despite innovative assignments such as these, and despite the efforts of researchers such as Allen, Morgan, and Atkinson, and Paré and colleagues to develop meticulously structured and empirically tested assignments, we are left with many unanswered questions.

1. How should the teacher's role in any particular collaborative classroom be conceived and carried out?

2. What constitutes empowerment of students, both as individuals and as members of a group, in a collaborative project or a classroom?

3. How does—and should—collaboration challenge or re-situate the attitudes, values, beliefs, and ideological assumptions students and teachers bring to the writing class?

4. How do issues of gender, race, and class impinge on collaboration? To what extent can—or should—collaborative activities attempt to highlight or address inequities of gender, race, and class?

5. How are—and should—power and authority be constituted or achieved in collaborative work?

As we hope this discussion demonstrates, much important work has been done to address the pedagogical issues related to collaborative writing and to move toward a compelling pedagogy of collaboration. And yet many challenges remain. Perhaps the greatest—as Kolodny argues and as the set of questions listed above suggests— is to balance theory and practice, to face the full theoretical implications of our practices, to see those practices as embedded in a set of social, political, ideological situations, and to ask our students to attend to and to examine these situations with us. Thus we must not be content to develop—on our own—individual collaborative writing activities, no matter how carefully worked out and tested they may be. Nor can we be content to address—on our own—provocative unanswered questions. Rather, we must find ways, together with our students, of opening out, of interrogating such assignments, of tracing their implications and assumptions, of building a theory that can account for them and then testing that theory against our practices, and always of making this process part of the very fabric of our classes.

Such a pedagogy may well produce, from time to time, consensually derived singular texts—but singular texts always animated by a self-conscious plurality, a

The Pedagogy of Collaboration

polyphonic chorus of voices, whose difference—as well as sameness—speaks and is heard. Hannah Arendt has said that, "For excellence, the presence of others is always required." We agree. And so, in spite of our many unanswered questions, we believe that working toward a pedagogy of collaboration is worth our efforts, for it holds the potential for allowing, finally and fully, for the presence of others.

INTERTEXTS

Beware, my friend, of the signifier that would take you back to the authority of a signified! Beware of diagnoses that would reduce your generative powers.—Helene Cixous, "The Laugh of the Medusa"

* * * * *

Rooted in the traditions of the printing press, the old patent and copyright system may not be versatile enough to deal with the dilemmas posed by electronic machinery. Some of the problems OTA (Office of Technology Assessment) foresees are:

It may be hard to establish who an author is, or what percentage of the product he or she may rightly claim, when many people contribute simultaneously to a data-base or other computerized product. Many things, from newspaper articles to airplane designs, are created by joint efforts focused in a single computer's brain.

Existing laws may not be useful in sorting out conflicts that arise between man and machine. For example, if a computer music-writing program is modified by a musician and produces a popular song, is the computer (or its programmer) entitled to royalties? Present law is unclear on how to treat "interactive" programs, in which the computer and its user together create an original work.—Eliot Marshall, "Copyrights Obsolete in an Electronic Age, OTA Finds"

* * * * *

Quantitative and qualitative data from the social and natural sciences suggest that publication credit is not always accorded on the basis of universalistic principles. It was also found that females may have fewer opportunities in collaborative research to contribute to the same extent as do males and that when they do, they are frequently excluded from authorship.—Alan G. Heffner, "Authorship Recognition of Subordinates in Collaborative Research"

* * * * *

The overriding antiphonal structure of the spirituals—the call and response pattern which Negroes brought with them from Africa . . . placed the individual in continual dialogue with his community, allowing him at one and the same time to preserve his voice as a distinct entity and to blend it with those of his fellows. Here again slave music confronts us with evidence which indicates that however seriously the slave system may have diminished the strong sense of community that had bound Africans together, it never totally destroyed it or left the individual atomized and emotionally and psychically defenseless.—Lawrence W. Levine, "Slave Songs and the Slave Consciousness"

* * * * *

From democracy to revolution, just about every aspect of society involves cooperation with other people.—Robin DeRieux, "Brewing Up a Great Group Project"

* * * * *

What we have discovered in the process of composing the pieces is that, once freed from the restraints of individual authorship, we are also freed from the potentially debilitating effects of personal ownership in the work. Once we chose to separate ourselves from the personality of our own writing selves and personal agendas we could come to the creative space that [our poems] occupy.—Miriam May and Jamie Shepherd, "Collaboration as Subversion"

* * * * *

If I have any doubts about what a character would say or what a room would look like, I ask my wife. Perhaps I should have used "John and Joan Gardner" all along; I may do this in the future. But in modern times such work is regarded as not really art. The notion that art is an individual and unique vision is a very unmedieval and unclassical view. In the Middle Ages it was very common to have several people work on one thing: the thirteenth century Vulgate cycle of Arthurian romances had hundreds of writers. I feel comfortable with this approach, but I haven't felt comfortable telling people it's what I do. As I get more and more into the medieval mode, I'll probably admit how many writers I have.—John Gardner, Interviewed by Pat Ensworth and Joe David Bellamy in The New Fiction: Interviews with Innovative American Writers. Quoted in Le-Fevre, Invention as a Social Act

*   *   *   *   *

Although . . . challenges to individualism must be reflected in any adequate contemporary account of social relations, they by no means relieve us of the responsibility of reflecting anew on the status of the individual in our contemporary world. Consequently, the . . . animating assumption of the conference ["Reconstructing Individualism"] was that the concept of the individual, which has played such a central role in the formation of the post-Renaissance world, needs to be re-thought in the wake of the severe criticisms which have been directed against it. In the conference title, "Recon-structing Individualism," reconstruction does not imply a return to a lost state but rather an alternative conceptualization of the experi-ence of subjectivity, enriched by the chastening experiences of the last century.—Thomas C. Heller and David E. Wellbery, "Introduction." Reconstructing Individualism: Autonomy, Individuality, and the Self in Western Thought

*   *   *   *   *

This book is the product of all of us, and none of us could have done it alone. But, as subsequent individual monographs should make clear, we have not been homogenized. Each of us has learned to speak better in his or her own voice. Our experience together has confirmed for us one of the central arguments of our book, that the individual and society are not in a zero-sum situation, that a strong group that respects individual differences will strengthen autonomy as well as solidarity, that it is not in groups but in isolation that people are most apt to be homogenized.—Robert N. Bellah, Rich-ard Madsen, William M. Sullivan, Ann Swidler, Steven M. Tipton, Habits of the Heart

Let us try again. (A direct hit is not likely here. The best one can do is to try different approaches toward the same center, whenever the opportunity offers.)—Kenneth Burke (*Rhetoric* 137)

5 / New Beginnings

"And so," as Kenneth Burke is so fond of asking, "where are we now?" For us, and we hope for many readers who have joined the intertextual conversation represented in these pages, yet another new beginning beckons. When we began work on this book six years ago, we thought of ourselves as embarking on a fairly straightforward data gathering project, one in which we would collect enough empirical information to demonstrate that collaborative writing is a typical mode of discourse and thus deserves greater attention by teachers of composition. (The original title for this book, *The Theory and Practice of Co-and Group Authorship,* reflects the "neatness" of our original research design.) The conclusion to the book we then envisioned writing would, we assumed, sum up our findings and offer a conceptual model for collaborative writing.

RESEARCH METHODS REVISITED

This rather naive aim broke down almost immediately, however. We quickly realized that we could not (and should not) depend on empirical research methods alone to bring our subject into focus. Rather, we needed to draw upon historical, theoretical, and pedagogical sources as well. Perhaps even more importantly, we recognized that any attempt neatly to resolve the paradoxes and ambiguities that multiplied as our research progressed would radically oversimplify the phenomenon we were studying. Rather than attempting to dissolve or minimize these paradoxes and ambiguities, we have endeavored to heighten them in an effort to set into play a mutual interrogation of research methods and of the discourses through which this book has been constituted. Our "method," then, has been both exploratory and nontraditional. Far from proceeding in a linear, formally logical (or phallogocentric) manner, we have—in the Latin sense of *research, re + circare*—circled around and around the phenomenon of collaborative writing, seeing and re-seeing it from the vantage point of shifting terministic screens, striving to achieve a series of perspectives by incongruity.

In so doing, we have tried to join a number of different conversations—from group management theory to cognitive and social psychology, library science, medieval studies, history of science, literary and composition theory, and our own home disciplinary trope, rhetoric. Such an effort entails, we recognize, a number of potential dangers. The assumptions, methods, and concerns that characterize the discourse of library science differ substantially from those of group management theory or literary history. Researchers in these fields looking at the phenomenon called collaborative writing ask different questions, use different methods to attempt to answer their questions, and arrive at (often radically) different conclusions. Researchers engaged in interdisciplinary research must, we noted in chapter 1, take care not simply to pick and choose those methods and results which support their perspectives. We have tried to avoid such inappropriate use of sources. But we have attempted in this study not just to draw upon but to "push" or pressure these often incommensurable discourses. The risk entailed in such a method is, we believe, justified. For only by setting these discourses not so much in conversation as in debate and disputation have we been able to gain a rich, contextualized, multiperspective on our subject.

In our reading, research, and discussions of collaborative writing, we have faced another very considerable risk—that of overstating our case, of using our sources to deny the subject and hence also deny the very possibility or value of individual authorship and authority and thus of doing what Jim W. Corder calls "fading into the tribe, relinquishing authority and autonomy to the tribe" (303). As teachers of writing and rhetoricians, however, we can never take such a stance, and so our project has led us not to assent to the "death of the author" but to try to conceive new and more expansive ways of experiencing and representing authorship. Like the editors of the recently published *Reconstructing Individualism,* we want neither the death "of the subject or a return to a lost state but rather an alternative conceptualization of the experience of subjectivity, enriched by the chastening experiences of the last century" (Heller 2).

Some scholars in psychology, resisting the long domination of the solitary and knowing self in that discipline, are calling for much the same kind of re-situating of the subject. In a series of articles dealing with the concept of individualism and its various permutations (see Perloff 1987, Spence 1985, Smith 1978), Edward Sampson argues that a form of Western individualism that he calls "self-contained individualism" has so dominated our experience that we have failed to recognize the potential of another form that he calls "ensembled" individualism. Sampson argues, in fact, that a great deal of "cross-cultural, historical, and intercultural evidence . . . suggests that the dominant meaning of individualism in U.S. society today is by no means universal" and further that this form may actually "thwart the very benefits" normally thought to stem from American individualism (15). Finally, he suggests that ensembled individualism is actually "more capable of achieving democratic ideals of freedom, responsibility, and achievement than is radical or self-contained individualism" (21).

Other researchers in psychology are challenging univocal psychological theories of the self. On the basis of empirical research, for instance, M. Brinton Lykes argues that her subjects evidenced at least "two different notions of the self" (which she calls "autonomous individualism" and "social individuality"), and further that "differences between women's and men's notions of the self are grounded in their different experiences of power" (356). And she calls for more work in psychology which would give us a better understanding of "women's psycho-social reality and fundamental revisions of currently biased psychological theories about the self" (357). Lykes' call is currently being answered in a number of important works in women's studies, including Gilligan's *In a Different Voice,* Chodorow's *The Reproduction of Mothering,* Nodding's *Caring,* and Belenky, Clinchy, Goldberger, and Tarule's *Women's Ways of Knowing.* Such investigations may help us to reconceive and redefine the ways in which selfhood and subjectivity are achieved and experienced.

The result of our circling and recircling around the questions raised by an investigation of collaborative writing has led us, then, to problematize rather than neatly to define and to classify or to anatomize collaborative writing and collaborative writers. In particular, our reading and discussions with students and colleagues about issues of gender, race, and class took us back more than once to our reams of data and led us to look once again at what Derrida calls "hinges"—those places where language deconstructs, undermines, or radically challenges itself. Our examination of such junctures (such as the contradiction between our personal experience of collaboration and our colleagues' skeptical and suspicious view of it or the tension between the views of language as a transparent tool and as a mysterious source of power held simultaneously by those we interviewed) confirmed our sense that collaborative writing, like the "self," is not a stable or coherent construct, but rather that it appears in complex and multiple modalities. Two of these modes, which we have only recently come to call the hierarchical and the dialogic, have been of particular interest to us because of the dialectical tension they embody.

HIERARCHICAL AND DIALOGIC MODES OF COLLABORATION

In our research, the hierarchical mode of collaboration emerged early on; it is, in fact, such a widespread means of producing texts in all the professions we studied that we failed at first to see that it was but one mode, not the whole reality, in spite of the fact that this mode belied in many instances our own experience of collaboration. This form of collaboration is carefully, and often rigidly, structured, driven by highly specific goals, and carried out by people playing clearly defined and delimited roles. These goals are most often designated by someone outside of and hierarchically superior to the immediate collaborative group or by a senior member or leader of the group. Because productivity and efficiency are of the essence in this mode of collaboration, the realities of multiple voices and shifting *author*ity are seen as difficulties to be overcome or resolved. Knowledge in this mode is most often viewed as information to be found or a problem to be resolved. The activity of finding such information or solving such problems is closely tied to the efficient realization of a particular end product. This mode of collaborative writing is, we would argue, highly productive, typically conservative, and most often, in our experience, a masculine mode of discourse.

Along the highways and byways of our research and reading roads, however, we began to catch glimpses, perceive traces, of another mode of collaboration, one we came to call dialogic and one which, we ultimately realized, succeeded in naming our own mode of collaboration. This mode is not as widespread in the professions we studied as the hierarchical mode, and in fact, its practitioners had difficulty describing it, finding language within which to inscribe their felt realities. This dialogic mode is loosely structured and the roles enacted within it are fluid: one person may occupy multiple and shifting roles as a project progresses. In this mode, the process of articulating goals is often as important as the goals themselves and sometimes even more important. Furthermore, those participating in dialogic collaboration generally value the creative tension inherent in multivoiced and multivalent ventures. What those involved in hierarchical collaboration see as a problem to be solved, these individuals view as a strength to capitalize on and to emphasize. In dialogic collaboration, this group effort is seen as an essential part of the production— rather than the recovery—of knowledge and as a means of individual satisfaction within the group. This mode of collaboration can in some circumstances be deeply subversive. And because neither we nor our respondents had ready language with which to describe such an enterprise, because most who tried to describe it were women, and because it seemed so clearly "other," we think of this mode as predominantly feminine.

Both of these modes can be discerned in the interviews reported in chapter 2. In these interviews, the hierarchical mode of collaboration predominated: the twelve-year research project on food additives described by Dr. Irving is perhaps the clearest example of a strongly hierarchical collaborative effort. But dialogical modalities—if not pure examples of dialogic collaboration—were also evidenced, particularly by Dr. Bernstein and Dr. Chiogioji, who of all the persons we interviewed had most consciously and carefully considered the human and social potentialities of collaboration. These modes feature in the difference, in chapter 3, between the hierarchical concept of authorship operative in much scientific collaboration, where determining authorship is a pragmatic institutional and political problem, and that operative in the work of Bakhtin and some contemporary feminists. And they reappear in chapter 4 in the distinctions between cooperative learning (whose activities are highly structured and hierarchical) and the pedagogy of collaboration invoked at the close of that chapter.

It might be tempting, given these and other examples, to set these two modes, the hierarchical and the dialogic, in binary opposition and to argue for one (the dialogic) as liberatory and postmodern and for the other (hierarchical) as oppressive and phallogocentric. But such an opposition is both harmfully reductive in its oversimplification and false to our own experience as writers and teachers of writing.

The hierarchical mode can be, and indeed often is, realized in situations that locate power in structurally oppressive ways. Often the lowest-paid, least-recognized members of research teams perform most of the work on a project (including "writing up" the results). Yet these individuals often get no credit for their work or financial and professional rewards for their labor. But the hierarchical mode can also comprise scenes of shared power and authority and lead not only to efficiency but to great job satisfaction. During our two and one-half day visit with Bill Qualls and his team, for instance, we were struck by the sense of mutual respect, ease, and authority manifested by all the team members, not just by Bill Qualls.

It is not possible or desirable, in other words, to develop a set of binary opposites that would neatly characterize collaborative writing situations as either hierarchical or dialogic, conservative or subversive, masculine or feminine. Perhaps only fullfledged ethnographic studies could provide the depth of detail and critical perspective necessary for such judgments. Like gender roles, discourse situations are, Burke reminds us, inherently mixed and paradoxical; they defy easy analysis and categorization. And surely it seems reasonable to find inscribed in any piece of collaboration or any particular collaborator the same kind of risks and tensions that are generally inscribed in our culture.

Similarly, we would resist efforts automatically to equate dialogic collaboration with "good" student-centered, process-oriented teaching and hierarchical collaboration with "bad" teacher-centered, product-oriented teaching. The dialogic mode of collaboration can be used with surprising ease in a traditional teacher-centered class, particularly when student groups are encouraged to view consensus as an end in itself (just as many of those whom we interviewed thought of efficiency as an end in itself). But a carefully structured and thus hierarchical mode of collaboration—one that defines tasks carefully and presents a series of steps students must follow in working together—can also be used in the ways Hillocks calls "environmental"—ways which many have found conducive to student-centered learning.

Because the hierarchical mode of collaboration is dominant in our culture, however, dialogic collaboration can at least sometimes take the form of resistance and subversion. A number of acknowledgments and prefaces in recent books by women, for instance, have struck a markedly dialogic key. Belenky, Clinchy, Goldberger, and Tarule preface *Women's Ways of Knowing* by noting:

> As we steeped ourselves in the women's recorded and transcribed words we found ourselves drawing even closer to their frames of mind. We emerged from this long process with an extraordinary sense of intimacy and collaboration with all the women. . . . So, too, during our work together, the four of us developed . . . an intimacy and collaboration which we have come to prize. We believe that the collaborative, egalitarian spirit so often shared by women should be more carefully nurtured in the work lives of all men and women. We hope to find it in all our future work. (ix)

This mode can serve a subversive purpose, then, by pointing not only to plural or multiple authors but to the degree to which even single-authored texts comprise a plurality of voices. In her acknowledgments to *Man Made Language*, for example, Dale Spender asserts that: "There is an assumption I wish to challenge: it is that people sit in garrets and write books on their own. I sat in the Women's Resources Center at the University of Utah in Salt Lake City, and I was not on my own. . . . While this book may represent a 'sum total,' its many parts have been shaped . . . by many different people. . . . Not in isolation in a garret did this book come into existence, but in the co-operative and dynamic context of women's struggle. . . ." (xv, xvi).

Similar statements appear in the prefaces of works in composition studies, particularly, we find, among our colleagues interested in and sensitive to issues of class, race, and gender. Richard Coe's recent monograph *Toward a Grammar of Passages* provides a case in point.

> Although in traditional terms I am the author of this book, it is in fact very much a collaborative invention. With the exception of a very few paragraphs, I did all the "actual writing." . . . But if revision is really part of the "actual writing" process, the concepts you will read are not entirely "mine." They began as such, but were revised collaboratively whenever they proved inadequate for particular tasks. And the research presented to support and develop those revised concepts . . . was done by others, mostly graduate students. Although in traditional terms I wrote the book and in real terms I am the primary author, to count me as its only author would give the lie to our fine and important theories about writing as a social and collaborative process. (xii)

New Beginnings

It is far from clear, however, that the mode of collaboration suggested in such prefatory remarks can succeed in resisting traditional Western phallogocentrism. It is important to note that statements about the importance of dialogic collaboration, like those cited above, have thus far been in effect marginalized by appearing in the prefaces or acknowledgments rather than in the body of the texts. Though many writers are convinced of the crucial importance and benefits of dialogic collaboration, they generally have not yet found ways to incorporate these concerns in the body of their texts, which as a rule do not yet challenge the conventions of single-authored documents.

Those in composition studies have also begun to recognize the difficulties inherent in any effort to resist or subvert the traditional culture of schooling. While a number of teachers and theorists in composition have recently argued for a social constructionist pedagogy—one that is often presented as inherently liberating—the claims for this pedagogy, and at times the methods, have been challenged as amelioristic and accommodating. In "Reality, Consensus, and Reform in the Rhetoric of Composition Teaching," for instance, Myers criticizes advocates of collaborative learning for proffering a naive, idealistic vision of collaborative learning, one easily co-opted by the larger educational system. In his most recent work, Trimbur says that "it would be fatuous . . . to presume that collaborative learning can constitute more than momentarily an alternative to the present asymmetrical relations of power and distribution of knowledge and its means of production" ("Consensus" 29). Trimbur asks us, as a result, to interrogate closely our notion of consensus and to "rehabilitate" it as a "way to orchestrate dissensus." In a like manner, Harris challenges us to examine more carefully the way in which we use the term "community" in "sweeping and vague" ways and notes that doing so often polarizes talk about writing: "One seems asked to defend *either* the power of the discourse community *or* the imagination of the individual writer" (12).

The dialectical tension between hierarchical and dialogic modes of collaboration mirrors the historical tension between the individual and society; the psychological tension between individual cognition, with its traditional focus on the inner, and the relational, the recognition of an "ensembled" self; the pragmatic tension between goal-directed work and process-oriented play. Because the phenomenon of collaborative writing calls up all of these dialectical tensions, we find it a particularly fruitful site of paradox and of promise. To define this phenomenon, to say that collaborative writing should be *x* or *y*, should proceed in ways *a* or *b*, would be, in Burke's words, not only to reflect and select but to *de*flect and ultimately to limit the usefulness of the concept. What seems much more powerful to us, as to Trimbur, is to allow the free play of the paradoxes animating collaborative writing to raise questions of power, politics, historiography, and ideology—questions of profound importance at the close of this century.

Borrowing "overstanding" from Wayne Booth's *Critical Understanding*, James Phelan defines the term as the "critical evaluation of what we have understood" (165). We wish to attempt here a bit of overstanding, for our study of collaborative writing has led us, finally, to embrace the full complexity of collaborative acts and, as a result, to dissolve the traditional boundaries between collaborative writing and writing. And contemplating the complex nature of this dissolution has led us to re-examine or overstand issues raised earlier in this book about the work-related, theoretical, and pedagogical implications of the construct we call collaborative writing.

In "Scenes of Collaboration: Reflections," chapter 2, we offered a beginning critique of the interviews we had conducted, noting that those with whom we spoke took an essentially pragmatic approach to language and to collaboration. These writers spoke eloquently to us about what makes collaborative writing work for them and about the personal and professional benefits of collaborative writing. But except for Dr. Chiogioji and Dr. Bernstein, they seemed generally unconcerned with questions of power and ideology. Collaborative writing for these individuals, then, is largely unproblematic and untheorized. Our surveys and interviews, our review of the history of the traditional concept of authorship and of contemporary theoretical and pragmatic challenges to this concept, and our investigation of pedagogical issues raised by collaborative learning and writing all confirm the necessity of a more critical perspective.

The relationship between power and *author*ity is, for example, more complex than that described in much research on work-related writing. Limited as it has been, our research on collaborative writing in the workplace suggests that, contrary to what we might have thought, power and *author*ity do not necessarily stand in isomorphic relationship to one another. An example may illustrate the unstable nature of this relationship. Early in our research, we had an opportunity to talk with a group of women involved in a FIPSE-funded program aimed at getting more women into government. These women, all lawyers or law students, were doing collaborative writing as part of an apprenticeship with various congressional committees and agencies. They reported that they were able to wield remarkable power in constructing the documents (often legislation) they worked on, but in no case did they have "authorship" or "authority." In fact, their power was effective, they felt, in proportion to their lack of authorship.

In our interviews, we saw the same principle at work, most notably in the case of Glenna Johnston. It was only during a second follow-up interview that Dick Miller, her supervisor, mentioned Johnston's contribution to the writing done by him and other team members. His comments emphasized the significant nature of her contribution—Johnston not only coordinates the team's efforts but also critiques his drafts and writes documents that draw heavily on boilerplate materials—yet as executive secretary Johnston bears little authority, much less even minimal claims to authorship, for this work.

These findings support what many feminist critics of the workplace suspect—that in collaborative situations, women often play the "secretarial" role, one that by definition devalues their contributions. To the extent that rewards, both financial and professional, are associated with authorship, this conclusion seems to hold and may in fact constitute an ironic Catch-22 for many women working in collaborative teams. Power may be distributed and shared, may even be the province of these women. But such power is not necessarily tied to authority, on the basis of which traditional rewards most typically accrue.

Issues of gender raise other important questions about collaborative writing in the professional work world. We have commented earlier on the overwhelming male, Anglo-Saxonness of the large representative sample we studied. The fact that collaborative writing is so readily accepted in this world may be connected to this world's homogeneity. What, we wonder, will result when such a context changes, when the professional work scene is populated much more by women and people of color? In spite of its apparent embrace of collaborative writing and its ability, in the current context, to use it to fulfill its goals, America's professional work force may well not be prepared for the day-to-day implications such a demographic shift will have. But in a transformed context, collaborative writing and the pragmatic necessity to use it well will tend, we believe, necessarily to foreground issues of power, ideology, and difference—issues the collaborative writers we studied are now largely able to ignore.

If collaborative writers in the professional world tend not to reflect on or to recognize the theoretical implications and problems raised by their practice, many of the theorists with whose texts we were in conversation in chapter 3 tend to lean in the opposite direction. Too often, that is, they seem not to recognize the practical implications of or the need to develop methods consonant with their theories. The latter tendency occurs most glaringly perhaps in the case of research in the sociology of science, where one method used in this research—counting the first author of studies and using this information to indicate the importance of a particular article or to derive maps of the structure of influence in disciplines—conflicts with one of this field's major theoretical assumptions: that modern science is inherently and necessarily a collaborative venture.

The failure to recognize the practical implications of theory also characterizes many literary theorists today. (There are, of course, exceptions to this trend: Richard Ohmann, Annette Kolodny, Gerald Graff, Wayne Booth, Robert Scholes, and others.) As we read and studied the theoretical texts discussed in chapter 3, and as we saw theoretical issues concerning the nature of the subject and of the author as privileged subject of the text, of power, ideology, and the situated nature of all discourse raised over and over again, we failed to find any sustained attention to a practical pedagogy that would enact such theoretical positions.

When we had an opportunity to speak personally with theorists about their research or their teaching, they seemed most often startled or irritated by questions about the pedagogical implications of their theories. One prominent feminist theorist answered our queries, for example, by saying that she could draw no pedagogical implications from her theory. A traditional classroom, in which the teacher/authority dispenses information to students/receivers seemed efficient, viable, and even necessary to her. In another instance, a noted reader-response critic refused to entertain a student's interpretation, even as a starting point of discussion, and was irritated when another student pointed out that such pedagogical practice seemed to confound—if not to deny—the critic's theoretical tenets. Theorists of various deconstructionist stripes have of course been roundly criticized for failing to face up to or to explore the political and pedagogical implications (and possible contradictions) of their theories, but these illustrative anecdotes suggest that it is not only deconstructionists who need to put their own pedagogical houses in order.

A study of the history of authorship also raises other questions about the relationship between theory and practice. Our investigations demonstrate that this history is heavily imbricated in material, technological change. Elizabeth Eisenstein's massive study of *The Printing Press as an Agent of Change* emphasizes the role that this technology played in establishing that "both the eponymous inventor and personal authorship appeared at the same time and as a consequence of the same process" (121). Similarly, later changes in the concept of revision are closely related to changes in the technology for text production (see Elizabeth Larsen's fascinating study of such changes in the eighteenth and the nineteenth centuries). So too, we believe, are shifts in and challenges to the traditional concept of authorship closely related to material changes in technology. Yet we—as well as many of the critical theorists we have studied—are too often ignorant of such material changes taking place all around us. Changes in copyright laws, in corporate authorship, in library cataloging systems, in artificial intelligence, in computer-generated discourse, in mixed-media texts, in networking systems, and in even more vast information storage, retrieval, and sharing systems seem necessarily related to theoretical challenges to the "author" construct and indeed to the whole notion of the codex book.

Just as many of the theorists we discussed in chapter 3 fail to articulate and examine the pedagogical implications of their theory, so many teachers of writing fail to articulate and examine the theoretical implications of their practice. Too often we are content—as the collaborative writers whose interviews we presented in chapter 2 were content—to focus simply on what works for us as teachers. Indeed, as noted in chapter 4, theory and practice are often in radical disjunction, as they are in the classrooms of those who espouse collaborative learning and writing yet enact a theory of the author as originary, autonomous, and radically individual.

Toril Moi has recently charged Anglo-American feminists with a similar disjunction:

> If we are truly to reject the model of the author as God the Father of the text, it is surely not enough to reject the patriarchal ideology implied in the paternal metaphor. It is equally necessary to reject the *critical practice* it leads to, a critical practice that relies on the author as the transcendental signified of his or her text. For the patriarchal critic, the author is the source, origin, and meaning of the text. If we are to undo this patriarchal practice of *authority*, we must take one further step and proclaim with Roland Barthes the death of the author. (62–63)

Moi's criticism of Anglo-American feminists and the implied criticism of many in composition studies who espouse collaborative learning or writing yet continue to view the individual author as the sole "source, origin, and meaning of the text" seems to us trenchant. Yet composition teachers face a difficulty that Moi and other theorists do not necessarily face: when we ask our students to free write, to plan an essay, or to revise, we observe these students striving to create and share their own felt meanings, and we participate in their acts of realizing intentions and purposes in their discourse. Theorists in composition may agree with Barthes or Moi about the need to replace or displace the traditional concept of the author, but the pedagogical implications of this "death" are hardly clear or simple. One possible response—replacing the concept of "author" with that of "writer"—is fraught with problems, as Barthes' discussion of "Authors and Writers" and the traditional academic distinction between literary "authors" and student "writers" suggest.

In fact, the challenge of responding to contemporary critiques of the author and of the subject comprises one of the most important tasks faced by those in composition in the coming years. In the meantime, we must focus even more insistently on critiquing our own practices, uncovering theoretical blind spots. As Tori Haring-Smith and others have shown, collaborative practices uncritically imposed on a classroom can yield merely a disguised version of the same old teacher-centered, authoritarian theory of learning, a version that confuses students with the mixed and contradictory messages it sends. Harris and Trimbur suggest, however, that such practices are not the only ones possible, and that examining the theoretical implications of collaboration—particularly in the dialogic mode—can be valuable precisely because it throws these practices into high relief, thereby allowing us and our students to question them, to open up the classroom to the free play of difference. Thus rigorously pursued, a theory of collaborative writing must lead us to question, in fact, not only the structure and management of our classrooms but our curricular and institutional structures as well.

Such a theory would, of course, radically re-situate authority or power in the classroom and, as we note in chapter 4, our entire system of placing and testing students. But it would also challenge some of our most entrenched ways of rewarding academic progress through advancement and tenure. A theory of collaboration such as we envision would value community literacy work, for instance, or collaboratively conducted research as much as it would the single-authored codex book.

We have attempted in this last chapter to interrogate or overstand our own work, particularly those assumptions implicit in chapters 2, 3, and 4, because we see such mutual interrogation and self-reflective overstanding as necessary for those working in composition studies today. In addition, our explorations suggest several other generalizations we think may be of particular importance to our colleagues in composition:

1. Conducting any mode of research always calls on the researcher to acknowledge and to attend to that which it is not, that which is absent or silent. Such recognition will inevitably be difficult and partial, but it will also allow for contextualization (and a fuller critique) of the research.

2. Interdisciplinary research brings challenges and dangers but carries its own rewards. Writing this book, for example, has graphically demonstrated for us the relevance of critical theory, which has been remarkably important to us in spite of the difficulties of negotiating the minefields of contemporary theoretical language. In a similar way, our excursions into library science and the sociology of science have allowed us to see our subject in new and clarifying ways.

3. Only through a mutual interrogation of theory and practice can we resist the powerful seduction of oversimplifying solutions. Such solutions are especially pressing in an age of accountability and almost blind faith in the power of tests as empirical means of measuring practice and achievement.

The work reviewed in this text strongly suggests that we have only begun to scratch the surface of what it means to describe writing as a social or collaborative process. Every aspect we have touched on—in the work world and in technological practices, in theory, in pedagogy—calls for further investigation, exploration, elaboration.

GROUNDINGS

Finally, it has been this capacity of collaborative writing to open out, to open up, to explore both the experiential present and the theoretically possible that has so intrigued us. In retrospect, we realize that our earliest discussion of collaboration ("Why Write . . . Together?") was unique in our publishing experience for just this grounding of our theoretical interest in collaborative writing in our deeply personal experience as coauthors. Throughout our research—and even in our surveys and interviews—we have never lost this connection between our "public" discourse and our "private" personal grounding, which is apparent both in our decision to focus on productive, satisfied collaborative writers in our interviews and in our eventual recognition and exploration of dialogic elements in those interviews.

As we worked on our project, what began almost whimsically in "Why Write" with personal anecdotes about collaborative pesto-making binges and our contrary but complementary natures grew into a conviction that we no longer wish to—indeed we no longer can—rigidly separate the public and the personal in our own discourse. In "Me and My Shadow," Jane Tompkins writes of the two voices inside her—one of a critic who wants to critique, the other of a person who wants to be personal in her responses—and notes that "I'm tired of the convention that keeps discussions of epistemology, or James Joyce, segregated from meditations on what is happening outside my window or inside my heart. The public-private dichotomy, which is to say the public-private *hierarchy,* is a founding condition of female oppression. I say to hell with it" (169).

In our own halting ways, we have said to hell with it too (when readers told us parts of chapter 1 were too personal and really belonged in a preface or when others noted that the "voice" in this text changes from time to time), and we have been able to do so in and through our experience and our exploration of collaboration. For that experience has been for us finally not one of loss of self or subjectivity but instead a deeply enriching and multiplicitous sense of self, one that allows us to countenance and to speak our own voices—public and academic, personal and private—as well as to recognize, value, and credit the voices of others, many physically present, many others distantly echoed, which animate our text.

*   *   *   *   *

It is 6:00 P.M., 9 December 1988. We have been writing and talking and cooking and reading and listening and writing and talking and cooking and reading steadily for seven days now. We have before us a text, some 250 pages or so, one that looks physically solid, present, singular. The illusion still holds, but barely. For just these last few days, as has so often been the case during our work together, we have managed mutual negotiation of issues of power and control and paused to think upon them; we have rambled through discussions of a point only to turn a corner and suddenly see that point anew. We have read much, have imagined ourselves in deep conversation with Kenneth Burke, Luce Irigaray, Mikhail Bakhtin, Kenneth Bruffee, Carolyn Heilbrun. We have, in fact, been in conversation with our editor and with numerous friends and colleagues, and always with our students—and with each other and all the voices within. We will mail our draft next week, await reviewers' responses, and begin revising.

* * * * *

And it is 8:30 P.M., 15 May 1989. Lisa is on a consulting trip in the east and Andrea is in her office, feet up, gathering notes for one more marathon telephone conversation. The months of revising have been long ones, full of helpful and generous critiques, express mail and Fax exchanges, public presentations and private dreamings, and always the long-distance talking in which the "real" revisions have taken place, regardless of which of us "writes" the actual words. And once those words are written, of course, yet another collaboration begins, as we work with copy-, line-, and production editors to produce our *Singular Text* with *Plural*—indeed polyphonous—*Authors*.

* * * * *

We began this book, this project, with a glimpse of Poe's purloined letter embedded in our intellectual landscape, a sudden sighting of James' indistinct figure in the rug. Throughout our work, this figure—of a multivocal, multiplicitous, collaborative writer/text—has shifted in and out of view, in and out of focus. It is shifting still, in what for us is another beginning, a chance to continue the conversation pursued in and between these pages with you.

Appendixes / Bibliography / Name Index / Subject Index

Appendix A / Survey of Writing in the Professions

Moreland Hall 238
Corvallis, OR 97331-5302

(503) 754-3244

November 8, 1984

Dear Member of the American Institute of Chemists:

Our experience as writers, researchers, and teachers of writing has convinced us that we know too little about the demands of professional writing. The consequences of this lack of knowledge are evident both in the schools, where students often receive inadequate or ineffective training, and on the job, where poor writing skills may result in decreased productivity and satisfaction. To help correct this problem, we are conducting a study of the writing done by members of the following major professional associations: the American Consulting Engineers Council, the American Institute of Chemists, the American Psychological Association, the International City Management Association, the Professional Services Management Association, and the Society for Technical Communication. This study, which is supported by a grant from the U.S. Fund for the Improvement of Post-Secondary Education, will result in an important report that will help us better prepare high school and college students for on-the-job writing tasks. We hope that you will agree to join us in this effort by completing the enclosed questionnaire.

Your name has been selected at random from the membership list of your professional association, the American Institute of Chemists. In order to obtain a truly representative sample of your profession, it is important that you complete and return the enclosed questionnaire. We assure you that all information will be completely confidential. The enclosed questionnaire has an identification number only so that we may check your name off the mailing list when your questionnaire is returned.

This research project, the first of its kind, will result in a major report, which we will share with your professional association. Please complete the questionnaire and return it to us in the enclosed stamped envelope within the next few days. (You may note that the return envelope is addressed to Oregon State University's Survey Research Center; the Center is collecting completed questionnaires for us.) If you would like a summary of the results of this survey, please include the enclosed response sheet with your questionnaire.

We will be happy to answer any questions you may have. Please write us or call (503) 754-3244.

Thank you for your help.

Sincerely,

Lisa S. Ede
Coordinator of Composition
Director, Communication Skills Center
Oregon State University

Andrea A. Lunsford
Director of Composition
University of British Columbia

LE/AL
Enclosures

SURVEY OF WRITING IN THE PROFESSIONS

RESPONSE SHEET

1. Please check below if you would like to receive a summary of the results
    of this survey.

    _____ YES, PLEASE SEND ME A SUMMARY OF THIS SURVEY.

2. Please check below if you would consider participating in the next stage
    of this research project, a slightly longer (6-8 page) questionnaire
    focusing on co- and group authorship in your profession. Participants
    in this second survey will be sent free copies of our brief manual,
    Writing with Power in Groups, to thank them for their time and effort.

    _____ YES, I WOULD CONSIDER PARTICIPATING IN THE NEXT STAGE OF THIS
              RESEARCH PROJECT.

              NAME   _____

              ADDRESS   _____

                        _____

                        _____

              WORK
              PHONE   _____

Department of English **Oregon State University** Corvallis, Oregon 97331-5302 (503) 754-3244

April 22, 1985

Dear Member of the American Consulting Engineers Council:

Thank you very much for responding to our Survey of Writing in the Professions. The enclosed copy of the survey questionnaire includes a summary of the responses provided by members of your professional organization. Specifically, each figure we have given represents the mean. Therefore, for example, question one indicates that members of the American Consulting Engineers Council spend a mean of 43% of their professional time on some kind of writing activity.

In general, the overall results of this survey document the significant role writing plays in each of the organizations studied. Ninety-eight per cent of all of the respondents, for instance, reported that effective writing was either "important" or "very important" to the successful execution of their jobs. In addition, the results indicate that a significant number of respondents from all the professions (87%) sometimes write as part of a team or group. This figure was a difficult one to establish because of a problem in interpreting question four. A large number of our respondents answered that question by saying that they did all of their writing alone but then contradicted this answer in questions six and seven where they specified a number of documents which they regularly wrote with one or more persons. The figure of 87% is based on a summative analysis of all responses to question six. We hope this explains what seems to be an anomalous response to question four.

The second stage of our research project, now under way, is based on the information you provided in the initial questionnaire. If we can provide any further information or answer any questions about the enclosed summary of our research or our research in general, please contact us at the addresses provided below.

Thank you again for your cooperation.

Sincerely yours,

Lisa S. Ede
Coordinator of Composition
Director, Communication Skills Center
Oregon State University

Andrea A. Lunsford
Director of Composition
University of British Columbia

LE/AL
Enclosure

Appendix A   151

AMERICAN CONSULTING ENGINEERS COUNCIL

SURVEY OF WRITING IN THE PROFESSIONS

This survey is intended to identify and define the nature, types, and frequency of writing done in your profession. For the purposes of this survey, <u>writing</u> <u>includes</u> any of the activities that lead to a completed written product. These activities include written or spoken brainstorming, outlining or note-taking, organizational planning, drafting, revising, and editing. <u>Written</u> <u>products</u> <u>include</u> any piece of writing, from notes, directions, or forms to reports and published materials.

1. In general, what percentage of your professional time is spent in some kind of writing activity?
    43 percent

2. What percentage of the time you spend in writing activities is devoted to each of the following? (Your figures should total 100 percent.)

		PERCENT
a.	Brainstorming and similar idea-generating activities	13 %
b.	Note-taking	10 %
c.	Organizational planning	13 %
d.	Drafting (including dictating) . . .	38 %
e.	Revising	14 %
f.	Editing (including proofreading) . .	12 %
	TOTAL	100 %

3. Technology is changing the way many people write. Please indicate the percentage of the time spent in writing activities that you use a word processor.
    20 percent

4. The situations in which people in the professions write may vary considerably. Please indicate the percentage of the time you spend in writing activities that is spent writing alone or as part of a team or group. (Your figures should total 100 percent.)

		PERCENT
a.	Writing alone	84 %
b.	Writing with one other person . . .	10 %
c.	Writing with a small group (2-5 persons)	4 %
d.	Writing with a large group (6 or more persons)	2 %
	TOTAL	100 %

5. How important do you think effective writing is to the successful execution of your job? (Circle one number.)
   (85%) 1 VERY IMPORTANT
   (15%) 2 IMPORTANT
   (0%) 3 NOT TOO IMPORTANT
   (0%) 4 NOT AT ALL IMPORTANT

6. Please indicate how frequently, in general, you work on the following types of writing, distinguishing between writing done alone and with one or more persons. (Circle one number for each.)

		VERY OFTEN	OFTEN	OCCASION-ALLY	NEVER
A.	LETTERS				
a.	Alone	1 (74%)	2 (18%)	3 (8%)	4 (0%)
b.	With one or more persons	1 (3%)	2 (4%)	3 (58%)	4 (35%)
B.	MEMOS				
a.	Alone	1 (54%)	2 (23%)	3 (19%)	4 (4%)
b.	With one or more persons	1 (0%)	2 (7%)	3 (40%)	4 (53%)
C.	SHORT REPORTS				
a.	Alone	1 (45%)	2 (38%)	3 (17%)	4 (0%)
b.	With one or more persons	1 (1%)	2 (19%)	3 (54%)	4 (26%)
D.	LONG REPORTS				
a.	Alone	1 (27%)	2 (27%)	3 (42%)	4 (4%)
b.	With one or more persons	1 (4%)	2 (25%)	3 (47%)	4 (24%)
E.	PROFESSIONAL ARTICLES AND ESSAYS				
a.	Alone	1 (13%)	2 (3%)	3 (35%)	4 (49%)
b.	With one or more persons	1 (0%)	2 (6%)	3 (30%)	4 (64%)
F.	POPULAR ARTICLES AND ESSAYS				
a.	Alone	1 (7%)	2 (0%)	3 (10%)	4 (83%)
b.	With one or more persons	1 (0%)	2 (1%)	3 (8%)	4 (91%)
G.	USER MANUALS OR OTHER DETAILED INSTRUCTIONS				
a.	Alone	1 (16%)	2 (15%)	3 (34%)	4 (35%)
b.	With one or more persons	1 (1%)	2 (12%)	3 (41%)	4 (46%)
H.	NEWSLETTERS, BULLETINS, OR IN-HOUSE PUBLICATIONS				
a.	Alone	1 (8%)	2 (12%)	3 (35%)	4 (45%)
b.	With one or more persons	1 (4%)	2 (4%)	3 (28%)	4 (64%)
I.	CASE STUDIES				
a.	Alone	1 (8%)	2 (15%)	3 (18%)	4 (59%)
b.	With one or more persons	1 (0%)	2 (14%)	3 (22%)	4 (64%)
J.	PROPOSALS FOR CONTRACTS AND GRANTS				
a.	Alone	1 (35%)	2 (34%)	3 (27%)	4 (4%)
b.	With one or more persons	1 (12%)	2 (39%)	3 (32%)	4 (17%)
K.	LECTURE/ORAL PRESENTATION NOTES				
a.	Alone	1 (22%)	2 (15%)	3 (41%)	4 (22%)
b.	With one or more persons	1 (0%)	2 (8%)	3 (34%)	4 (58%)
L.	INSTRUCTIONAL OR COURSE-RELATED MATERIALS				
a.	Alone	1 (4%)	2 (5%)	3 (41%)	4 (50%)
b.	With one or more persons	1 (0%)	2 (4%)	3 (28%)	4 (68%)

M.   BOOKS AND MONOGRAPHS
a.   Alone 1 (5%) 2 (0%) 3 (8%) 4 (87%)
b.   With one or more persons 1 (0%) 2 (0%) 3 (8%) 4 (92%)
N.   OTHER
a.   Alone (Please specify
    _____)   1 (50%) 2 (22%) 3 (6%) 4 (22%)
b.   With one or more persons
  (Please specify _____) 1 (11%) 2 (44%) 3 (17%) 4 (28%)

7.   Collaboration in writing can, of course, take many
forms. If you have written with a co-author or as part
of a group, please indicate how frequently you use each
of the following organizational patterns for that
writing. (Circle one number for each.) IF YOU NEVER
WRITE WITH ONE OR MORE PERSONS, PLEASE SKIP TO QUESTION
11.

	VERY OFTEN	OFTEN	OCCASION- ALLY	NEVER

ORGANIZATIONAL PATTERNS
A.   Team or group plans and
outlines. Each member drafts
a part. Team or group
compiles the parts and
revises the whole 1 (4%) 2 (22%) 3 (52%) 4 (22%)
B.   Team or group plans
and outlines. One member
writes the entire draft.
Team or group revises . . . 1 (4%) 2 (22%) 3 (46%) 4 (28%)
C.   One member plans and
writes draft. Group or
team revises 1 (4%) 2 (26%) 3 (55%) 4 (15%)
D.   One person plans and
writes draft. This draft
is submitted to one or more
persons who revise the draft
without consulting the writer
of the first draft 1 (2%) 2 (9%) 3 (11%) 4 (78%)
E.   Team or group plans and
writes draft. This draft is
submitted to one or more
persons who revise the draft
without consulting the writers
of the first draft 1 (2%) 2 (2%) 3 (11%) 4 (85%)
F.   One member assigns writing
tasks. Each member carries out
individual tasks. One member
compiles the parts and revises
the whole 1 (4%) 2 (22%) 3 (41%) 4 (33%)
G.   One person dictates.
Another person transcribes
and revises 1 (2%) 2 (8%) 3 (20%) 4 (70%)

8.   The list of organizational patterns described in
     question 7 is not exhaustive. If you use another
     organizational pattern, please describe it in the
     following space.

9.   In general, how productive do you find writing as part
     of a team or group as compared to writing alone?
     (Circle one number.)
     (15%) 1 VERY PRODUCTIVE
     (46%) 2 PRODUCTIVE
     (39%) 3 NOT TOO PRODUCTIVE
     (0%) 4 NOT AT ALL PRODUCTIVE

10. If you write with one or more persons, who most often
     assumes final responsibility for the written product?
     (Circle one number.)
     (9%) 1   EACH MEMBER OF THE GROUP OR TEAM SHARES EQUAL
                RESPONSIBILITY.
     (38%) 2   ONE MEMBER OF THE GROUP OR TEAM TAKES
                RESPONSIBILITY.
     (48%) 3   THE HEAD OF THE GROUP TAKES RESPONSIBILITY.
     (4%) 4   A SUPERIOR OR GROUP OF SUPERIORS OUTSIDE THE
                GROUP TAKES RESPONSIBILITY.
     (2%) 5   OTHER (Please specify _____)

11. Which one of the following best describes the type of
     employer for whom you work? (Circle one number.)
     (63%) 1   BUSINESS AND INDUSTRY
     (0%) 2   COLLEGE OR UNIVERSITY
     (4%) 3   LOCAL, STATE, OR FEDERAL GOVERNMENT
     (29%) 4   SELF-EMPLOYED
     (4%) 5   OTHER (Please specify _____)

12. About how many people are employed by your institution
     or company?
     _____148_____ NUMBER

13. And how many are employed at your branch, division, or
     department of that institution or company?
     _____34_____ NUMBER

14. How many years have you been doing the type of work
     characteristic of your present job?
     _____19_____ YEARS

15. Please state your title and briefly describe your major
     job responsibilities.
     _____ TITLE
     _____RESPONSIBILITIES

16. Please give the year of your birth.
    _____1934_____ YEAR

17. Are you: (Circle one.)
    (99%) 1 MALE
    (1%) 2 FEMALE

18. Is there anything else you can tell us about the
    writing you do in your profession that will help us
    better understand the nature, types, or frequency of
    that writing?

    (THANK YOU VERY MUCH FOR YOUR COOPERATION)

AMERICAN INSTITUTE OF CHEMISTS

SURVEY OF WRITING IN THE PROFESSIONS

This survey is intended to identify and define the nature, types, and frequency of writing done in your profession. For the purposes of this survey, <u>writing includes</u> any of the activities that lead to a completed written product. These activities include written or spoken brainstorming, outlining or note-taking, organizational planning, drafting, revising, and editing. <u>Written products include</u> any piece of writing, from notes, directions, or forms to reports and published materials.

1.   In general, what percentage of your professional time
     is spent in some kind of writing activity?
     41   percent

2.   What percentage of the time you spend in writing
     activities is devoted to each of the following? (Your
     figures should total 100 percent.)

                                                        PERCENT
     a.   Brainstorming and similar idea-
          generating activities . . . .   17 %
     b.   Note-taking . . . .   11 %
     c.   Organizational planning . . . . . .   11 %
     d.   Drafting (including dictating) . . .   34 %
     e.   Revising . . . .   15 %
     f.   Editing (including proofreading) . .   12 %
          TOTAL . . . .   100 %

3.   Technology is changing the way many people write.
     Please indicate the percentage of the time spent in
     writing activities that you use a word processor.
     20   percent

4.   The situations in which people in the professions write
     may vary considerably. Please indicate the percentage
     of the time you spend in writing activities that is
     spent writing alone or as part of a team or group.
     (Your figures should total 100 percent.)

                                                        PERCENT
     a.   Writing alone . . . .   84 %
     b.   Writing with one other person . . .   8 %
     c.   Writing with a small group
          (2-5 persons) . . . .   7 %
     d.   Writing with a large group
          (6 or more persons) . . . .   1 %
          TOTAL . . . .   100 %

Appendix A   157

5. How important do you think effective writing is to the successful execution of your job? (Circle one number.)
    (86%) 1   VERY IMPORTANT
    (12%) 2   IMPORTANT
    (2%) 3   NOT TOO IMPORTANT
    (0%) 4   NOT AT ALL IMPORTANT

6. Please indicate how frequently, in general, you work on the following types of writing, distinguishing between writing done alone and with one or more persons. (Circle one number for each.)

		VERY OFTEN	OFTEN	OCCASION-ALLY	NEVER
A.	LETTERS				
a.	Alone	1 (55%)	2 (24%)	3 (20%)	4 (1%)
b.	With one or more persons	1 (3%)	2 (5%)	3 (36%)	4 (56%)
B.	MEMOS				
a.	Alone	1 (52%)	2 (29%)	3 (17%)	4 (2%)
b.	With one or more persons	1 (2%)	2 (10%)	3 (41%)	4 (47%)
C.	SHORT REPORTS				
a.	Alone	1 (51%)	2 (34%)	3 (11%)	4 (4%)
b.	With one or more persons	1 (5%)	2 (15%)	3 (45%)	4 (35%)
D.	LONG REPORTS				
a.	Alone	1 (37%)	2 (27%)	3 (32%)	4 (4%)
b.	With one or more persons	1 (6%)	2 (9%)	3 (51%)	4 (34%)
E.	PROFESSIONAL ARTICLES AND ESSAYS				
a.	Alone	1 (23%)	2 (22%)	3 (41%)	4 (14%)
b.	With one or more persons	1 (4%)	2 (16%)	3 (41%)	4 (39%)
F.	POPULAR ARTICLES AND ESSAYS				
a.	Alone	1 (15%)	2 (0%)	3 (31%)	4 (54%)
b.	With one or more persons	1 (1%)	2 (0%)	3 (18%)	4 (81%)
G.	USER MANUALS OR OTHER DETAILED INSTRUCTIONS				
a.	Alone	1 (17%)	2 (14%)	3 (42%)	4 (27%)
b.	With one or more persons	1 (4%)	2 (6%)	3 (42%)	4 (48%)
H.	NEWSLETTERS, BULLETINS, OR IN-HOUSE PUBLICATIONS				
a.	Alone	1 (15%)	2 (14%)	3 (32%)	4 (39%)
b.	With one or more persons	1 (4%)	2 (10%)	3 (31%)	4 (55%)
I.	CASE STUDIES				
a.	Alone	1 (11%)	2 (8%)	3 (25%)	4 (56%)
b.	With one or more persons	1 (3%)	2 (5%)	3 (17%)	4 (75%)
J.	PROPOSALS FOR CONTRACTS AND GRANTS				
a.	Alone	1 (8%)	2 (24%)	3 (28%)	4 (40%)
b.	With one or more persons	1 (6%)	2 (16%)	3 (28%)	4 (50%)
K.	LECTURE/ORAL PRESENTATION NOTES				
a.	Alone	1 (33%)	2 (28%)	3 (34%)	4 (5%)
b.	With one or more persons	1 (1%)	2 (4%)	3 (33%)	4 (62%)
L.	INSTRUCTIONAL OR COURSE-RELATED MATERIALS				
a.	Alone	1 (20%)	2 (17%)	3 (28%)	4 (35%)
b.	With one or more persons	1 (1%)	2 (10%)	3 (23%)	4 (66%)

M. BOOKS AND MONOGRAPHS
a. Alone 1 (6%) 2 (7%) 3 (30%) 4 (57%)
b. With one or more persons 1 (3%) 2 (5%) 3 (24%) 4 (68%)
N. OTHER
a. Alone (Please specify
_____) 1 (0%) 2 (33%) 3 (0%) 4 (67%)
b. With one or more persons
(Please specify _____) 1 (0%) 2 (10%) 3 (40%) 4 (50%)

7. Collaboration in writing can, of course, take many
forms. If you have written with a co-author or as part
of a group, please indicate how frequently you use each
of the following organizational patterns for that
writing. (Circle one number for each.) IF YOU NEVER
WRITE WITH ONE OR MORE PERSONS, PLEASE SKIP TO QUESTION
11.

	VERY OFTEN	OFTEN	OCCASION-ALLY	NEVER

ORGANIZATIONAL PATTERNS
A. Team or group plans and
outlines. Each member drafts
a part. Team or group
compiles the parts and
revises the whole 1 (5%) 2 (25%) 3 (40%) 4 (30%)
B. Team or group plans
and outlines. One member
writes the entire draft.
Team or group revises . . . 1 (5%) 2 (21%) 3 (45%) 4 (29%)
C. One member plans and
writes draft. Group or
team revises 1 (8%) 2 (20%) 3 (45%) 4 (27%)
D. One person plans and
writes draft. This draft
is submitted to one or more
persons who revise the draft
without consulting the writer
of the first draft 1 (8%) 2 (6%) 3 (19%) 4 (67%)
E. Team or group plans and
writes draft. This draft is
submitted to one or more
persons who revise the draft
without consulting the writers
of the first draft 1 (2%) 2 (2%) 3 (14%) 4 (82%)
F. One member assigns writing
tasks. Each member carries out
individual tasks. One member
compiles the parts and revises
the whole 1 (10%) 2 (16%) 3 (36%) 4 (38%)
G. One person dictates.
Another person transcribes
and revises 1 (3%) 2 (3%) 3 (14%) 4 (80%)

8. The list of organizational patterns described in question 7 is not exhaustive. If you use another organizational pattern, please describe it in the following space.

9. In general, how productive do you find writing as part of a team or group as compared to writing alone? (Circle one number.)
   (10%) 1 VERY PRODUCTIVE
   (41%) 2 PRODUCTIVE
   (44%) 3 NOT TOO PRODUCTIVE
   (5%) 4 NOT AT ALL PRODUCTIVE

10. If you write with one or more persons, who <u>most</u> <u>often</u> assumes final responsibility for the written product? (Circle one number.)
   (14%) 1 EACH MEMBER OF THE GROUP OR TEAM SHARES EQUAL RESPONSIBILITY.
   (37%) 2 ONE MEMBER OF THE GROUP OR TEAM TAKES RESPONSIBILITY.
   (38%) 3 THE HEAD OF THE GROUP TAKES RESPONSIBILITY.
   (8%) 4 A SUPERIOR OR GROUP OF SUPERIORS OUTSIDE THE GROUP TAKES RESPONSIBILITY.
   (3%) 5 OTHER (Please specify _____)

11. Which one of the following best describes the type of employer for whom you work? (Circle one number.)
   (52%) 1 BUSINESS AND INDUSTRY
   (15%) 2 COLLEGE OR UNIVERSITY
   (20%) 3 LOCAL, STATE, OR FEDERAL GOVERNMENT
   (11%) 4 SELF-EMPLOYED
   (2%) 5 OTHER (Please specify _____)

12. About how many people are employed by your institution or company?
   ____6082____ NUMBER

13. And how many are employed at your branch, division, or department of that institution or company?
   ____394____ NUMBER

14. How many years have you been doing the type of work characteristic of your present job?
   ____17____ YEARS

15. Please state your title and briefly describe your major job responsibilities.
   _____ TITLE
   _____RESPONSIBILITIES

16. Please give the year of your birth.
    _____1931_____ YEAR

17. Are you: (Circle one.)
    (91%) 1 MALE
    (9%) 2 FEMALE

18. Is there anything else you can tell us about the writing you do in your profession that will help us better understand the nature, types, or frequency of that writing?

(THANK YOU VERY MUCH FOR YOUR COOPERATION)

AMERICAN PSYCHOLOGICAL ASSOCIATION

SURVEY OF WRITING IN THE PROFESSIONS

This survey is intended to identify and define the nature, types, and frequency of writing done in your profession. For the purposes of this survey, writing includes any of the activities that lead to a completed written product. These activities include written or spoken brainstorming, outlining or note-taking, organizational planning, drafting, revising, and editing. Written products include any piece of writing, from notes, directions, or forms to reports and published materials.

1. In general, what percentage of your professional time is spent in some kind of writing activity?
    28   percent

2. What percentage of the time you spend in writing activities is devoted to each of the following? (Your figures should total 100 percent.)

		PERCENT
a.	Brainstorming and similar idea-generating activities	10 %
b.	Note-taking	20 %
c.	Organizational planning	9 %
d.	Drafting (including dictating) . . .	36 %
e.	Revising	14 %
f.	Editing (including proofreading) . .	11 %
	TOTAL	100 %

3. Technology is changing the way many people write. Please indicate the percentage of the time spent in writing activities that you use a word processor.
    17   percent

4. The situations in which people in the professions write may vary considerably. Please indicate the percentage of the time you spend in writing activities that is spent writing alone or as part of a team or group. (Your figures should total 100 percent.)

		PERCENT
a.	Writing alone	86 %
b.	Writing with one other person . . .	7 %
c.	Writing with a small group (2-5 persons)	6 %
d.	Writing with a large group (6 or more persons)	1 %
	TOTAL	100 %

5. How important do you think effective writing is to the successful execution of your job? (Circle one number.)
    (70%) 1   VERY IMPORTANT
    (26%) 2   IMPORTANT
    (3%) 3   NOT TOO IMPORTANT
    (1%) 4   NOT AT ALL IMPORTANT

6. Please indicate how frequently, in general, you work on the following types of writing, distinguishing between writing done alone and with one or more persons. (Circle one number for each.)

		VERY OFTEN	OFTEN	OCCASION- ALLY	NEVER
A.	LETTERS				
a.	Alone	1 (49%)	2 (21%)	3 (30%)	4 (0%)
b.	With one or more persons	1 (1%)	2 (5%)	3 (34%)	4 (60%)
B.	MEMOS				
a.	Alone	1 (41%)	2 (22%)	3 (32%)	4 (5%)
b.	With one or more persons	1 (0%)	2 (6%)	3 (39%)	4 (55%)
C.	SHORT REPORTS				
a.	Alone	1 (47%)	2 (25%)	3 (26%)	4 (2%)
b.	With one or more persons	1 (2%)	2 (14%)	3 (30%)	4 (54%)
D.	LONG REPORTS				
a.	Alone	1 (39%)	2 (22%)	3 (30%)	4 (9%)
b.	With one or more persons	1 (4%)	2 (14%)	3 (29%)	4 (53%)
E.	PROFESSIONAL ARTICLES AND ESSAYS				
a.	Alone	1 (26%)	2 (16%)	3 (38%)	4 (20%)
b.	With one or more persons	1 (6%)	2 (16%)	3 (37%)	4 (41%)
F.	POPULAR ARTICLES AND ESSAYS				
a.	Alone	1 (7%)	2 (6%)	3 (28%)	4 (59%)
b.	With one or more persons	1 (1%)	2 (0%)	3 (22%)	4 (77%)
G.	USER MANUALS OR OTHER DETAILED INSTRUCTIONS				
a.	Alone	1 (1%)	2 (14%)	3 (35%)	4 (50%)
b.	With one or more persons	1 (1%)	2 (9%)	3 (23%)	4 (67%)
H.	NEWSLETTERS, BULLETINS, OR IN-HOUSE PUBLICATIONS				
a.	Alone	1 (9%)	2 (14%)	3 (27%)	4 (50%)
b.	With one or more persons	1 (1%)	2 (9%)	3 (29%)	4 (61%)
I.	CASE STUDIES				
a.	Alone	1 (27%)	2 (23%)	3 (33%)	4 (17%)
b.	With one or more persons	1 (1%)	2 (5%)	3 (36%)	4 (58%)
J.	PROPOSALS FOR CONTRACTS AND GRANTS				
a.	Alone	1 (6%)	2 (22%)	3 (33%)	4 (39%)
b.	With one or more persons	1 (6%)	2 (16%)	3 (37%)	4 (41%)
K.	LECTURE/ORAL PRESENTATION NOTES				
a.	Alone	1 (43%)	2 (15%)	3 (40%)	4 (2%)
b.	With one or more persons	1 (0%)	2 (2%)	3 (33%)	4 (65%)
L.	INSTRUCTIONAL OR COURSE-RELATED MATERIALS				
a.	Alone	1 (31%)	2 (21%)	3 (31%)	4 (17%)
b.	With one or more persons	1 (0%)	2 (4%)	3 (37%)	4 (59%)

M. BOOKS AND MONOGRAPHS
a. Alone 1 (6%) 2 (13%) 3 (22%) 4 (59%)
b. With one or more persons 1 (4%) 2 (10%) 3 (23%) 4 (63%)
N. OTHER
a. Alone (Please specify
    _____)   1 (25%) 2 (33%) 3 (17%) 4 (25%)
b. With one or more persons
    (Please specify _____) 1 (20%) 2 (0%) 3 (20%) 4 (60%)

7. Collaboration in writing can, of course, take many
    forms. If you have written with a co-author or as part
    of a group, please indicate how frequently you use each
    of the following organizational patterns for that
    writing. (Circle one number for each.) IF YOU NEVER
    WRITE WITH ONE OR MORE PERSONS, PLEASE SKIP TO QUESTION
    11.

	VERY OFTEN	OFTEN	OCCASION- ALLY	NEVER

ORGANIZATIONAL PATTERNS
A. Team or group plans and
outlines. Each member drafts
a part. Team or group
compiles the parts and
revises the whole 1 (8%) 2 (3%) 3 (65%) 4 (24%)
B. Team or group plans
and outlines. One member
writes the entire draft.
Team or group revises . . . 1 (6%) 2 (14%) 3 (53%) 4 (27%)
C. One member plans and
writes draft. Group or
team revises 1 (5%) 2 (21%) 3 (41%) 4 (33%)
D. One person plans and
writes draft. This draft
is submitted to one or more
persons who revise the draft
without consulting the writer
of the first draft 1 (2%) 2 (6%) 3 (25%) 4 (67%)
E. Team or group plans and
writes draft. This draft is
submitted to one or more
persons who revise the draft
without consulting the writers
of the first draft 1 (0%) 2 (2%) 3 (24%) 4 (74%)
F. One member assigns writing
tasks. Each member carries out
individual tasks. One member
compiles the parts and revises
the whole 1 (5%) 2 (11%) 3 (51%) 4 (33%)
G. One person dictates.
Another person transcribes
and revises 1 (0%) 2 (8%) 3 (18%) 4 (74%)

8. The list of organizational patterns described in question 7 is not exhaustive. If you use another organizational pattern, please describe it in the following space.

9. In general, how productive do you find writing as part of a team or group as compared to writing alone? (Circle one number.)
    (15%) 1 VERY PRODUCTIVE
    (42%) 2 PRODUCTIVE
    (40%) 3 NOT TOO PRODUCTIVE
    (3%) 4 NOT AT ALL PRODUCTIVE

10. If you write with one or more persons, who most often assumes final responsibility for the written product? (Circle one number.)
    (17%) 1 EACH MEMBER OF THE GROUP OR TEAM SHARES EQUAL RESPONSIBILITY.
    (53%) 2 ONE MEMBER OF THE GROUP OR TEAM TAKES RESPONSIBILITY.
    (24%) 3 THE HEAD OF THE GROUP TAKES RESPONSIBILITY.
    (5%) 4 A SUPERIOR OR GROUP OF SUPERIORS OUTSIDE THE GROUP TAKES RESPONSIBILITY.
    (1%) 5 OTHER (Please specify _____)

11. Which one of the following best describes the type of employer for whom you work? (Circle one number.)
    (4%) 1 BUSINESS AND INDUSTRY
    (27%) 2 COLLEGE OR UNIVERSITY
    (14%) 3 LOCAL, STATE, OR FEDERAL GOVERNMENT
    (39%) 4 SELF-EMPLOYED
    (16%) 5 OTHER (Please specify _____)

12. About how many people are employed by your institution or company?
    ___1704___ NUMBER

13. And how many are employed at your branch, division, or department of that institution or company?
    ___69___ NUMBER

14. How many years have you been doing the type of work characteristic of your present job?
    ___15___ YEARS

15. Please state your title and briefly describe your major job responsibilities.
    _____ TITLE
    _____RESPONSIBILITIES

16. Please give the year of your birth.
    _____1934_____ YEAR

17. Are you: (Circle one.)
    (84%) 1 MALE
    (16%) 2 FEMALE

18. Is there anything else you can tell us about the writing you do in your profession that will help us better understand the nature, types, or frequency of that writing?

(THANK YOU VERY MUCH FOR YOUR COOPERATION)

INTERNATIONAL CITY MANAGEMENT ASSOCIATION

SURVEY OF WRITING IN THE PROFESSIONS

This survey is intended to identify and define the nature,
types, and frequency of writing done in your profession.
For the purposes of this survey, <u>writing</u> <u>includes</u> any of the
activities that lead to a completed written product. These
activities include written or spoken brainstorming,
outlining or note-taking, organizational planning, drafting,
revising, and editing. <u>Written</u> <u>products</u> <u>include</u> any piece
of writing, from notes, directions, or forms to reports and
published materials.

1.   In general, what percentage of your professional time
     is spent in some kind of writing activity?
     36   percent

2.   What percentage of the time you spend in writing
     activities is devoted to each of the following? (Your
     figures should total 100 percent.)

		PERCENT
a.	Brainstorming and similar idea-generating activities	17 %
b.	Note-taking	14 %
c.	Organizational planning	15 %
d.	Drafting (including dictating) . . .	33 %
e.	Revising	11 %
f.	Editing (including proofreading) . .	10 %
	TOTAL	100 %

3.   Technology is changing the way many people write.
     Please indicate the percentage of the time spent in
     writing activities that you use a word processor.
     13   percent

4.   The situations in which people in the professions write
     may vary considerably. Please indicate the percentage
     of the time you spend in writing activities that is
     spent writing alone or as part of a team or group.
     (Your figures should total 100 percent.)

		PERCENT
a.	Writing alone	79 %
b.	Writing with one other person . . .	11 %
c.	Writing with a small group (2-5 persons)	6 %
d.	Writing with a large group (6 or more persons)	4 %
	TOTAL	100 %

5. How important do you think effective writing is to the successful execution of your job? (Circle one number.)
    (88%) 1   VERY IMPORTANT
    (12%) 2   IMPORTANT
    (0%) 3   NOT TOO IMPORTANT
    (0%) 4   NOT AT ALL IMPORTANT

6. Please indicate how frequently, in general, you work on the following types of writing, distinguishing between writing done alone and with one or more persons. (Circle one number for each.)

		VERY OFTEN	OFTEN	OCCASION-ALLY	NEVER
A.	LETTERS				
a.	Alone	1 (75%)	2 (17%)	3 (8%)	4 (0%)
b.	With one or more persons	1 (0%)	2 (9%)	3 (53%)	4 (38%)
B.	MEMOS				
a.	Alone	1 (72%)	2 (22%)	3 (6%)	4 (0%)
b.	With one or more persons	1 (3%)	2 (10%)	3 (50%)	4 (37%)
C.	SHORT REPORTS				
a.	Alone	1 (45%)	2 (40%)	3 (15%)	4 (0%)
b.	With one or more persons	1 (3%)	2 (24%)	3 (49%)	4 (24%)
D.	LONG REPORTS				
a.	Alone	1 (28%)	2 (26%)	3 (42%)	4 (4%)
b.	With one or more persons	1 (4%)	2 (29%)	3 (46%)	4 (21%)
E.	PROFESSIONAL ARTICLES AND ESSAYS				
a.	Alone	1 (15%)	2 (11%)	3 (40%)	4 (34%)
b.	With one or more persons	1 (0%)	2 (8%)	3 (31%)	4 (61%)
F.	POPULAR ARTICLES AND ESSAYS				
a.	Alone	1 (9%)	2 (6%)	3 (21%)	4 (64%)
b.	With one or more persons	1 (0%)	2 (4%)	3 (20%)	4 (76%)
G.	USER MANUALS OR OTHER DETAILED INSTRUCTIONS				
a.	Alone	1 (8%)	2 (15%)	3 (42%)	4 (35%)
b.	With one or more persons	1 (1%)	2 (18%)	3 (39%)	4 (42%)
H.	NEWSLETTERS, BULLETINS, OR IN-HOUSE PUBLICATIONS				
a.	Alone	1 (14%)	2 (27%)	3 (39%)	4 (20%)
b.	With one or more persons	1 (3%)	2 (22%)	3 (40%)	4 (35%)
I.	CASE STUDIES				
a.	Alone	1 (4%)	2 (7%)	3 (27%)	4 (62%)
b.	With one or more persons	1 (0%)	2 (9%)	3 (33%)	4 (58%)
J.	PROPOSALS FOR CONTRACTS AND GRANTS				
a.	Alone	1 (10%)	2 (39%)	3 (38%)	4 (13%)
b.	With one or more persons	1 (4%)	2 (46%)	3 (28%)	4 (22%)
K.	LECTURE/ORAL PRESENTATION NOTES				
a.	Alone	1 (33%)	2 (32%)	3 (33%)	4 (2%)
b.	With one or more persons	1 (1%)	2 (8%)	3 (46%)	4 (45%)
L.	INSTRUCTIONAL OR COURSE-RELATED MATERIALS				
a.	Alone	1 (12%)	2 (7%)	3 (37%)	4 (44%)
b.	With one or more persons	1 (1%)	2 (8%)	3 (40%)	4 (51%)

M. BOOKS AND MONOGRAPHS
a. Alone 1 (2%) 2 (4%) 3 (9%) 4 (85%)
b. With one or more persons 1 (0%) 2 (1%) 3 (10%) 4 (89%)
N. OTHER
a. Alone (Please specify
   _____)   1 (43%) 2 (29%) 3 (0%) 4 (28%)
b. With one or more persons
   (Please specify _____) 1 (20%) 2 (20%) 3 (20%) 4 (40%)

7.   Collaboration in writing can, of course, take many
     forms. If you have written with a co-author or as part
     of a group, please indicate how frequently you use each
     of the following organizational patterns for that
     writing. (Circle one number for each.) IF YOU NEVER
     WRITE WITH ONE OR MORE PERSONS, PLEASE SKIP TO QUESTION
     11.

	VERY OFTEN	OFTEN	OCCASION- ALLY	NEVER
ORGANIZATIONAL PATTERNS				
A. Team or group plans and outlines. Each member drafts a part. Team or group compiles the parts and revises the whole	1 (2%)	2 (12%)	3 (60%)	4 (26%)
B. Team or group plans and outlines. One member writes the entire draft. Team or group revises . . .	1 (3%)	2 (30%)	3 (53%)	4 (14%)
C. One member plans and writes draft. Group or team revises	1 (5%)	2 (33%)	3 (51%)	4 (11%)
D. One person plans and writes draft. This draft is submitted to one or more persons who revise the draft without consulting the writer of the first draft	1 (2%)	2 (11%)	3 (26%)	4 (61%)
E. Team or group plans and writes draft. This draft is submitted to one or more persons who revise the draft without consulting the writers of the first draft	1 (0%)	2 (5%)	3 (23%)	4 (72%)
F. One member assigns writing tasks. Each member carries out individual tasks. One member compiles the parts and revises the whole	1 (4%)	2 (22%)	3 (41%)	4 (33%)
G. One person dictates. Another person transcribes and revises	1 (5%)	2 (18%)	3 (32%)	4 (45%)

8. The list of organizational patterns described in question 7 is not exhaustive. If you use another organizational pattern, please describe it in the following space.

9. In general, how productive do you find writing as part of a team or group as compared to writing alone? (Circle one number.)
   (6%) 1 VERY PRODUCTIVE
   (60%) 2 PRODUCTIVE
   (34%) 3 NOT TOO PRODUCTIVE
   (0%) 4 NOT AT ALL PRODUCTIVE

10. If you write with one or more persons, who <u>most</u> <u>often</u> assumes final responsibility for the written product? (Circle one number.)
    (3%) 1 EACH MEMBER OF THE GROUP OR TEAM SHARES EQUAL RESPONSIBILITY.
    (37%) 2 ONE MEMBER OF THE GROUP OR TEAM TAKES RESPONSIBILITY.
    (52%) 3 THE HEAD OF THE GROUP TAKES RESPONSIBILITY.
    (5%) 4 A SUPERIOR OR GROUP OF SUPERIORS OUTSIDE THE GROUP TAKES RESPONSIBILITY.
    (3%) 5 OTHER (Please specify _____)

11. Which one of the following best describes the type of employer for whom you work? (Circle one number.)
    (3%) 1 BUSINESS AND INDUSTRY
    (1%) 2 COLLEGE OR UNIVERSITY
    (90%) 3 LOCAL, STATE, OR FEDERAL GOVERNMENT
    (5%) 4 SELF-EMPLOYED
    (1%) 5 OTHER (Please specify _____)

12. About how many people are employed by your institution or company?
    ____369____ NUMBER

13. And how many are employed at your branch, division, or department of that institution or company?
    ____88____ NUMBER

14. How many years have you been doing the type of work characteristic of your present job?
    ____15____ YEARS

15. Please state your title and briefly describe your major job responsibilities.
    _____ TITLE
    _____RESPONSIBILITIES

16. Please give the year of your birth.
    _____1939_____ YEAR

17. Are you: (Circle one.)
    (93%) 1 MALE
    (7%) 2 FEMALE

18. Is there anything else you can tell us about the
    writing you do in your profession that will help us
    better understand the nature, types, or frequency of
    that writing?

(THANK YOU VERY MUCH FOR YOUR COOPERATION)

MODERN LANGUAGE ASSOCIATION

SURVEY OF WRITING IN THE PROFESSIONS

This survey is intended to identify and define the nature,
types, and frequency of writing done in your profession.
For the purposes of this survey, <u>writing</u> <u>includes</u> any of the
activities that lead to a completed written product. These
activities include written or spoken brainstorming,
outlining or note-taking, organizational planning, drafting,
revising, and editing. <u>Written</u> <u>products</u> <u>include</u> any piece
of writing, from notes, directions, or forms to reports and
published materials.

1.   In general, what percentage of your professional time
     is spent in some kind of writing activity?
     42   percent

2.   What percentage of the time you spend in writing
     activities is devoted to each of the following? (Your
     figures should total 100 percent.)

		PERCENT
a.	Brainstorming and similar idea-generating activities	15 %
b.	Note-taking	18 %
c.	Organizational planning	11 %
d.	Drafting (including dictating) . . .	28 %
e.	Revising	18 %
f.	Editing (including proofreading) . .	10 %
	TOTAL	100 %

3.   Technology is changing the way many people write.
     Please indicate the percentage of the time spent in
     writing activities that you use a word processor.
     36   percent

4.   The situations in which people in the professions write
     may vary considerably. Please indicate the percentage
     of the time you spend in writing activities that is
     spent writing alone or as part of a team or group.
     (Your figures should total 100 percent.)

		PERCENT
a.	Writing alone	90 %
b.	Writing with one other person . . .	5 %
c.	Writing with a small group (2-5 persons)	3 %
d.	Writing with a large group (6 or more persons)	2 %
	TOTAL	100 %

5. How important do you think effective writing is to the successful execution of your job? (Circle one number.)
    (89%) 1   VERY IMPORTANT
    (7%) 2   IMPORTANT
    (4%) 3   NOT TOO IMPORTANT
    (0%) 4   NOT AT ALL IMPORTANT

6. Please indicate how frequently, in general, you work on the following types of writing, distinguishing between writing done alone and with one or more persons. (Circle one number for each.)

		VERY OFTEN	OFTEN	OCCASION- ALLY	NEVER
A.	LETTERS				
a.	Alone	1 (46%)	2 (34%)	3 (20%)	4 (0%)
b.	With one or more persons	1 (0%)	2 (0%)	3 (30%)	4 (70%)
B.	MEMOS				
a.	Alone	1 (39%)	2 (29%)	3 (28%)	4 (4%)
b.	With one or more persons	1 (0%)	2 (5%)	3 (32%)	4 (63%)
C.	SHORT REPORTS				
a.	Alone	1 (21%)	2 (26%)	3 (43%)	4 (10%)
b.	With one or more persons	1 (0%)	2 (7%)	3 (40%)	4 (53%)
D.	LONG REPORTS				
a.	Alone	1 (18%)	2 (14%)	3 (46%)	4 (22%)
b.	With one or more persons	1 (2%)	2 (6%)	3 (39%)	4 (53%)
E.	PROFESSIONAL ARTICLES AND ESSAYS				
a.	Alone	1 (46%)	2 (22%)	3 (26%)	4 (6%)
b.	With one or more persons	1 (2%)	2 (2%)	3 (25%)	4 (71%)
F.	POPULAR ARTICLES AND ESSAYS				
a.	Alone	1 (14%)	2 (6%)	3 (36%)	4 (44%)
b.	With one or more persons	1 (1%)	2 (2%)	3 (6%)	4 (91%)
G.	USER MANUALS OR OTHER DETAILED INSTRUCTIONS				
a.	Alone	1 (5%)	2 (3%)	3 (27%)	4 (65%)
b.	With one or more persons	1 (0%)	2 (4%)	3 (7%)	4 (89%)
H.	NEWSLETTERS, BULLETINS, OR IN-HOUSE PUBLICATIONS				
a.	Alone	1 (8%)	2 (7%)	3 (42%)	4 (43%)
b.	With one or more persons	1 (5%)	2 (5%)	3 (18%)	4 (72%)
I.	CASE STUDIES				
a.	Alone	1 (3%)	2 (1%)	3 (5%)	4 (91%)
b.	With one or more persons	1 (0%)	2 (0%)	3 (3%)	4 (97%)
J.	PROPOSALS FOR CONTRACTS AND GRANTS				
a.	Alone	1 (13%)	2 (12%)	3 (51%)	4 (24%)
b.	With one or more persons	1 (6%)	2 (5%)	3 (31%)	4 (58%)
K.	LECTURE/ORAL PRESENTATION NOTES				
a.	Alone	1 (65%)	2 (23%)	3 (9%)	4 (3%)
b.	With one or more persons	1 (1%)	2 (2%)	3 (19%)	4 (78%)
L.	INSTRUCTIONAL OR COURSE-RELATED MATERIALS				
a.	Alone	1 (59%)	2 (24%)	3 (10%)	4 (7%)
b.	With one or more persons	1 (2%)	2 (6%)	3 (32%)	4 (60%)

M. BOOKS AND MONOGRAPHS
a. Alone 1 (32%) 2 (22%) 3 (27%) 4 (19%)
b. With one or more persons 1 (1%) 2 (4%) 3 (19%) 4 (76%)
N. OTHER
a. Alone (Please specify
   _____) 1 (25%) 2 (25%) 3 (40%) 4 (10%)
b. With one or more persons
   (Please specify _____) 1 (7%) 2 (20%) 3 (27%) 4 (46%)

7. Collaboration in writing can, of course, take many
    forms. If you have written with a co-author or as part
    of a group, please indicate how frequently you use each
    of the following organizational patterns for that
    writing. (Circle one number for each.) IF YOU NEVER
    WRITE WITH ONE OR MORE PERSONS, PLEASE SKIP TO QUESTION
    11.

	VERY OFTEN	OFTEN	OCCASION-ALLY	NEVER
ORGANIZATIONAL PATTERNS				
A. Team or group plans and outlines. Each member drafts a part. Team or group compiles the parts and revises the whole	1 (9%)	2 (5%)	3 (33%)	4 (53%)
B. Team or group plans and outlines. One member writes the entire draft. Team or group revises	1 (3%)	2 (16%)	3 (25%)	4 (56%)
C. One member plans and writes draft. Group or team revises	1 (3%)	2 (11%)	3 (26%)	4 (60%)
D. One person plans and writes draft. This draft is submitted to one or more persons who revise the draft without consulting the writer of the first draft	1 (1%)	2 (3%)	3 (12%)	4 (84%)
E. Team or group plans and writes draft. This draft is submitted to one or more persons who revise the draft without consulting the writers of the first draft	1 (0%)	2 (2%)	3 (8%)	4 (90%)
F. One member assigns writing tasks. Each member carries out individual tasks. One member compiles the parts and revises the whole	1 (3%)	2 (4%)	3 (33%)	4 (60%)
G. One person dictates. Another person transcribes and revises	1 (0%)	2 (1%)	3 (8%)	4 (91%)

8. The list of organizational patterns described in
    question 7 is not exhaustive. If you use another
    organizational pattern, please describe it in the
    following space.

9. In general, how productive do you find writing as part
    of a team or group as compared to writing alone?
    (Circle one number.)
    (6%) 1 VERY PRODUCTIVE
    (41%) 2 PRODUCTIVE
    (41%) 3 NOT TOO PRODUCTIVE
    (12%) 4 NOT AT ALL PRODUCTIVE

10. If you write with one or more persons, who _most often_
    assumes final responsibility for the written product?
    (Circle one number.)
    (30%) 1 EACH MEMBER OF THE GROUP OR TEAM SHARES EQUAL
              RESPONSIBILITY.
    (32%) 2 ONE MEMBER OF THE GROUP OR TEAM TAKES
              RESPONSIBILITY.
    (33%) 3 THE HEAD OF THE GROUP TAKES RESPONSIBILITY.
    (2%) 4 A SUPERIOR OR GROUP OF SUPERIORS OUTSIDE THE
              GROUP TAKES RESPONSIBILITY.
    (3%) 5 OTHER (Please specify _____)

11. Which one of the following best describes the type of
    employer for whom you work? (Circle one number.)
    (0%) 1 BUSINESS AND INDUSTRY
    (95%) 2 COLLEGE OR UNIVERSITY
    (1%) 3 LOCAL, STATE, OR FEDERAL GOVERNMENT
    (2%) 4 SELF-EMPLOYED
    (2%) 5 OTHER (Please specify _____)

12. About how many people are employed by your institution
    or company?
    ___3,319___ NUMBER

13. And how many are employed at your branch, division, or
    department of that institution or company?
    ___201___ NUMBER

14. How many years have you been doing the type of work
    characteristic of your present job?
    ___16___ YEARS

15. Please state your title and briefly describe your major
    job responsibilities.
    _____ TITLE
    _____RESPONSIBILITIES

16. Please give the year of your birth.
    _____1939_____ YEAR

17. Are you: (Circle one.)
    (55%) 1 MALE
    (45%) 2 FEMALE

18. Is there anything else you can tell us about the writing you do in your profession that will help us better understand the nature, types, or frequency of that writing?

(THANK YOU VERY MUCH FOR YOUR COOPERATION)

PROFESSIONAL SERVICES MANAGEMENT ASSOCIATION

SURVEY OF WRITING IN THE PROFESSIONS

This survey is intended to identify and define the nature, types, and frequency of writing done in your profession. For the purposes of this survey, writing includes any of the activities that lead to a completed written product. These activities include written or spoken brainstorming, outlining or note-taking, organizational planning, drafting, revising, and editing. Written products include any piece of writing, from notes, directions, or forms to reports and published materials.

1. In general, what percentage of your professional time is spent in some kind of writing activity?
    37 percent

2. What percentage of the time you spend in writing activities is devoted to each of the following? (Your figures should total 100 percent.)

		PERCENT
a.	Brainstorming and similar idea-generating activities	16 %
b.	Note-taking	13 %
c.	Organizational planning	14 %
d.	Drafting (including dictating) . . .	33 %
e.	Revising	13 %
f.	Editing (including proofreading) . .	11 %
	TOTAL	100 %

3. Technology is changing the way many people write. Please indicate the percentage of the time spent in writing activities that you use a word processor.
    26 percent

4. The situations in which people in the professions write may vary considerably. Please indicate the percentage of the time you spend in writing activities that is spent writing alone or as part of a team or group. (Your figures should total 100 percent.)

		PERCENT
a.	Writing alone	80 %
b.	Writing with one other person . . .	12 %
c.	Writing with a small group (2-5 persons)	6 %
d.	Writing with a large group (6 or more persons)	2 %
	TOTAL	100 %

5. How important do you think effective writing is to the
    successful execution of your job? (Circle one number.)
    (89%) 1   VERY IMPORTANT
    (10%) 2   IMPORTANT
    (1%) 3   NOT TOO IMPORTANT
    (0%) 4   NOT AT ALL IMPORTANT

6. Please indicate how frequently, in general, you work on
    the following types of writing, distinguishing between
    writing done alone and with one or more persons.
    (Circle one number for each.)

		VERY OFTEN	OFTEN	OCCASION- ALLY	NEVER
A.	LETTERS				
a.	Alone	1 (67%)	2 (28%)	3 (5%)	4 (0%)
b.	With one or more persons	1 (1%)	2 (14%)	3 (56%)	4 (29%)
B.	MEMOS				
a.	Alone	1 (63%)	2 (25%)	3 (12%)	4 (0%)
b.	With one or more persons	1 (0%)	2 (9%)	3 (47%)	4 (44%)
C.	SHORT REPORTS				
a.	Alone	1 (39%)	2 (28%)	3 (32%)	4 (1%)
b.	With one or more persons	1 (3%)	2 (20%)	3 (57%)	4 (20%)
D.	LONG REPORTS				
a.	Alone	1 (20%)	2 (18%)	3 (53%)	4 (9%)
b.	With one or more persons	1 (5%)	2 (18%)	3 (55%)	4 (22%)
E.	PROFESSIONAL ARTICLES AND ESSAYS				
a.	Alone	1 (15%)	2 (2%)	3 (49%)	4 (34%)
b.	With one or more persons	1 (0%)	2 (5%)	3 (30%)	4 (65%)
F.	POPULAR ARTICLES AND ESSAYS				
a.	Alone	1 (4%)	2 (0%)	3 (17%)	4 (79%)
b.	With one or more persons	1 (0%)	2 (3%)	3 (11%)	4 (86%)
G.	USER MANUALS OR OTHER DETAILED INSTRUCTIONS				
a.	Alone	1 (6%)	2 (9%)	3 (43%)	4 (42%)
b.	With one or more persons	1 (5%)	2 (5%)	3 (35%)	4 (55%)
H.	NEWSLETTERS, BULLETINS, OR IN-HOUSE PUBLICATIONS				
a.	Alone	1 (9%)	2 (9%)	3 (43%)	4 (39%)
b.	With one or more persons	1 (4%)	2 (7%)	3 (37%)	4 (52%)
I.	CASE STUDIES				
a.	Alone	1 (5%)	2 (5%)	3 (27%)	4 (63%)
b.	With one or more persons	1 (1%)	2 (6%)	3 (19%)	4 (74%)
J.	PROPOSALS FOR CONTRACTS AND GRANTS				
a.	Alone	1 (30%)	2 (26%)	3 (24%)	4 (20%)
b.	With one or more persons	1 (22%)	2 (29%)	3 (27%)	4 (22%)
K.	LECTURE/ORAL PRESENTATION NOTES				
a.	Alone	1 (16%)	2 (20%)	3 (51%)	4 (13%)
b.	With one or more persons	1 (1%)	2 (7%)	3 (36%)	4 (56%)
L.	INSTRUCTIONAL OR COURSE-RELATED MATERIALS				
a.	Alone	1 (5%)	2 (13%)	3 (34%)	4 (48%)
b.	With one or more persons	1 (0%)	2 (8%)	3 (25%)	4 (67%)

M.   <u>BOOKS AND MONOGRAPHS</u>
a.   Alone 1 (4%) 2 (1%) 3 (7%) 4 (88%)
b.   With one or more persons 1 (0%) 2 (0%) 3 (13%) 4 (87%)
N.   <u>OTHER</u>
a.   Alone (Please specify
    _____) 1 (10%) 2 (50%) 3 (0%) 4 (40%)
b.   With one or more persons
    (Please specify _____) 1 (0%) 2 (27%) 3 (37%) 4 (36%)

7.   Collaboration in writing can, of course, take many
    forms. If you have written with a co-author or as part
    of a group, please indicate how frequently you use each
    of the following organizational patterns for that
    writing. (Circle one number for each.) IF YOU NEVER
    WRITE WITH ONE OR MORE PERSONS, PLEASE SKIP TO QUESTION
    11.

	VERY OFTEN	OFTEN	OCCASION- ALLY	NEVER
<u>ORGANIZATIONAL PATTERNS</u>				
A. Team or group plans and outlines. Each member drafts a part. Team or group compiles the parts and revises the whole	1 (3%)	2 (26%)	3 (31%)	4 (40%)
B. Team or group plans and outlines. One member writes the entire draft. Team or group revises . . .	1 (5%)	2 (26%)	3 (36%)	4 (33%)
C. One member plans and writes draft. Group or team revises	1 (12%)	2 (29%)	3 (38%)	4 (21%)
D. One person plans and writes draft. This draft is submitted to one or more persons who revise the draft without consulting the writer of the first draft	1 (3%)	2 (10%)	3 (28%)	4 (59%)
E. Team or group plans and writes draft. This draft is submitted to one or more persons who revise the draft without consulting the writers of the first draft	1 (2%)	2 (5%)	3 (10%)	4 (83%)
F. One member assigns writing tasks. Each member carries out individual tasks. One member compiles the parts and revises the whole	1 (10%)	2 (10%)	3 (43%)	4 (37%)
G. One person dictates. Another person transcribes and revises	1 (2%)	2 (9%)	3 (22%)	4 (67%)

8. The list of organizational patterns described in question 7 is not exhaustive. If you use another organizational pattern, please describe it in the following space.

9. In general, how productive do you find writing as part of a team or group as compared to writing alone? (Circle one number.)
   (14%) 1 VERY PRODUCTIVE
   (37%) 2 PRODUCTIVE
   (44%) 3 NOT TOO PRODUCTIVE
   (5%) 4 NOT AT ALL PRODUCTIVE

10. If you write with one or more persons, who <u>most often</u> assumes final responsibility for the written product? (Circle one number.)
   (3%) 1 EACH MEMBER OF THE GROUP OR TEAM SHARES EQUAL RESPONSIBILITY.
   (48%) 2 ONE MEMBER OF THE GROUP OR TEAM TAKES RESPONSIBILITY.
   (44%) 3 THE HEAD OF THE GROUP TAKES RESPONSIBILITY.
   (5%) 4 A SUPERIOR OR GROUP OF SUPERIORS OUTSIDE THE GROUP TAKES RESPONSIBILITY.
   (0%) 5 OTHER (Please specify _____)

11. Which one of the following best describes the type of employer for whom you work? (Circle one number.)
   (76%) 1 BUSINESS AND INDUSTRY
   (0%) 2 COLLEGE OR UNIVERSITY
   (0%) 3 LOCAL, STATE, OR FEDERAL GOVERNMENT
   (19%) 4 SELF-EMPLOYED
   (5%) 5 OTHER (Please specify _____)

12. About how many people are employed by your institution or company?
   ____301____ NUMBER

13. And how many are employed at your branch, division, or department of that institution or company?
   ____79____ NUMBER

14. How many years have you been doing the type of work characteristic of your present job?
   ____15____ YEARS

15. Please state your title and briefly describe your major job responsibilities.
   _____ TITLE
   _____RESPONSIBILITIES

16. Please give the year of your birth.
    _____1937_____ YEAR

17. Are you: (Circle one.)
    (90%) 1 MALE
    (10%) 2 FEMALE

18. Is there anything else you can tell us about the
    writing you do in your profession that will help us
    better understand the nature, types, or frequency of
    that writing?

(THANK YOU VERY MUCH FOR YOUR COOPERATION)

SOCIETY FOR TECHNICAL COMMUNICATION

SURVEY OF WRITING IN THE PROFESSIONS

This survey is intended to identify and define the nature,
types, and frequency of writing done in your profession.
For the purposes of this survey, writing includes any of the
activities that lead to a completed written product. These
activities include written or spoken brainstorming,
outlining or note-taking, organizational planning, drafting,
revising, and editing. Written products include any piece
of writing, from notes, directions, or forms to reports and
published materials.

1. In general, what percentage of your professional time
   is spent in some kind of writing activity?
   70   percent

2. What percentage of the time you spend in writing
   activities is devoted to each of the following? (Your
   figures should total 100 percent.)

		PERCENT
a.	Brainstorming and similar idea-generating activities	11 %
b.	Note-taking	9 %
c.	Organizational planning	14 %
d.	Drafting (including dictating) . . .	25 %
e.	Revising	19 %
f.	Editing (including proofreading) . .	22 %
	TOTAL	100 %

3. Technology is changing the way many people write.
   Please indicate the percentage of the time spent in
   writing activities that you use a word processor.
   51   percent

4. The situations in which people in the professions write
   may vary considerably. Please indicate the percentage
   of the time you spend in writing activities that is
   spent writing alone or as part of a team or group.
   (Your figures should total 100 percent.)

		PERCENT
a.	Writing alone	73 %
b.	Writing with one other person . . .	11 %
c.	Writing with a small group (2-5 persons)	13 %
d.	Writing with a large group (6 or more persons)	3 %
	TOTAL	100 %

5. How important do you think effective writing is to the successful execution of your job? (Circle one number.)
    (93%) 1   VERY IMPORTANT
    (6%) 2   IMPORTANT
    (1%) 3   NOT TOO IMPORTANT
    (0%) 4   NOT AT ALL IMPORTANT

6. Please indicate how frequently, in general, you work on the following types of writing, distinguishing between writing done alone and with one or more persons. (Circle one number for each.)

		VERY OFTEN	OFTEN	OCCASION- ALLY	NEVER
A.	LETTERS				
a.	Alone	1 (23%)	2 (18%)	3 (47%)	4 (12%)
b.	With one or more persons	1 (2%)	2 (2%)	3 (40%)	4 (56%)
B.	MEMOS				
a.	Alone	1 (33%)	2 (22%)	3 (37%)	4 (8%)
b.	With one or more persons	1 (1%)	2 (6%)	3 (35%)	4 (58%)
C.	SHORT REPORTS				
a.	Alone	1 (27%)	2 (19%)	3 (40%)	4 (14%)
b.	With one or more persons	1 (2%)	2 (16%)	3 (35%)	4 (47%)
D.	LONG REPORTS				
a.	Alone	1 (13%)	2 (16%)	3 (37%)	4 (34%)
b.	With one or more persons	1 (4%)	2 (13%)	3 (37%)	4 (46%)
E.	PROFESSIONAL ARTICLES AND ESSAYS				
a.	Alone	1 (8%)	2 (11%)	3 (31%)	4 (50%)
b.	With one or more persons	1 (1%)	2 (6%)	3 (19%)	4 (74%)
F.	POPULAR ARTICLES AND ESSAYS				
a.	Alone	1 (3%)	2 (8%)	3 (17%)	4 (72%)
b.	With one or more persons	1 (0%)	2 (1%)	3 (6%)	4 (93%)
G.	USER MANUALS OR OTHER DETAILED INSTRUCTIONS				
a.	Alone	1 (41%)	2 (17%)	3 (25%)	4 (17%)
b.	With one or more persons	1 (18%)	2 (20%)	3 (31%)	4 (31%)
H.	NEWSLETTERS, BULLETINS, OR IN-HOUSE PUBLICATIONS				
a.	Alone	1 (10%)	2 (19%)	3 (32%)	4 (39%)
b.	With one or more persons	1 (11%)	2 (8%)	3 (27%)	4 (54%)
I.	CASE STUDIES				
a.	Alone	1 (3%)	2 (5%)	3 (11%)	4 (81%)
b.	With one or more persons	1 (1%)	2 (2%)	3 (9%)	4 (88%)
J.	PROPOSALS FOR CONTRACTS AND GRANTS				
a.	Alone	1 (5%)	2 (11%)	3 (19%)	4 (65%)
b.	With one or more persons	1 (8%)	2 (11%)	3 (21%)	4 (60%)
K.	LECTURE/ORAL PRESENTATION NOTES				
a.	Alone	1 (16%)	2 (9%)	3 (45%)	4 (30%)
b.	With one or more persons	1 (2%)	2 (7%)	3 (31%)	4 (60%)
L.	INSTRUCTIONAL OR COURSE-RELATED MATERIALS				
a.	Alone	1 (20%)	2 (12%)	3 (42%)	4 (26%)
b.	With one or more persons	1 (6%)	2 (10%)	3 (35%)	4 (49%)

Appendix A

M. BOOKS AND MONOGRAPHS
a. Alone 1 (3%) 2 (3%) 3 (14%) 4 (80%)
b. With one or more persons 1 (2%) 2 (2%) 3 (10%) 4 (86%)
N. OTHER
a. Alone (Please specify
   _____) 1 (40%) 2 (13%) 3 (13%) 4 (34%)
b. With one or more persons
   (Please specify _____) 1 (11%) 2 (11%) 3 (39%) 4 (39%)

7. Collaboration in writing can, of course, take many
    forms. If you have written with a co-author or as part
    of a group, please indicate how frequently you use each
    of the following organizational patterns for that
    writing. (Circle one number for each.) IF YOU NEVER
    WRITE WITH ONE OR MORE PERSONS, PLEASE SKIP TO QUESTION
    11.

	VERY OFTEN	OFTEN	OCCASION-ALLY	NEVER

ORGANIZATIONAL PATTERNS
A. Team or group plans and
outlines. Each member drafts
a part. Team or group
compiles the parts and
revises the whole 1 (13%) 2 (19%) 3 (42%) 4 (26%)
B. Team or group plans
and outlines. One member
writes the entire draft.
Team or group revises . . . 1 (7%) 2 (22%) 3 (33%) 4 (38%)
C. One member plans and
writes draft. Group or
team revises 1 (14%) 2 (27%) 3 (38%) 4 (21%)
D. One person plans and
writes draft. This draft
is submitted to one or more
persons who revise the draft
without consulting the writer
of the first draft 1 (6%) 2 (6%) 3 (18%) 4 (70%)
E. Team or group plans and
writes draft. This draft is
submitted to one or more
persons who revise the draft
without consulting the writers
of the first draft 1 (0%) 2 (0%) 3 (23%) 4 (77%)
F. One member assigns writing
tasks. Each member carries out
individual tasks. One member
compiles the parts and revises
the whole 1 (7%) 2 (26%) 3 (37%) 4 (30%)
G. One person dictates.
Another person transcribes
and revises 1 (0%) 2 (2%) 3 (12%) 4 (86%)

8. The list of organizational patterns described in question 7 is not exhaustive. If you use another organizational pattern, please describe it in the following space.

9. In general, how productive do you find writing as part of a team or group as compared to writing alone? (Circle one number.)
   (22%) 1 VERY PRODUCTIVE
   (46%) 2 PRODUCTIVE
   (28%) 3 NOT TOO PRODUCTIVE
   (4%) 4 NOT AT ALL PRODUCTIVE

10. If you write with one or more persons, who <u>most</u> <u>often</u> assumes final responsibility for the written product? (Circle one number.)
   (17%) 1 EACH MEMBER OF THE GROUP OR TEAM SHARES EQUAL RESPONSIBILITY.
   (36%) 2 ONE MEMBER OF THE GROUP OR TEAM TAKES RESPONSIBILITY.
   (29%) 3 THE HEAD OF THE GROUP TAKES RESPONSIBILITY.
   (9%) 4 A SUPERIOR OR GROUP OF SUPERIORS OUTSIDE THE GROUP TAKES RESPONSIBILITY.
   (9%) 5 OTHER (Please specify _____)

11. Which one of the following best describes the type of employer for whom you work? (Circle one number.)
   (69%) 1 BUSINESS AND INDUSTRY
   (11%) 2 COLLEGE OR UNIVERSITY
   (1%) 3 LOCAL, STATE, OR FEDERAL GOVERNMENT
   (9%) 4 SELF-EMPLOYED
   (10%) 5 OTHER (Please specify _____)

12. About how many people are employed by your institution or company?
   ___14,834___ NUMBER

13. And how many are employed at your branch, division, or department of that institution or company?
   ___286___ NUMBER

14. How many years have you been doing the type of work characteristic of your present job?
   ___8___ YEARS

15. Please state your title and briefly describe your major job responsibilities.
   _____ TITLE
   _____RESPONSIBILITIES

16. Please give the year of your birth.
    _____1945_____ YEAR

17. Are you: (Circle one.)
    (38%) 1 MALE
    (62%) 2 FEMALE

18. Is there anything else you can tell us about the
    writing you do in your profession that will help us
    better understand the nature, types, or frequency of
    that writing?

(THANK YOU VERY MUCH FOR YOUR COOPERATION)

Appendix B / Survey of Writing in the Professions: Stage Two/Group Writing

| Department of English | Oregon State University | Moreland Hall 238
Corvallis, OR 97331-5302 | (503) 754-3244 |

March 14, 1985

Dear Member of the American Consulting Engineers Council:

Thank you very much for your thorough and informed response to our Survey of Writing in the Professions; you will soon receive a summary of the results. Thank you also for agreeing to participate in the second stage of our research, an additional questionnaire (enclosed) that will yield more detailed information about group writing in the professions.

Because you are one of only twelve members of the American Consulting Engineers Council to whom this questionnaire is being sent, your response is of great importance. You and the other eleven respondents from your association have been carefully identified as those most likely to provide substantive information about group writing in your profession. (Members of six major professional associations are participating in this research. These associations include the American Consulting Engineers Council, the American Institute of Chemists, the American Psychological Association, the International City Management Association, the Professional Services Management Association, and the Society for Technical Communication.) The information gained by this study will help us better understand the demands of writing in your profession and thus better prepare future colleagues who will work in your field.

Please complete the enclosed questionnaire at your earliest convenience and return it in the envelope provided. In addition, please attach any other materials or information that would help clarify your answers to the questionnaire or other details about group writing in your profession. To thank you for participating in this study, we will send you a copy of our Writing with Power in Groups, an analysis of the results of this research, immediately upon publication. If you have any questions about the questionnaire or about our research in general, please call or write us at the phone numbers and addresses provided below.

Thank you very much for your help.

Sincerely,

Lisa S. Ede
Coordinator of Composition
Director, Communication Skills Center
Oregon State University
503-754-3244

Andrea A. Lunsford
Director of Composition
University of British Columbia
604-228-5506

LE/AL
Enclosures

AMERICAN CONSULTING ENGINEERS COUNCIL

SURVEY OF WRITING IN THE PROFESSIONS
STAGE II: GROUP WRITING

This survey explores the dynamics and demands of group writing in your profession. For the purposes of this survey, <u>writing</u> includes any of the activities that lead to a completed written product. These activities include written and spoken brainstorming, outlining, note-taking, organizational planning, drafting, revising, and editing. <u>Written</u> products include any piece of writing, from notes, directions, and forms to reports and published materials. <u>Group writing</u> includes any writing done in collaboration with one or more persons.

1. In general, do you work with the same person or persons in producing a written document? (Circle one number.)
1   YES ---->   (Please indicate the number of persons in this group.)
    (27%)   __3-10__ NUMBER OF PERSONS IN GROUP
2   NO   ---->   (Please indicate the number of persons in the three groups with which you most regularly work.)
    (73%)   __1-3__ NUMBER OF PERSONS IN FIRST GROUP
                   __1-8__ NUMBER OF PERSONS IN SECOND GROUP
                   __1-20__ NUMBER OF PERSONS IN THIRD GROUP

2. Please add any additional comments about the groups with which you work.

3. From the following list, please indicate the four kinds of documents that you most typically work on as part of a group, rank ordering them in terms of frequency written. (Place one letter in each of the appropriate boxes.)

_J/H*_	MOST FREQUENTLY WRITTEN	A.	Memos
		B.	Short reports
		C.	Long reports
_C_	SECOND MOST FREQUENTLY WRITTEN	D.	Professional articles and essays
		E.	Popular articles and essays
		F.	User manuals or other detailed instructions
		G.	Newsletters, bulletins, or other in-house publications
_J_	THIRD MOST FREQUENTLY	H.	Letters
		I.	Case Studies

	WRITTEN	J.	Proposals for contracts or grants
H*	FOURTH MOST FREQUENTLY WRITTEN	K.	Lecture/oral presentation notes
		L.	Instructional or other course-related materials
		M.	Books and monographs
		N.	Other (Please specify__)

* This response is anomalous, since respondents later identified letters as one of the documents <u>least</u> productive to work on collaboratively. Our interviews suggest that a number of respondents may have misread this question and simply marked the documents most frequently written, whether alone or in collaboration with others.

4. In general, which of the documents cited in question 3 do you find <u>most</u> <u>productive</u> to work on as part of a group, and why? Please refer to all of these documents, not just the four documents you most frequently write.

5. In general, which of the documents cited in question 3 do you find <u>least</u> <u>productive</u> to work on as part of a group, and why? Please refer to all of these documents, not just the four documents you most frequently write.

6. When you participate in a group writing project, do you generally carry out each of the following activities alone, with other group members, or partly alone and partly with the group? If you are generally not involved in one or more of these activities, please circle 4 for not applicable. (Circle one number for each.)

	GENERALLY ALONE	GENERALLY AS PART OF GROUP	PARTLY ALONE AND PARTLY WITH GROUP	NOT APPLIC-ABLE
a. Brainstorming and similar idea-generating activities	1 (0%)	2 (18%)	3 (82%)	4 (0%)
b. Information gathering	1 (18%)	2 (18%)	3 (64%)	4 (0%)
c. Organizational planning	1 (45%)	2 (46%)	3 (9%)	4 (0%)
d. Drafting (including dictating)	1 (73%)	2 (0%)	3 (27%)	4 (0%)
e. Revising . . .	1 (36%)	2 (0%)	3 (64%)	4 (0%)
f. Editing (including proofreading . . .	1 (55%)	2 (0%)	3 (36%)	4 (9%)

7. Which of these activities (brainstorming, information-gathering, organizational planning, drafting, revising, editing) do you find _most_ _productive_ to perform as part of a group, and why?

8. Which of these activities (brainstorming, information-gathering, organizational planning, drafting, revising, editing) do you find _least_ _productive_ to perform as part of a group, and why?

9. Please indicate the frequency of use of prepared in-house or other "boilerplate" materials used in documents your group or groups produce. Such materials might include standard descriptions of equipment, facilities, staff, processes, or methods that are regularly included in various documents. (Circle one number.)

        1 NEVER   (PLEASE SKIP TO QUESTION #10)   (9%)
    --2 SELDOM USED   (18%)
    --3 OFTEN USED   (55%)
    --4 VERY OFTEN USED   (18%)

    ------> 9a. Approximately how many "boilerplate materials" do you use in a typical document? (Circle one number.)

    (10%)   1   "BOILERPLATE MATERIALS" COMPRISE 75-100% OF A TYPICAL DOCUMENT
    (30%)   2   "BOILERPLATE MATERIALS" COMPRISE 50%-74% OF A TYPICAL DOCUMENT
    (40%)   3   "BOILERPLATE MATERIALS" COMPRISE 25%-49% OF A TYPICAL DOCUMENT
    (20%)   4   "BOILERPLATE MATERIALS" COMPRISE 0%-24% OF A TYPICAL DOCUMENT

             9b. How productive do you find the use of such in-house or "boilerplate" materials? (Circle one number.)
    (40%)   1   VERY PRODUCTIVE
    (50%)   2   PRODUCTIVE
    (10%)   3   NOT TOO PRODUCTIVE
    (0%)   4   NOT AT ALL PRODUCTIVE

             9c. Do you have any additional comments about the use or productivity of in-house or "boilerplate" materials in group writing?

10. How often do the group or groups with which you work assign duties for completing a project according to a set plan? (The set plan might specify, for instance, that the group will plan and outline a proposed document together, then divide writing tasks so that each member drafts a part, and then reconvene so that the group can compile and revise the entire document.) (Circle one number.)

```
       1    NEVER    (PLEASE SKIP TO QUESTION #11)  ( 0%)
  --   2    SELDOM                                   (36%)
  --   3    OFTEN                                    (46%)
  --   4    VERY OFTEN                               ( 9%)
  --   5    ALWAYS                                   ( 9%)

  -------> 10a.   When your group or groups follow a set plan
                  to divide duties, who typically assigns the
                  tasks each member of the group will
                  accomplish?  (Circle one number.)
```

```
(100%)    1    GROUP LEADER
(  0%)    2    SUPERIOR OUTSIDE THE GROUP
(  0%)    3    GROUP MEMBER OTHER THAN LEADER
(  0%)    4    THE ENTIRE GROUP
(  0%)    5    OTHER (Please specify_____)
```

10b. When your group or groups follow a set plan, how productive do you find its use? (Circle one number.)

```
(27%)    1    VERY PRODUCTIVE
(73%)    2    PRODUCTIVE
( 0%)    3    NOT TOO PRODUCTIVE
( 0%)    4    NOT AT ALL PRODUCTIVE
```

10C. Please briefly describe the set plan your group or groups most often use in assigning duties, or attach a copy of the plan with this questionnaire. (After describing this set plan, please skip to question #12.)

11. If the group or groups you write with do not follow a set plan to assign duties, how do you decide how those duties will be divided?

12. When you write as part of a group, how is authorship or credit most often assigned? (Circle one number.)

(9%)   1   TO ALL THOSE WHO PARTICIPATED IN THE
              PROJECT
(9%)   2   TO THE MAIN WRITER(S)
(27%)   3   TO THE GROUP LEADER
(9%)   4   TO THE WRITERS OF EACH SECTION
              OF THE DOCUMENT
(0%)   5   TO A SUPERIOR OUTSIDE THE GROUP
(46%)   6   TO THE COMPANY ONLY (NO PERSON
              IS CITED AS THE AUTHOR)
(7%)   7   OTHER (Please specify_____)

13. Are you satisfied or dissatisfied with the way
    authorship or credit is typically assigned in group
    writing projects in which you participate?

         | --   1   SATISFIED   (91%)
         | --   2   DISSATISFIED   (9%)
         |
         |----> 13a. Please explain why you are satisfied
                      or dissatisfied with the way
                      authorship or credit is typically
                      assigned in group writing projects in
                      which you participate.

14. In your experience, to what extent are members of the
    group or groups with which you work likely to agree
    about each of the following areas? If you are
    generally not involved with one or more of these areas,
    please circle 5 for not applicable. (Circle one number
    for each.)

	VERY LIKELY TO AGREE	LIKELY TO AGREE	LIKELY TO DISAGREE	VERY LIKELY TO DISAGREE	NOT APPLIC-ABLE
a. Division of duties . .	1 (36%)	2 (55%)	3 (0%)	4 (0%)	5 (9%)
b. Research methodology . .	1 (9%)	2 (55%)	3 (9%)	4 (0%)	5 (27%)
c. Content or substance . .	1 (9%)	2 (64%)	3 (0%)	4 (27%)	5 (0%)
d. Format or organization of document . . .	1 (27%)	2 (55%)	3 (18%)	4 (0%)	5 (0%)
e. Style . .	1 (18%)	2 (37%)	3 (27%)	4 (9%)	5 (9%)
f. Grammar, punctuation or usage . . .	1 (9%)	2 (46%)	3 (18%)	4 (18%)	5 (9%)

g. credit or
responsibility
for document   1 (27%) 2 (37%) 3 (9%) 4 (0%) 5 (27%)
h. other
Please specify 1   2   3   4   5

_____

_____

15. When the group or groups with which you work come to
    the revision stage of a project, who most often does
    the actual revision? (Circle one number.)

    (82%)   1   GROUP LEADER
    (9%)   2   GROUP MEMBER OTHER THAN LEADER
    (0%)   3   ENTIRE GROUP
    (9%)   4   SEVERAL MEMBERS OF THE GROUP
    (0%)   5   TECHNICAL WRITER OR EDITOR
                    WITHIN THE GROUP
    (0%)   6   TECHNICAL WRITER OR EDITOR
                    OUTSIDE THE GROUP
    (0%)   7   OTHER (Please specify _____)

16. Please briefly describe the stages of review a group-
    written document typically goes through from the time
    the initial draft is complete to the time it is
    delivered to the intended receiver. (Please include
    all levels of review--legal, editorial, scientific,
    technical, etc.)

17. When you are working on a group writing project, how
    often do you use the following technologies? (Circle
    one number for each.)

	VERY OFTEN	OFTEN	OCCASION- ALLY	NEVER
a. Photocopying . . .	1 (91%)	2 (9%)	3 (0%)	4 (0%)
b. Conference phone calls	1 (18%)	2 (0%)	3 (64%)	4 (18%)
c. Teleconferencing . .	1 (0%)	2 (9%)	3 (18%)	4 (73%)
d. Electronic mail . .	1 (0%)	2 (18%)	3 (18%)	4 (64%)
e. Computer links . . .	1 (0%)	2 (18%)	3 (55%)	4 (27%)
f. Word processing . . .	1 (91%)	2 (9%)	3 (0%)	4 (0%)
g. Dictaphones	1 (27%)	2 (27%)	3 (9%)	4 (37%)
h. Other (Please specify _____)	1	2	3	4

18. Have any of the technologies listed in the preceding question affected the writing you typically do as part of a group? (Circle one number.)

```
    1    NO        (27%)
|-- 2    YES       (73%)
|
|------> 18a.  Please describe how any of these
              technologies have affected your writing.
```

19. In your experience, what are the three greatest <u>advantages</u> of group writing in your profession?

20. In your experience, what are the three greatest <u>disadvantages</u> of group writing in your profession?

21. Please comment on how your participation in group writing contributes or does not contribute to your overall job satisfaction.

22. What advice would you give to someone in your field about how to write effectively as part of a group?

23. Were you given any on-the-job training to prepare you for the group writing you do? (Circle one number.)

```
    1    NO    (73%)
|-- 2    YES   (27%)
|
|------>  23a.  Please describe this training and comment on
              its effectiveness.
```

24. Do you feel that your high school and college English classes adequately prepared you for the group writing you do in your profession? (Circle one number.)

1 YES (36%)
-- 2 NO (64%)

------> 24a. Please comment on how your high school or college English classes might have better prepared you for professional group writing tasks.

25. What degrees, if any, do you hold? Please list the degree (BA, MA, etc.), the major, the year awarded, and the awarding institution.

DEGREE	MAJOR	YEAR	INSTITUTION
_____	_____	_____	_____
_____	_____	_____	_____

26. Please add any additional comments that will help us better understand group writing in your profession.

(THANK YOU FOR YOUR COOPERATION)

AMERICAN INSTITUTE OF CHEMISTS

SURVEY OF WRITING IN THE PROFESSIONS
STAGE II: GROUP WRITING

This survey explores the dynamics and demands of group
writing in your profession. For the purposes of this
survey, <u>writing</u> includes any of the activities that lead to
a completed written product. These activities include
written and spoken brainstorming, outlining, note-taking,
organizational planning, drafting, revising, and editing.
<u>Written</u> products include any piece of writing, from notes,
directions, and forms to reports and published materials.
<u>Group</u> <u>writing</u> includes any writing done in collaboration
with one or more persons.

1. In general, do you work with the same person or persons
    in producing a written document? (Circle one number.)

    1   YES ---->   (Please indicate the number of persons
                          in this group.)
        (57%)   __2-25__ NUMBER OF PERSONS IN GROUP
    2   NO ---->   (Please indicate the number of persons
                          in the three groups with which you most
                          regularly work.)
        (43%)   __2-7__ NUMBER OF PERSONS IN FIRST GROUP
                          __1-8__ NUMBER OF PERSONS IN SECOND
                                   GROUP
                          __1-6__ NUMBER OF PERSONS IN THIRD GROUP

2. Please add any additional comments about the groups
    with which you work.

3. From the following list, please indicate the four kinds
    of documents that you most typically work on as part of
    a group, rank ordering them in terms of frequency
    written. (Place one letter in each of the appropriate
    boxes.)

__B__	MOST FREQUENTLY	A.	Memos
	WRITTEN	B.	Short reports
		C.	Long reports
__B__	SECOND MOST	D.	Professional articles and
	FREQUENTLY		essays
	WRITTEN	E.	Popular articles and
			essays
		F.	User manuals or other
			detailed instructions
		G.	Newsletters, bulletins, or
			other in-house
			publications
__D__	THIRD MOST	H.	Letters
	FREQUENTLY	I.	Case Studies

```
          WRITTEN              J.  Proposals for contracts
                                   or grants
          FOURTH MOST          K.  Lecture/oral presentation
    C     FREQUENTLY               notes
          WRITTEN              L.  Instructional or other
                                   course-related materials
                               M.  Books and monographs
                               N.  Other (Please specify__)
```

4. In general, which of the documents cited in question 3
    do you find <u>most productive</u> to work on as part of a
    group, and why? Please refer to all of these
    documents, not just the four documents you most
    frequently write.

5. In general, which of the documents cited in question 3
    do you find <u>least productive</u> to work on as part of a
    group, and why? Please refer to all of these
    documents, not just the four documents you most
    frequently write.

6. When you participate in a group writing project, do you
    generally carry out each of the following activities
    alone, with other group members, or partly alone and
    partly with the group? If you are generally not
    involved in one or more of these activities, please
    circle 4 for not applicable. (Circle one number for
    each.)

	GENERALLY ALONE	GENERALLY AS PART OF GROUP	PARTLY ALONE AND PARTLY WITH GROUP	NOT APPLIC- ABLE
a. Brainstorming and similar idea-generating activities	1 (14%)	2 (72%)	3 (14%)	4 (0%)
b. Information gathering	1 (36%)	2 (0%)	3 (64%)	4 (0%)
c. Organizational planning	1 (21%)	2 (43%)	3 (29%)	4 (7%)
d. Drafting (including dictating)	1 (71%)	2 (7%)	3 (22%)	4 (0%)
e. Revising . . .	1 (43%)	2 (36%)	3 (21%)	4 (0%)
f. Editing (including proofreading . . .	1 (57%)	2 (7%)	3 (29%)	4 (7%)

7. Which of these activities (brainstorming, information-
    gathering, organizational planning, drafting, revising,
    editing) do you find <u>most productive</u> to perform as part
    of a group, and why?

8. Which of these activities (brainstorming, information-gathering, organizational planning, drafting, revising, editing) do you find _least_ productive to perform as part of a group, and why?

9. Please indicate the frequency of use of prepared in-house or other "boilerplate" materials used in documents your group or groups produce. Such materials might include standard descriptions of equipment, facilities, staff, processes, or methods that are regularly included in various documents. (Circle one number.)

     1 NEVER   (PLEASE SKIP TO QUESTION #10)   (31%)
    --2 SELDOM USED   (46%)
    --3 OFTEN USED   (23%)
    --4 VERY OFTEN USED   (0%)

    ------> 9a. Approximately how many "boilerplate" materials" do you use in a typical document? (Circle one number.)

    (0%)   1   "BOILERPLATE MATERIALS" COMPRISE 75-100% OF A TYPICAL DOCUMENT
    (0%)   2   "BOILERPLATE MATERIALS" COMPRISE 50%-74% OF A TYPICAL DOCUMENT
    (30%)   3   "BOILERPLATE MATERIALS" COMPRISE 25%-49% OF A TYPICAL DOCUMENT
    (70%)   4   "BOILERPLATE MATERIALS" COMPRISE 0%-24% OF A TYPICAL DOCUMENT

             9b. How productive do you find the use of such in-house or "boilerplate" materials? (Circle one number.)
    (20%)   1   VERY PRODUCTIVE
    (70%)   2   PRODUCTIVE
    (10%)   3   NOT TOO PRODUCTIVE
    (0%)   4   NOT AT ALL PRODUCTIVE

             9c. Do you have any additional comments about the use or productivity of in-house or "boilerplate" materials in group writing?

10. How often do the group or groups with which you work
    assign duties for completing a project according to a
    set plan? (The set plan might specify, for instance,
    that the group will plan and outline a proposed
    document together, then divide writing tasks so that
    each member drafts a part, and then reconvene so that
    the group can compile and revise the entire document.)
    (Circle one number.)

     1   NEVER   (PLEASE SKIP TO QUESTION #11)   (14%)
  -- 2   SELDOM   (7%)
  -- 3   OFTEN   (57%)
  -- 4   VERY OFTEN   (22%)
  -- 5   ALWAYS   (0%)

------> 10a. When your group or groups follow a set plan
            to divide duties, who typically assigns the
            tasks each member of the group will
            accomplish? (Circle one number.)

  (75%)   1   GROUP LEADER
  (8%)   2   SUPERIOR OUTSIDE THE GROUP
  (0%)   3   GROUP MEMBER OTHER THAN LEADER
  (17%)   4   THE ENTIRE GROUP
  (3%)   5   OTHER (Please specify_____)

        10b. When your group or groups follow a set plan,
            how productive do you find its use? (Circle
            one number.)

  (25%)   1   VERY PRODUCTIVE
  (75%)   2   PRODUCTIVE
  (0%)   3   NOT TOO PRODUCTIVE
  (0%)   4   NOT AT ALL PRODUCTIVE

        10C. Please briefly describe the set plan your
            group or groups most often use in assigning
            duties, or attach a copy of the plan with
            this questionnaire. (After describing this
            set plan, please skip to question #12.)

11. If the group or groups you write with do <u>not</u> follow a
    set plan to assign duties, how do you decide how those
    duties will be divided?

12. When you write as part of a group, how is authorship or credit most often assigned? (Circle one number.)

(64%)	1	TO ALL THOSE WHO PARTICIPATED IN THE PROJECT
(7%)	2	TO THE MAIN WRITER(S)
(0%)	3	TO THE GROUP LEADER
(0%)	4	TO THE WRITERS OF EACH SECTION OF THE DOCUMENT
(0%)	5	TO A SUPERIOR OUTSIDE THE GROUP
(29%)	6	TO THE COMPANY ONLY (NO PERSON IS CITED AS THE AUTHOR)
(0%)	7	OTHER (Please specify_____)

13. Are you satisfied or dissatisfied with the way authorship or credit is typically assigned in group writing projects in which you participate?

```
|-- 1    SATISFIED      (85%)
|-- 2    DISSATISFIED   (15%)
|
|----> 13a.  Please explain why you are satisfied
             or dissatisfied with the way
             authorship or credit is typically
             assigned in group writing projects in
             which you participate.
```

14. In your experience, to what extent are members of the group or groups with which you work likely to agree about each of the following areas? If you are generally not involved with one or more of these areas, please circle 5 for not applicable. (Circle one number for each.)

	VERY LIKELY TO AGREE	LIKELY TO AGREE	LIKELY TO DISAGREE	VERY LIKELY TO DISAGREE	NOT APPLIC- ABLE
a. Division of duties . .	1 (36%)	2 (57%)	3 (0%)	4 (0%)	5 (7%)
b. Research methodology . .	1 (21%)	2 (43%)	3 (29%)	4 (0%)	5 (7%)
c. Content or substance . .	1 (0%)	2 (71%)	3 (22%)	4 (7%)	5 (0%)
d. Format or organization of document . . .	1 (21%)	2 (50%)	3 (22%)	4 (0%)	5 (7%)
e. Style . .	1 (7%)	2 (50%)	3 (29%)	4 (7%)	5 (7%)
f. Grammar, punctuation or usage . . .	1 (29%)	2 (43%)	3 (14%)	4 (7%)	5 (7%)

g. credit or
responsibility
for document   1 (36%) 2 (43%) 3 (14%) 4 (0%) 5 (7%)
h. other
Please specify 1   2   3   4   5

_____

_____

15.   When the group or groups with which you work come to
      the revision stage of a project, who most often does
      the actual revision? (Circle one number.)

         (14%)   1   GROUP LEADER
         (22%)   2   GROUP MEMBER OTHER THAN LEADER
         (14%)   3   ENTIRE GROUP
         (29%)   4   SEVERAL MEMBERS OF THE GROUP
         (7%)   5   TECHNICAL WRITER OR EDITOR
                         WITHIN THE GROUP
         (0%)   6   TECHNICAL WRITER OR EDITOR
                         OUTSIDE THE GROUP
         (14%)   7   OTHER (Please specify _____)

16.   Please briefly describe the stages of review a group-
      written document typically goes through from the time
      the initial draft is complete to the time it is
      delivered to the intended receiver. (Please include
      all levels of review--legal, editorial, scientific,
      technical, etc.)

17.   When you are working on a group writing project, how
      often do you use the following technologies? (Circle
      one number for each.)

	VERY OFTEN	OFTEN	OCCASION- ALLY	NEVER
a. Photocopying . . .	1 (93%)	2 (7%)	3 (0%)	4 (0%)
b. Conference phone calls	1 (16%)	2 (23%)	3 (46%)	4 (15%)
c. Teleconferencing . .	1 (0%)	2 (0%)	3 (15%)	4 (85%)
d. Electronic mail . .	1 (7%)	2 (21%)	3 (29%)	4 (43%)
e. Computer links . . .	1 (7%)	2 (21%)	3 (36%)	4 (36%)
f. Word processing . . .	1 (86%)	2 (14%)	3 (0%)	4 (0%)
g. Dictaphones	1 (0%)	2 (0%)	3 (46%)	4 (54%)
h. Other (Please specify _____)	1	2	3	4

18. Have any of the technologies listed in the preceding question affected the writing you typically do as part of a group? (Circle one number.)

```
    1   NO        (17%)
|-- 2   YES       (83%)
|
|------> 18a.  Please describe how any of these
              technologies have affected your writing.
```

19. In your experience, what are the three greatest advantages of group writing in your profession?

20. In your experience, what are the three greatest disadvantages of group writing in your profession?

21. Please comment on how your participation in group writing contributes or does not contribute to your overall job satisfaction.

22. What advice would you give to someone in your field about how to write effectively as part of a group?

23. Were you given any on-the-job training to prepare you for the group writing you do? (Circle one number.)

```
    1   NO   (79%)
|-- 2   YES  (21%)
|
|------> 23a.  Please describe this training and comment on
              its effectiveness.
```

24. Do you feel that your high school and college English classes adequately prepared you for the group writing you do in your profession? (Circle one number.)

```
    1    YES  (64%)
--  2    NO   (36%)

------>  24a.  Please comment on how your high school or
               college English classes might have better
               prepared you for professional group writing
               tasks.
```

25. What degrees, if any, do you hold? Please list the degree (BA, MA, etc.), the major, the year awarded, and the awarding institution.

DEGREE	MAJOR	YEAR	INSTITUTION
_____	_____	_____	_____
_____	_____	_____	_____
_____	_____	_____	_____

26. Please add any additional comments that will help us better understand group writing in your profession.

(THANK YOU FOR YOUR COOPERATION)

AMERICAN PSYCHOLOGICAL ASSOCIATION

SURVEY OF WRITING IN THE PROFESSIONS
STAGE II: GROUP WRITING

This survey explores the dynamics and demands of group writing in your profession. For the purposes of this survey, <u>writing</u> includes any of the activities that lead to a completed written product. These activities include written and spoken brainstorming, outlining, note-taking, organizational planning, drafting, revising, and editing. <u>Written</u> products include any piece of writing, from notes, directions, and forms to reports and published materials. <u>Group writing</u> includes any writing done in collaboration with one or more persons.

1.   In general, do you work with the same person or persons in producing a written document? (Circle one number.)

1   YES ---->   (Please indicate the number of persons in this group.)
      (27%)   <u>1-3</u> NUMBER OF PERSONS IN GROUP
2   NO ---->   (Please indicate the number of persons in the three groups with which you most regularly work.)
      (73%)   <u>2-3</u> NUMBER OF PERSONS IN FIRST GROUP
                      <u>2-12</u> NUMBER OF PERSONS IN SECOND GROUP
                      <u>2-8</u> NUMBER OF PERSONS IN THIRD GROUP

2.   Please add any additional comments about the groups with which you work.

3.   From the following list, please indicate the four kinds of documents that you most typically work on as part of a group, rank ordering them in terms of frequency written. (Place one letter in each of the appropriate boxes.)

<u>A/D</u>	MOST FREQUENTLY WRITTEN	A.	Memos
		B.	Short reports
		C.	Long reports
<u>B</u>	SECOND MOST FREQUENTLY WRITTEN	D.	Professional articles and essays
		E.	Popular articles and essays
		F.	User manuals or other detailed instructions
		G.	Newsletters, bulletins, or other in-house publications
<u>G</u>	THIRD MOST FREQUENTLY	H.	Letters
		I.	Case Studies

```
        WRITTEN           J.   Proposals for contracts
                               or grants
        FOURTH MOST       K.   Lecture/oral presentation
  D     FREQUENTLY             notes
        WRITTEN           L.   Instructional or other
                               course-related materials
                          M.   Books and monographs
                          N.   Other (Please specify__)
```

4.   In general, which of the documents cited in question 3 do you find <u>most</u> <u>productive</u> to work on as part of a group, and why? Please refer to all of these documents, not just the four documents you most frequently write.

5.   In general, which of the documents cited in question 3 do you find <u>least</u> <u>productive</u> to work on as part of a group, and why? Please refer to all of these documents, not just the four documents you most frequently write.

6.   When you participate in a group writing project, do you generally carry out each of the following activities alone, with other group members, or partly alone and partly with the group? If you are generally not involved in one or more of these activities, please circle 4 for not applicable. (Circle one number for each.)

	GENERALLY ALONE	GENERALLY AS PART OF GROUP	PARTLY ALONE AND PARTLY WITH GROUP	NOT APPLIC- ABLE
a. Brainstorming and similar idea-generating activities	1 (0%)	2 (50%)	3 (50%)	4 (0%)
b. Information gathering	1 (67%)	2 (0%)	3 (33%)	4 (0%)
c. Organizational planning	1 (0%)	2 (17%)	3 (75%)	4 (8%)
d. Drafting (including dictating)	1 (67%)	2 (8%)	3 (25%)	4 (0%)
e. Revising . . .	1 (25%)	2 (17%)	3 (58%)	4 (0%)
f. Editing (including proofreading . . .	1 (50%)	2 (0%)	3 (42%)	4 (8%)

7.   Which of these activities (brainstorming, information-gathering, organizational planning, drafting, revising, editing) do you find <u>most</u> <u>productive</u> to perform as part of a group, and why?

8. Which of these activities (brainstorming, information-gathering, organizational planning, drafting, revising, editing) do you find least productive to perform as part of a group, and why?

9. Please indicate the frequency of use of prepared in-house or other "boilerplate" materials used in documents your group or groups produce. Such materials might include standard descriptions of equipment, facilities, staff, processes, or methods that are regularly included in various documents. (Circle one number.)

```
  1 NEVER    (PLEASE SKIP TO QUESTION #10)    (33%)
--2 SELDOM USED                               (50%)
--3 OFTEN USED                                (17%)
--4 VERY OFTEN USED                           ( 0%)

------>  9a.  Approximately how many "boilerplate
              materials" do you use in a typical document?
              (Circle one number.)
```

(0%)   1   "BOILERPLATE MATERIALS" COMPRISE 75-100% OF A TYPICAL DOCUMENT

(0%)   2   "BOILERPLATE MATERIALS" COMPRISE 50%-74% OF A TYPICAL DOCUMENT

(25%)   3   "BOILERPLATE MATERIALS" COMPRISE 25%-49% OF A TYPICAL DOCUMENT

(75%)   4   "BOILERPLATE MATERIALS" COMPRISE 0%-24% OF A TYPICAL DOCUMENT

9b. How productive do you find the use of such in-house or "boilerplate" materials? (Circle one number.)

(25%)   1   VERY PRODUCTIVE
(25%)   2   PRODUCTIVE
(38%)   3   NOT TOO PRODUCTIVE
(12%)   4   NOT AT ALL PRODUCTIVE

9c. Do you have any additional comments about the use or productivity of in-house or "boilerplate" materials in group writing?

10. How often do the group or groups with which you work assign duties for completing a project according to a set plan? (The set plan might specify, for instance, that the group will plan and outline a proposed document together, then divide writing tasks so that each member drafts a part, and then reconvene so that the group can compile and revise the entire document.) (Circle one number.)

	1	NEVER	(PLEASE SKIP TO QUESTION #11)	(17%)
--	2	SELDOM		(8%)
--	3	OFTEN		(42%)
--	4	VERY OFTEN		(25%)
--	5	ALWAYS		(8%)

-------> 10a. When your group or groups follow a set plan to divide duties, who typically assigns the tasks each member of the group will accomplish? (Circle one number.)

(50%)	1	GROUP LEADER
(0%)	2	SUPERIOR OUTSIDE THE GROUP
(0%)	3	GROUP MEMBER OTHER THAN LEADER
(50%)	4	THE ENTIRE GROUP
(0%)	5	OTHER (Please specify_____)

10b. When your group or groups follow a set plan, how productive do you find its use? (Circle one number.)

(30%)	1	VERY PRODUCTIVE
(70%)	2	PRODUCTIVE
(0%)	3	NOT TOO PRODUCTIVE
(0%)	4	NOT AT ALL PRODUCTIVE

10C. Please briefly describe the set plan your group or groups most often use in assigning duties, or attach a copy of the plan with this questionnaire. (After describing this set plan, please skip to question #12.)

11. If the group or groups you write with do not follow a set plan to assign duties, how do you decide how those duties will be divided?

12. When you write as part of a group, how is authorship or credit most often assigned? (Circle one number.)

(84%)	1	TO ALL THOSE WHO PARTICIPATED IN THE PROJECT
(0%)	2	TO THE MAIN WRITER(S)
(0%)	3	TO THE GROUP LEADER
(8%)	4	TO THE WRITERS OF EACH SECTION OF THE DOCUMENT
(0%)	5	TO A SUPERIOR OUTSIDE THE GROUP
(8%)	6	TO THE COMPANY ONLY (NO PERSON IS CITED AS THE AUTHOR)
(0%)	7	OTHER (Please specify_____)

13. Are you satisfied or dissatisfied with the way authorship or credit is typically assigned in group writing projects in which you participate?

    | -- 1   SATISFIED   (100%)
    | -- 2   DISSATISFIED

    |----> 13a. Please explain why you are satisfied
    | or dissatisfied with the way
    | authorship or credit is typically
    | assigned in group writing projects in
    | which you participate.

14. In your experience, to what extent are members of the group or groups with which you work likely to agree about each of the following areas? If you are generally not involved with one or more of these areas, please circle 5 for not applicable. (Circle one number for each.)

	VERY LIKELY TO AGREE	LIKELY TO AGREE	LIKELY TO DISAGREE	VERY LIKELY TO DISAGREE	NOT APPLIC- ABLE
a. Division of duties . .	1 (42%)	2 (58%)	3 (0%)	4 (0%)	5 (0%)
b. Research methodology . .	1 (8%)	2 (76%)	3 (8%)	4 (0%)	5 (8%)
c. Content or substance . .	1 (25%)	2 (59%)	3 (8%)	4 (8%)	5 (0%)
d. Format or organization of document . . .	1 (8%)	2 (75%)	3 (17%)	4 (0%)	5 (0%)
e. Style . .	1 (8%)	2 (67%)	3 (25%)	4 (0%)	5 (0%)
f. Grammar, punctuation or usage . . .	1 (25%)	2 (58%)	3 (17%)	4 (0%)	5 (0%)

g. credit or
responsibility
for document   1 (58%) 2 (42%) 3 (0%) 4 (0%) 5 (0%)
h. other
Please specify 1   2   3   4   5

_____

_____

15. When the group or groups with which you work come to
     the revision stage of a project, who most often does
     the actual revision? (Circle one number.)

     (50%)   1   GROUP LEADER
     (17%)   2   GROUP MEMBER OTHER THAN LEADER
     (8%)   3   ENTIRE GROUP
     (25%)   4   SEVERAL MEMBERS OF THE GROUP
     (0%)   5   TECHNICAL WRITER OR EDITOR
                      WITHIN THE GROUP
     (0%)   6   TECHNICAL WRITER OR EDITOR
                      OUTSIDE THE GROUP
     (0%)   7   OTHER (Please specify _____)

16. Please briefly describe the stages of review a group-
     written document typically goes through from the time
     the initial draft is complete to the time it is
     delivered to the intended receiver. (Please include
     all levels of review--legal, editorial, scientific,
     technical, etc.)

17. When you are working on a group writing project, how
     often do you use the following technologies? (Circle
     one number for each.)

	VERY OFTEN	OFTEN	OCCASION-ALLY	NEVER
a. Photocopying . . .	1 (75%)	2 (25%)	3 (0%)	4 (0%)
b. Conference phone calls	1 (8%)	2 (25%)	3 (25%)	4 (42%)
c. Teleconferencing . .	1 (0%)	2 (8%)	3 (8%)	4 (84%)
d. Electronic mail . .	1 (0%)	2 (8%)	3 (0%)	4 (92%)
e. Computer links . . .	1 (0%)	2 (8%)	3 (17%)	4 (75%)
f. Word processing . . .	1 (50%)	2 (8%)	3 (17%)	4 (25%)
g. Dictaphones	1 (42%)	2 (33%)	3 (8%)	4 (17%)
h. Other (Please specify _____)	1	2	3	4

18. Have any of the technologies listed in the preceding question affected the writing you typically do as part of a group? (Circle one number.)

```
     1   NO       (40%)
 --  2   YES      (60%)

 ------> 18a.  Please describe how any of these
               technologies have affected your writing.
```

19. In your experience, what are the three greatest <u>advantages</u> of group writing in your profession?

20. In your experience, what are the three greatest <u>disadvantages</u> of group writing in your profession?

21. Please comment on how your participation in group writing contributes or does not contribute to your overall job satisfaction.

22. What advice would you give to someone in your field about how to write effectively as part of a group?

23. Were you given any on-the-job training to prepare you for the group writing you do? (Circle one number.)

```
     1   NO    (92%)
 --  2   YES   ( 8%)

 ------>  23a.  Please describe this training and comment on
               its effectiveness.
```

24. Do you feel that your high school and college English classes adequately prepared you for the group writing you do in your profession? (Circle one number.)

```
     1    YES   (27%)
--   2    NO    (73%)

------>  24a.  Please comment on how your high school or
               college English classes might have better
               prepared you for professional group writing
               tasks.
```

25. What degrees, if any, do you hold? Please list the degree (BA, MA, etc.), the major, the year awarded, and the awarding institution.

DEGREE	MAJOR	YEAR	INSTITUTION
_____	_____	_____	_____
_____	_____	_____	_____
_____	_____	_____	_____

26. Please add any additional comments that will help us better understand group writing in your profession.

(THANK YOU FOR YOUR COOPERATION)

INTERNATIONAL CITY MANAGEMENT ASSOCIATION

SURVEY OF WRITING IN THE PROFESSIONS
STAGE II: GROUP WRITING

This survey explores the dynamics and demands of group
writing in your profession. For the purposes of this
survey, <u>writing</u> includes any of the activities that lead to
a completed written product. These activities include
written and spoken brainstorming, outlining, note-taking,
organizational planning, drafting, revising, and editing.
<u>Written</u> products include any piece of writing, from notes,
directions, and forms to reports and published materials.
<u>Group</u> <u>writing</u> includes any writing done in collaboration
with one or more persons.

1.   In general, do you work with the same person or persons
      in producing a written document? (Circle one number.)
1.   YES ---->   (Please indicate the number of persons
                       in this group.)
      (40%)   <u>3-4</u> NUMBER OF PERSONS IN GROUP
2   NO   ---->   (Please indicate the number of persons
                       in the three groups with which you most
                       regularly work.)
      (60%)   <u>1-2</u> NUMBER OF PERSONS IN FIRST GROUP
                       <u>3-7</u> NUMBER OF PERSONS IN SECOND
                              GROUP
                      <u>5-10</u> NUMBER OF PERSONS IN THIRD GROUP

2.   Please add any additional comments about the groups
      with which you work.

3.   From the following list, please indicate the four kinds
      of documents that you most typically work on as part of
      a group, rank ordering them in terms of frequency
      written. (Place one letter in each of the appropriate
      boxes.)

	MOST FREQUENTLY	A.	Memos
<u>J/H</u>	WRITTEN	B.	Short reports
		C.	Long reports
	SECOND MOST	D.	Professional articles and
<u>B/C</u>	FREQUENTLY		essays
	WRITTEN	E.	Popular articles and
			essays
		F.	User manuals or other
			detailed instructions
		G.	Newsletters, bulletins, or
			other in-house
			publications
	THIRD MOST	H.	Letters
<u>B</u>	FREQUENTLY	I.	Case Studies

	WRITTEN	J.	Proposals for contracts or grants
__G__	FOURTH MOST FREQUENTLY WRITTEN	K.	Lecture/oral presentation notes
		L.	Instructional or other course-related materials
		M.	Books and monographs
		N.	Other (Please specify__)

4. In general, which of the documents cited in question 3 do you find __most__ productive to work on as part of a group, and why? Please refer to all of these documents, not just the four documents you most frequently write.

5. In general, which of the documents cited in question 3 do you find __least__ productive to work on as part of a group, and why? Please refer to all of these documents, not just the four documents you most frequently write.

6. When you participate in a group writing project, do you generally carry out each of the following activities alone, with other group members, or partly alone and partly with the group? If you are generally not involved in one or more of these activities, please circle 4 for not applicable. (Circle one number for each.)

	GENERALLY ALONE	GENERALLY AS PART OF GROUP	PARTLY ALONE AND PARTLY WITH GROUP	NOT APPLIC-ABLE
a. Brainstorming and similar idea-generating activities	1 (0%)	2 (33%)	3 (67%)	4 (0%)
b. Information gathering	1 (11%)	2 (11%)	3 (78%)	4 (0%)
c. Organizational planning	1 (11%)	2 (33%)	3 (56%)	4 (0%)
d. Drafting (including dictating)	1 (56%)	2 (11%)	3 (33%)	4 (0%)
e. Revising	1 (22%)	2 (67%)	3 (11%)	4 (0%)
f. Editing (including proofreading	1 (56%)	2 (11%)	3 (33%)	4 (0%)

7. Which of these activities (brainstorming, information-gathering, organizational planning, drafting, revising, editing) do you find __most__ productive to perform as part of a group, and why?

Appendix B   215

8. Which of these activities (brainstorming, information-gathering, organizational planning, drafting, revising, editing) do you find <u>least</u> <u>productive</u> to perform as part of a group, and why?

9. Please indicate the frequency of use of prepared in-house or other "boilerplate" materials used in documents your group or groups produce. Such materials might include standard descriptions of equipment, facilities, staff, processes, or methods that are regularly included in various documents. (Circle one number.)

```
   1 NEVER   (PLEASE SKIP TO QUESTION #10)    (25%)
 --2 SELDOM USED                              (62%)
 --3 OFTEN USED                               (13%)
 --4 VERY OFTEN USED                          ( 0%)
```

------> 9a. Approximately how many "boilerplate" materials" do you use in a typical document? (Circle one number.)

(0%) 1 "BOILERPLATE MATERIALS" COMPRISE 75-100% OF A TYPICAL DOCUMENT

(0%) 2 "BOILERPLATE MATERIALS" COMPRISE 50%-74% OF A TYPICAL DOCUMENT

(13%) 3 "BOILERPLATE MATERIALS" COMPRISE 25%-49% OF A TYPICAL DOCUMENT

(87%) 4 "BOILERPLATE MATERIALS" COMPRISE 0%-24% OF A TYPICAL DOCUMENT

9b. How productive do you find the use of such in-house or "boilerplate" materials? (Circle one number.)

(13%) 1 VERY PRODUCTIVE
(50%) 2 PRODUCTIVE
(37%) 3 NOT TOO PRODUCTIVE
(0%) 4 NOT AT ALL PRODUCTIVE

9c. Do you have any additional comments about the use or productivity of in-house or "boilerplate" materials in group writing?

10. How often do the group or groups with which you work assign duties for completing a project according to a set plan? (The set plan might specify, for instance, that the group will plan and outline a proposed document together, then divide writing tasks so that each member drafts a part, and then reconvene so that the group can compile and revise the entire document.) (Circle one number.)

```
    1    NEVER     (PLEASE SKIP TO QUESTION #11)   (11%)
--  2    SELDOM                                    (45%)
--  3    OFTEN                                     (33%)
--  4    VERY OFTEN                                (11%)
--  5    ALWAYS                                    ( 0%)

-------> 10a. When your group or groups follow a set plan
              to divide duties, who typically assigns the
              tasks each member of the group will
              accomplish?  (Circle one number.)

    (78%)    1    GROUP LEADER
    ( 0%)    2    SUPERIOR OUTSIDE THE GROUP
    ( 0%)    3    GROUP MEMBER OTHER THAN LEADER
    (11%)    4    THE ENTIRE GROUP
    (11%)    5    OTHER (Please specify_____)
```

10b. When your group or groups follow a set plan, how productive do you find its use? (Circle one number.)

```
    (38%)    1    VERY PRODUCTIVE
    (37%)    2    PRODUCTIVE
    (25%)    3    NOT TOO PRODUCTIVE
    ( 0%)    4    NOT AT ALL PRODUCTIVE
```

10C. Please briefly describe the set plan your group or groups most often use in assigning duties, or attach a copy of the plan with this questionnaire. (After describing this set plan, please skip to question #12.)

11. If the group or groups you write with do not follow a set plan to assign duties, how do you decide how those duties will be divided?

12. When you write as part of a group, how is authorship or credit most often assigned? (Circle one number.)

   (30%)   1   TO ALL THOSE WHO PARTICIPATED IN THE PROJECT
   (30%)   2   TO THE MAIN WRITER(S)
   (0%)   3   TO THE GROUP LEADER
   (0%)   4   TO THE WRITERS OF EACH SECTION OF THE DOCUMENT
   (0%)   5   TO A SUPERIOR OUTSIDE THE GROUP
   (20%)   6   TO THE COMPANY ONLY (NO PERSON IS CITED AS THE AUTHOR)
   (20%)   7   OTHER (Please specify_____)

13. Are you satisfied or dissatisfied with the way authorship or credit is typically assigned in group writing projects in which you participate?

    -- 1   SATISFIED   (100%)
    -- 2   DISSATISFIED

    ----> 13a. Please explain why you are satisfied or dissatisfied with the way authorship or credit is typically assigned in group writing projects in which you participate.

14. In your experience, to what extent are members of the group or groups with which you work likely to agree about each of the following areas? If you are generally not involved with one or more of these areas, please circle 5 for not applicable. (Circle one number for each.)

	VERY LIKELY TO AGREE	LIKELY TO AGREE	LIKELY TO DISAGREE	VERY LIKELY TO DISAGREE	NOT APPLIC-ABLE
a. Division of duties . .	1 (20%)	2 (50%)	3 (10%)	4 (0%)	5 (20%)
b. Research methodology . .	1 (20%)	2 (70%)	3 (0%)	4 (0%)	5 (10%)
c. Content or substance . .	1 (11%)	2 (67%)	3 (11%)	4 (11%)	5 (0%)
d. Format or organization of document . . .	1 (10%)	2 (80%)	3 (10%)	4 (0%)	5 (0%)
e. Style . .	1 (22%)	2 (45%)	3 (33%)	4 (0%)	5 (0%)
f. Grammar, punctuation or usage . . .	1 (20%)	2 (50%)	3 (20%)	4 (10%)	5 (0%)

g. credit or
responsibility
for document   1 (30%) 2 (50%) 3 (10%) 4 (10%) 5 (0%)
h. other
Please specify 1   2   3   4   5
_____
_____

15. When the group or groups with which you work come to
     the revision stage of a project, who most often does
     the actual revision? (Circle one number.)

     (33%)   1   GROUP LEADER
     (0%)   2   GROUP MEMBER OTHER THAN LEADER
     (23%)   3   ENTIRE GROUP
     (11%)   4   SEVERAL MEMBERS OF THE GROUP
     (11%)   5   TECHNICAL WRITER OR EDITOR
                    WITHIN THE GROUP
     (0%)   6   TECHNICAL WRITER OR EDITOR
                    OUTSIDE THE GROUP
     (22%)   7   OTHER (Please specify _____)

16. Please briefly describe the stages of review a group-
     written document typically goes through from the time
     the initial draft is complete to the time it is
     delivered to the intended receiver. (Please include
     all levels of review--legal, editorial, scientific,
     technical, etc.)

17. When you are working on a group writing project, how
     often do you use the following technologies? (Circle
     one number for each.)

	VERY OFTEN	OFTEN	OCCASION-ALLY	NEVER
a. Photocopying . . .	1 (67%)	2 (33%)	3 (0%)	4 (0%)
b. Conference phone calls	1 (0%)	2 (11%)	3 (67%)	4 (22%)
c. Teleconferencing . .	1 (0%)	2 (0%)	3 (22%)	4 (78%)
d. Electronic mail . .	1 (0%)	2 (0%)	3 (0%)	4 (100%)
e. Computer links . . .	1 (0%)	2 (11%)	3 (22%)	4 (67%)
f. Word processing . . .	1 (56%)	2 (22%)	3 (11%)	4 (11%)
g. Dictaphones	1 (0%)	2 (22%)	3 (45%)	4 (33%)
h. Other (Please specify _____)	1 (17%)	2 (6%)	3 (12%)	4 (65%)

18. Have any of the technologies listed in the preceding
     question affected the writing you typically do as part
     of a group? (Circle one number.)

         1   NO   (33%)
     -- 2   YES   (67%)

     ------> 18a. Please describe how any of these
                   technologies have affected your writing.

19. In your experience, what are the three greatest
     <u>advantages</u> of group writing in your profession?

20. In your experience, what are the three greatest
     <u>disadvantages</u> of group writing in your profession?

21. Please comment on how your participation in group
     writing contributes or does not contribute to your
     overall job satisfaction.

22. What advice would you give to someone in your field
     about how to write effectively as part of a group?

23. Were you given any on-the-job training to prepare you
     for the group writing you do? (Circle one number.)

         1   NO   (80%)
     -- 2   YES   (20%)

     ------>   23a. Please describe this training and comment on
                     its effectiveness.

24. Do you feel that your high school and college English classes adequately prepared you for the group writing you do in your profession? (Circle one number.)

```
     1   YES (50%)
--   2   NO  (50%)

----->  24a.  Please comment on how your high school or
              college English classes might have better
              prepared you for professional group writing
              tasks.
```

25. What degrees, if any, do you hold? Please list the degree (BA, MA, etc.), the major, the year awarded, and the awarding institution.

DEGREE	MAJOR	YEAR	INSTITUTION
_____	_____	_____	_____
_____	_____	_____	_____
_____	_____	_____	_____

26. Please add any additional comments that will help us better understand group writing in your profession.

(THANK YOU FOR YOUR COOPERATION)

MODERN LANGUAGE ASSOCIATION

SURVEY OF WRITING IN THE PROFESSIONS
STAGE II: GROUP WRITING

This survey explores the dynamics and demands of group writing in your profession. For the purposes of this survey, <u>writing</u> includes any of the activities that lead to a completed written product. These activities include written and spoken brainstorming, outlining, note-taking, organizational planning, drafting, revising, and editing. <u>Written</u> products include any piece of writing, from notes, directions, and forms to reports and published materials. <u>Group writing</u> includes any writing done in collaboration with one or more persons.

1. In general, do you work with the same person or persons in producing a written document? (Circle one number.)

1   YES ---->   (Please indicate the number of persons in this group.)
    (9%)   __2__ NUMBER OF PERSONS IN GROUP
2   NO   ---->   (Please indicate the number of persons in the three groups with which you most regularly work.)
    (91%)   _1-8_ NUMBER OF PERSONS IN FIRST GROUP
                    _2-12_ NUMBER OF PERSONS IN SECOND GROUP
                    _2-10_ NUMBER OF PERSONS IN THIRD GROUP

2. Please add any additional comments about the groups with which you work.

3. From the following list, please indicate the four kinds of documents that you most typically work on as part of a group, rank ordering them in terms of frequency written. (Place one letter in each of the appropriate boxes.)

	MOST FREQUENTLY WRITTEN	A. Memos
__A__		B. Short reports
		C. Long reports
	SECOND MOST FREQUENTLY WRITTEN	D. Professional articles and essays
__J__		
		E. Popular articles and essays
		F. User manuals or other detailed instructions
		G. Newsletters, bulletins, or other in-house publications
	THIRD MOST FREQUENTLY	H. Letters
__B__		I. Case Studies

		J.	Proposals for contracts or grants
WRITTEN		K.	Lecture/oral presentation notes
	FOURTH MOST	L.	Instructional or other course-related materials
__G__	FREQUENTLY	M.	Books and monographs
	WRITTEN	N.	Other (Please specify__)

4. In general, which of the documents cited in question 3 do you find __most__ __productive__ to work on as part of a group, and why? Please refer to all of these documents, not just the four documents you most frequently write.

5. In general, which of the documents cited in question 3 do you find __least__ __productive__ to work on as part of a group, and why? Please refer to all of these documents, not just the four documents you most frequently write.

6. When you participate in a group writing project, do you generally carry out each of the following activities alone, with other group members, or partly alone and partly with the group? If you are generally not involved in one or more of these activities, please circle 4 for not applicable. (Circle one number for each.)

	GENERALLY ALONE	GENERALLY AS PART OF GROUP	PARTLY ALONE AND PARTLY WITH GROUP	NOT APPLIC-ABLE
a. Brainstorming and similar idea-generating activities	1 (0%)	2 (25%)	3 (75%)	4 (0%)
b. Information gathering	1 (36%)	2 (27%)	3 (37%)	4 (0%)
c. Organizational planning	1 (8%)	2 (42%)	3 (50%)	4 (0%)
d. Drafting (including dictating)	1 (50%)	2 (17%)	3 (33%)	4 (0%)
e. Revising . . .	1 (25%)	2 (33%)	3 (42%)	4 (0%)
f. Editing (including proofreading . . .	1 (58%)	2 (0%)	3 (42%)	4 (0%)

7. Which of these activities (brainstorming, information-gathering, organizational planning, drafting, revising, editing) do you find __most__ __productive__ to perform as part of a group, and why?

8. Which of these activities (brainstorming, information-gathering, organizational planning, drafting, revising, editing) do you find <u>least</u> <u>productive</u> to perform as part of a group, and why?

9. Please indicate the frequency of use of prepared in-house or other "boilerplate" materials used in documents your group or groups produce. Such materials might include standard descriptions of equipment, facilities, staff, processes, or methods that are regularly included in various documents. (Circle one number.)

```
  1 NEVER     (PLEASE SKIP TO QUESTION #10)    (17%)
|--2 SELDOM USED                                (67%)
|--3 OFTEN USED                                 (16%)
|--4 VERY OFTEN USED                            ( 0%)
|
|------>  9a.  Approximately how many "boilerplate
              materials" do you use in a typical document?
              (Circle one number.)
```

(0%)   1   "BOILERPLATE MATERIALS" COMPRISE 75-100% OF A TYPICAL DOCUMENT

(0%)   2   "BOILERPLATE MATERIALS" COMPRISE 50%-74% OF A TYPICAL DOCUMENT

(0%)   3   "BOILERPLATE MATERIALS" COMPRISE 25%-49% OF A TYPICAL DOCUMENT

(100%)   4   "BOILERPLATE MATERIALS" COMPRISE 0%-24% OF A TYPICAL DOCUMENT

9b. How productive do you find the use of such in-house or "boilerplate" materials? (Circle one number.)

(0%)   1   VERY PRODUCTIVE
(50%)   2   PRODUCTIVE
(50%)   3   NOT TOO PRODUCTIVE
(0%)   4   NOT AT ALL PRODUCTIVE

9c. Do you have any additional comments about the use or productivity of in-house or "boilerplate" materials in group writing?

10. How often do the group or groups with which you work assign duties for completing a project according to a set plan? (The set plan might specify, for instance, that the group will plan and outline a proposed document together, then divide writing tasks so that each member drafts a part, and then reconvene so that the group can compile and revise the entire document.) (Circle one number.)

```
    1    NEVER     (PLEASE SKIP TO QUESTION #11)   ( 8%)
--  2    SELDOM                                    ( 8%)
--  3    OFTEN                                     (84%)
--  4    VERY OFTEN                                ( 0%)
--  5    ALWAYS                                    ( 0%)

------->  10a.  When your group or groups follow a set plan
               to divide duties, who typically assigns the
               tasks each member of the group will
               accomplish?  (Circle one number.)

(55%)     1    GROUP LEADER
( 0%)     2    SUPERIOR OUTSIDE THE GROUP
( 0%)     3    GROUP MEMBER OTHER THAN LEADER
(45%)     4    THE ENTIRE GROUP
( 0%)     5    OTHER (Please specify_____)
```

        10b. When your group or groups follow a set plan, how productive do you find its use? (Circle one number.)

```
( 9%)     1    VERY PRODUCTIVE
(91%)     2    PRODUCTIVE
( 0%)     3    NOT TOO PRODUCTIVE
( 0%)     4    NOT AT ALL PRODUCTIVE
```

        10C. Please briefly describe the set plan your group or groups most often use in assigning duties, or attach a copy of the plan with this questionnaire. (After describing this set plan, please skip to question #12.)

11. If the group or groups you write with do <u>not</u> follow a set plan to assign duties, how do you decide how those duties will be divided?

12. When you write as part of a group, how is authorship or credit most often assigned? (Circle one number.)

(58%)	1	TO ALL THOSE WHO PARTICIPATED IN THE PROJECT
(25%)	2	TO THE MAIN WRITER(S)
(8%)	3	TO THE GROUP LEADER
(0%)	4	TO THE WRITERS OF EACH SECTION OF THE DOCUMENT
(0%)	5	TO A SUPERIOR OUTSIDE THE GROUP
(9%)	6	TO THE COMPANY ONLY (NO PERSON IS CITED AS THE AUTHOR)
(0%)	7	OTHER (Please specify_____)

13. Are you satisfied or dissatisfied with the way authorship or credit is typically assigned in group writing projects in which you participate?

```
|-- 1    SATISFIED       (100%)
|-- 2    DISSATISFIED
|
|----> 13a.  Please explain why you are satisfied
             or dissatisfied with the way
             authorship or credit is typically
             assigned in group writing projects in
             which you participate.
```

14. In your experience, to what extent are members of the group or groups with which you work likely to agree about each of the following areas? If you are generally not involved with one or more of these areas, please circle 5 for not applicable. (Circle one number for each.)

	VERY LIKELY TO AGREE	LIKELY TO AGREE	LIKELY TO DISAGREE	VERY LIKELY TO DISAGREE	NOT APPLIC- ABLE
a. Division of duties . .	1 (67%)	2 (33%)	3 (0%)	4 (0%)	5 (0%)
b. Research methodology . .	1 (17%)	2 (83%)	3 (0%)	4 (0%)	5 (0%)
c. Content or substance . .	1 (17%)	2 (50%)	3 (33%)	4 (0%)	5 (0%)
d. Format or organization of document . . .	1 (33%)	2 (67%)	3 (0%)	4 (0%)	5 (0%)
e. Style . .	1 (17%)	2 (75%)	3 (8%)	4 (0%)	5 (0%)
f. Grammar, punctuation or usage . . .	1 (50%)	2 (42%)	3 (8%)	4 (0%)	5 (0%)

g. credit or
responsibility
for document   1 (58%) 2 (42%) 3 (0%) 4 (0%) 5 (0%)
h. other
Please specify 1   2   3   4   5

15.   When the group or groups with which you work come to
      the revision stage of a project, who most often does
      the actual revision? (Circle one number.)

      (17%)   1   GROUP LEADER
      (8%)   2   GROUP MEMBER OTHER THAN LEADER
      (17%)   3   ENTIRE GROUP
      (58%)   4   SEVERAL MEMBERS OF THE GROUP
      (0%)   5   TECHNICAL WRITER OR EDITOR
                        WITHIN THE GROUP
      (0%)   6   TECHNICAL WRITER OR EDITOR
                        OUTSIDE THE GROUP
      (0%)   7   OTHER (Please specify _____)

16.   Please briefly describe the stages of review a group-
      written document typically goes through from the time
      the initial draft is complete to the time it is
      delivered to the intended receiver. (Please include
      all levels of review--legal, editorial, scientific,
      technical, etc.)

17.   When you are working on a group writing project, how
      often do you use the following technologies? (Circle
      one number for each.)

	VERY OFTEN	OFTEN	OCCASION- ALLY	NEVER
a. Photocopying . . .	1 (42%)	2 (58%)	3 (0%)	4 (0%)
b. Conference phone calls	1 (0%)	2 (8%)	3 (33%)	4 (59%)
c. Teleconferencing . .	1 (0%)	2 (0%)	3 (8%)	4 (92%)
d. Electronic mail . .	1 (0%)	2 (0%)	3 (25%)	4 (75%)
e. Computer links . . .	1 (0%)	2 (17%)	3 (8%)	4 (75%)
f. Word processing . . .	1 (92%)	2 (0%)	3 (8%)	4 (0%)
g. Dictaphones	1 (0%)	2 (8%)	3 (33%)	4 (59%)
h. Other (Please specify _____)	1	2	3	4

18. Have any of the technologies listed in the preceding
     question affected the writing you typically do as part
     of a group? (Circle one number.)

         1   NO   (17%)
     | -- 2   YES   (83%)
     |
     |------> 18a. Please describe how any of these
                    technologies have affected your writing.

19. In your experience, what are the three greatest
     <u>advantages</u> of group writing in your profession?

20. In your experience, what are the three greatest
     <u>disadvantages</u> of group writing in your profession?

21. Please comment on how your participation in group
     writing contributes or does not contribute to your
     overall job satisfaction.

22. What advice would you give to someone in your field
     about how to write effectively as part of a group?

23. Were you given any on-the-job training to prepare you
     for the group writing you do? (Circle one number.)

         1   NO   (92%)
     | -- 2   YES (8%)
     |
     |------> 23a. Please describe this training and comment on
                     its effectiveness.

24. Do you feel that your high school and college English classes adequately prepared you for the group writing you do in your profession? (Circle one number.)

```
   1   YES  (25%)
-- 2   NO   (75%)
```

------> 24a. Please comment on how your high school or college English classes might have better prepared you for professional group writing tasks.

25. What degrees, if any, do you hold? Please list the degree (BA, MA, etc.), the major, the year awarded, and the awarding institution.

DEGREE	MAJOR	YEAR	INSTITUTION
_____	_____	_____	_____
_____	_____	_____	_____
_____	_____	_____	_____

26. Please add any additional comments that will help us better understand group writing in your profession.

(THANK YOU FOR YOUR COOPERATION)

Appendix B   229

PROFESSIONAL SERVICES MANAGEMENT ASSOCIATION

SURVEY OF WRITING IN THE PROFESSIONS
STAGE II: GROUP WRITING

This survey explores the dynamics and demands of group
writing in your profession. For the purposes of this
survey, <u>writing</u> includes any of the activities that lead to
a completed written product. These activities include
written and spoken brainstorming, outlining, note-taking,
organizational planning, drafting, revising, and editing.
<u>Written</u> products include any piece of writing, from notes,
directions, and forms to reports and published materials.
<u>Group</u> <u>writing</u> includes any writing done in collaboration
with one or more persons.

1.   In general, do you work with the same person or persons
     in producing a written document? (Circle one number.)

1.   YES ---->   (Please indicate the number of persons
                    in this group.)
     (36%)   __2-50__ NUMBER OF PERSONS IN GROUP
2   NO ---->   (Please indicate the number of persons
                    in the three groups with which you most
                    regularly work.)
     (64%)   __1-8__ NUMBER OF PERSONS IN FIRST GROUP
                    __2-10__ NUMBER OF PERSONS IN SECOND
                             GROUP
                    __2-20__ NUMBER OF PERSONS IN THIRD GROUP

2.   Please add any additional comments about the groups
     with which you work.

3.   From the following list, please indicate the four kinds
     of documents that you most typically work on as part of
     a group, rank ordering them in terms of frequency
     written. (Place one letter in each of the appropriate
     boxes.)

	MOST FREQUENTLY	A.	Memos
__F__	WRITTEN	B.	Short reports
		C.	Long reports
	SECOND MOST	D.	Professional articles and
__J__	FREQUENTLY		essays
	WRITTEN	E.	Popular articles and
			essays
		F.	User manuals or other
			detailed instructions
		G.	Newsletters, bulletins, or
			other in-house
			publications
	THIRD MOST	H.	Letters
__B__	FREQUENTLY	I.	Case Studies

```
        WRITTEN              J.  Proposals for contracts
                                 or grants
        FOURTH MOST          K.  Lecture/oral presentation
  C     FREQUENTLY               notes
        WRITTEN              L.  Instructional or other
                                 course-related materials
                             M.  Books and monographs
                             N.  Other (Please specify__)
```

4. In general, which of the documents cited in question 3
    do you find <u>most productive</u> to work on as part of a
    group, and why? Please refer to all of these
    documents, not just the four documents you most
    frequently write.

5. In general, which of the documents cited in question 3
    do you find <u>least productive</u> to work on as part of a
    group, and why? Please refer to all of these
    documents, not just the four documents you most
    frequently write.

6. When you participate in a group writing project, do you
    generally carry out each of the following activities
    alone, with other group members, or partly alone and
    partly with the group? If you are generally not
    involved in one or more of these activities, please
    circle 4 for not applicable. (Circle one number for
    each.)

	GENERALLY ALONE	GENERALLY AS PART OF GROUP	PARTLY ALONE AND PARTLY WITH GROUP	NOT APPLICABLE
a. Brainstorming and similar idea-generating activities	1 (0%)	2 (73%)	3 (27%)	4 (0%)
b. Information gathering	1 (27%)	2 (18%)	3 (55%)	4 (0%)
c. Organizational planning	1 (9%)	2 (36%)	3 (55%)	4 (0%)
d. Drafting (including dictating)	1 (64%)	2 (0%)	3 (36%)	4 (0%)
e. Revising . . .	1 (55%)	2 (36%)	3 (9%)	4 (0%)
f. Editing (including proofreading . . .	1 (55%)	2 (9%)	3 (36%)	4 (0%)

7. Which of these activities (brainstorming, information-
    gathering, organizational planning, drafting, revising,
    editing) do you find <u>most productive</u> to perform as part
    of a group, and why?

8. Which of these activities (brainstorming, information-gathering, organizational planning, drafting, revising, editing) do you find <u>least</u> <u>productive</u> to perform as part of a group, and why?

9. Please indicate the frequency of use of prepared in-house or other "boilerplate" materials used in documents your group or groups produce. Such materials might include standard descriptions of equipment, facilities, staff, processes, or methods that are regularly included in various documents. (Circle one number.)

```
  1 NEVER    (PLEASE SKIP TO QUESTION #10)    ( 0%)
--2 SELDOM USED                               (27%)
--3 OFTEN USED                                (55%)
--4 VERY OFTEN USED                           (18%)

------>  9a.  Approximately how many "boilerplate
              materials" do you use in a typical document?
              (Circle one number.)
```

(9%)   1   "BOILERPLATE MATERIALS" COMPRISE 75-100% OF A TYPICAL DOCUMENT

(27%)   2   "BOILERPLATE MATERIALS" COMPRISE 50%-74% OF A TYPICAL DOCUMENT

(18%)   3   "BOILERPLATE MATERIALS" COMPRISE 25%-49% OF A TYPICAL DOCUMENT

(46%)   4   "BOILERPLATE MATERIALS" COMPRISE 0%-24% OF A TYPICAL DOCUMENT

         9b. How productive do you find the use of such in-house or "boilerplate" materials? (Circle one number.)

(45%)   1   VERY PRODUCTIVE
(46%)   2   PRODUCTIVE
(9%)   3   NOT TOO PRODUCTIVE
(0%)   4   NOT AT ALL PRODUCTIVE

         9c. Do you have any additional comments about the use or productivity of in-house or "boilerplate" materials in group writing?

10. How often do the group or groups with which you work assign duties for completing a project according to a set plan? (The set plan might specify, for instance, that the group will plan and outline a proposed document together, then divide writing tasks so that each member drafts a part, and then reconvene so that the group can compile and revise the entire document.) (Circle one number.)

	1	NEVER	(PLEASE SKIP TO QUESTION #11)	(0%)
--	2	SELDOM		(18%)
--	3	OFTEN		(64%)
--	4	VERY OFTEN		(18%)
--	5	ALWAYS		(0%)

------> 10a. When your group or groups follow a set plan to divide duties, who typically assigns the tasks each member of the group will accomplish? (Circle one number.)

(73%)	1	GROUP LEADER
(0%)	2	SUPERIOR OUTSIDE THE GROUP
(0%)	3	GROUP MEMBER OTHER THAN LEADER
(27%)	4	THE ENTIRE GROUP
(0%)	5	OTHER (Please specify_____)

10b. When your group or groups follow a set plan, how productive do you find its use? (Circle one number.)

(46%)	1	VERY PRODUCTIVE
(45%)	2	PRODUCTIVE
(9%)	3	NOT TOO PRODUCTIVE
(0%)	4	NOT AT ALL PRODUCTIVE

10C. Please briefly describe the set plan your group or groups most often use in assigning duties, or attach a copy of the plan with this questionnaire. (After describing this set plan, please skip to question #12.)

11. If the group or groups you write with do not follow a set plan to assign duties, how do you decide how those duties will be divided?

12. When you write as part of a group, how is authorship or credit most often assigned? (Circle one number.)

(9%)   1   TO ALL THOSE WHO PARTICIPATED IN THE
                PROJECT
(9%)   2   TO THE MAIN WRITER(S)
(9%)   3   TO THE GROUP LEADER
(0%)   4   TO THE WRITERS OF EACH SECTION
                OF THE DOCUMENT
(9%)   5   TO A SUPERIOR OUTSIDE THE GROUP
(37%)   6   TO THE COMPANY ONLY   (NO PERSON
                IS CITED AS THE AUTHOR)
(27%)   7   OTHER (Please specify_____)

13. Are you satisfied or dissatisfied with the way authorship or credit is typically assigned in group writing projects in which you participate?

```
|-- 1    SATISFIED        (91%)
|-- 2    DISSATISFIED     ( 9%)
|
|----> 13a.  Please explain why you are satisfied
             or dissatisfied with the way
             authorship or credit is typically
             assigned in group writing projects in
             which you participate.
```

14. In your experience, to what extent are members of the group or groups with which you work likely to agree about each of the following areas? If you are generally not involved with one or more of these areas, please circle 5 for not applicable. (Circle one number for each.)

	VERY LIKELY TO AGREE	LIKELY TO AGREE	LIKELY TO DISAGREE	VERY LIKELY TO DISAGREE	NOT APPLICABLE
a. Division of duties . .	1 (9%)	2 (91%)	3 (0%)	4 (0%)	5 (0%)
b. Research methodology . .	1 (0%)	2 (82%)	3 (9%)	4 (0%)	5 (9%)
c. Content or substance . .	1 (9%)	2 (73%)	3 (18%)	4 (0%)	5 (0%)
d. Format or organization of document . . .	1 (9%)	2 (46%)	3 (45%)	4 (0%)	5 (0%)
e. Style . .	1 (0%)	2 (64%)	3 (36%)	4 (0%)	5 (0%)
f. Grammar, punctuation or usage . . .	1 (18%)	2 (73%)	3 (9%)	4 (0%)	5 (0%)

g. credit or
responsibility
for document   1 (27%) 2 (46%) 3 (9%) 4 (0%) 5 (18%)
h. other
Please specify 1   2   3   4   5

_____

_____

15. When the group or groups with which you work come to
     the revision stage of a project, who most often does
     the actual revision? (Circle one number.)

     (18%)   1   GROUP LEADER
     (0%)   2   GROUP MEMBER OTHER THAN LEADER
     (18%)   3   ENTIRE GROUP
     (18%)   4   SEVERAL MEMBERS OF THE GROUP
     (37%)   5   TECHNICAL WRITER OR EDITOR
                     WITHIN THE GROUP
     (0%)   6   TECHNICAL WRITER OR EDITOR
                     OUTSIDE THE GROUP
     (9%)   7   OTHER (Please specify _____)

16. Please briefly describe the stages of review a group-
     written document typically goes through from the time
     the initial draft is complete to the time it is
     delivered to the intended receiver. (Please include
     all levels of review--legal, editorial, scientific,
     technical, etc.)

17. When you are working on a group writing project, how
     often do you use the following technologies? (Circle
     one number for each.)

	VERY OFTEN	OFTEN	OCCASION- ALLY	NEVER
a. Photocopying . . .	1 (100%)	2 (0%)	3 (0%)	4 (0%)
b. Conference phone calls	1 (18%)	2 (27%)	3 (55%)	4 (0%)
c. Teleconferencing . .	1 (0%)	2 (0%)	3 (27%)	4 (73%)
d. Electronic mail . .	1 (0%)	2 (9%)	3 (27%)	4 (64%)
e. Computer links . . .	1 (10%)	2 (20%)	3 (30%)	4 (40%)
f. Word processing . . .	1 (91%)	2 (9%)	3 (0%)	4 (0%)
g. Dictaphones	1 (27%)	2 (27%)	3 (27%)	4 (19%)
h. Other (Please specify _____)	1	2	3	4

18. Have any of the technologies listed in the preceding
    question affected the writing you typically do as part
    of a group? (Circle one number.)

    ```
       1   NO      (36%)
    |-- 2   YES     (64%)
    |
    |------> 18a.  Please describe how any of these
                   technologies have affected your writing.
    ```

19. In your experience, what are the three greatest
    <u>advantages</u> of group writing in your profession?

20. In your experience, what are the three greatest
    <u>disadvantages</u> of group writing in your profession?

21. Please comment on how your participation in group
    writing contributes or does not contribute to your
    overall job satisfaction.

22. What advice would you give to someone in your field
    about how to write effectively as part of a group?

23. Were you given any on-the-job training to prepare you
    for the group writing you do? (Circle one number.)

    ```
       1   NO   (82%)
    |-- 2   YES  (18%)
    |
    |------>  23a.  Please describe this training and comment on
                    its effectiveness.
    ```

24. Do you feel that your high school and college English classes adequately prepared you for the group writing you do in your profession? (Circle one number.)

```
      1    YES   (36%)
 --   2    NO    (64%)
```

------> 24a. Please comment on how your high school or college English classes might have better prepared you for professional group writing tasks.

25. What degrees, if any, do you hold? Please list the degree (BA, MA, etc.), the major, the year awarded, and the awarding institution.

<u>DEGREE</u>   <u>MAJOR</u>   <u>YEAR</u>   <u>INSTITUTION</u>

_____   _____   _____   _____

_____   _____   _____   _____

_____   _____   _____   _____

26. Please add any additional comments that will help us better understand group writing in your profession.

(THANK YOU FOR YOUR COOPERATION)

SOCIETY FOR TECHNICAL COMMUNICATION

SURVEY OF WRITING IN THE PROFESSIONS
STAGE II: GROUP WRITING

This survey explores the dynamics and demands of group
writing in your profession. For the purposes of this
survey, <u>writing</u> includes any of the activities that lead to
a completed written product. These activities include
written and spoken brainstorming, outlining, note-taking,
organizational planning, drafting, revising, and editing.
<u>Written</u> products include any piece of writing, from notes,
directions, and forms to reports and published materials.
<u>Group</u> <u>writing</u> includes any writing done in collaboration
with one or more persons.

1. In general, do you work with the same person or persons
    in producing a written document? (Circle one number.)

1   YES ---->   (Please indicate the number of persons
                    in this group.)
    (40%)   _2-9_ NUMBER OF PERSONS IN GROUP
2   NO   ---->   (Please indicate the number of persons
                    in the three groups with which you most
                    regularly work.)
    (60%)   _2-20_ NUMBER OF PERSONS IN FIRST GROUP
                    _2-8_ NUMBER OF PERSONS IN SECOND
                          GROUP
                    _3-20_ NUMBER OF PERSONS IN THIRD GROUP

2. Please add any additional comments about the groups
    with which you work.

3. From the following list, please indicate the four kinds
    of documents that you most typically work on as part of
    a group, rank ordering them in terms of frequency
    written. (Place one letter in each of the appropriate
    boxes.)

_F_	MOST FREQUENTLY WRITTEN	A. Memos
		B. Short reports
		C. Long reports
_A/G_	SECOND MOST FREQUENTLY WRITTEN	D. Professional articles and essays
		E. Popular articles and essays
		F. User manuals or other detailed instructions
		G. Newsletters, bulletins, or other in-house publications
_L_	THIRD MOST FREQUENTLY	H. Letters
		I. Case Studies

```
         WRITTEN             J.  Proposals for contracts
                                 or grants
         FOURTH MOST         K.  Lecture/oral presentation
   H*    FREQUENTLY              notes
         WRITTEN             L.  Instructional or other
                                 course-related materials
                             M.  Books and monographs
                             N.  Other (Please specify___)
```

* This response is anomalous, since respondents later identified letters as one of the documents _least_ productive to work on collaboratively. Our interviews suggest that a number of respondents may have misread this question and simply marked the documents most frequently written, whether alone or in collaboration with others.

4. In general, which of the documents cited in question 3 do you find _most_ _productive_ to work on as part of a group, and why? Please refer to all of these documents, not just the four documents you most frequently write.

5. In general, which of the documents cited in question 3 do you find _least_ _productive_ to work on as part of a group, and why? Please refer to all of these documents, not just the four documents you most frequently write.

6. When you participate in a group writing project, do you generally carry out each of the following activities alone, with other group members, or partly alone and partly with the group? If you are generally not involved in one or more of these activities, please circle 4 for not applicable. (Circle one number for each.)

	GENERALLY ALONE	GENERALLY AS PART OF GROUP	PARTLY ALONE AND PARTLY WITH GROUP	NOT APPLIC-ABLE
a. Brainstorming and similar idea-generating activities	1 (20%)	2 (30%)	3 (40%)	4 (10%)
b. Information gathering	1 (30%)	2 (30%)	3 (40%)	4 (0%)
c. Organizational planning	1 (10%)	2 (30%)	3 (50%)	4 (10%)
d. Drafting (including dictating)	1 (60%)	2 (30%)	3 (10%)	4 (0%)
e. Revising . . .	1 (10%)	2 (20%)	3 (70%)	4 (0%)
f. Editing (including				

proofreading . . .   1 (60%)   2 (0%)   3 (40%)   4 (0%)

7.   Which of these activities (brainstorming, information-gathering, organizational planning, drafting, revising, editing) do you find <u>most</u> <u>productive</u> to perform as part of a group, and why?

8.   Which of these activities (brainstorming, information-gathering, organizational planning, drafting, revising, editing) do you find <u>least</u> <u>productive</u> to perform as part of a group, and why?

9.   Please indicate the frequency of use of prepared in-house or other "boilerplate" materials used in documents your group or groups produce. Such materials might include standard descriptions of equipment, facilities, staff, processes, or methods that are regularly included in various documents. (Circle one number.)

```
 | 1 NEVER    (PLEASE SKIP TO QUESTION #10)     (20%)
 |--2 SELDOM USED                               (20%)
 |--3 OFTEN USED                                (30%)
 |--4 VERY OFTEN USED                           (30%)
 |
 |------>  9a.  Approximately how many "boilerplate
 |             materials" do you use in a typical document?
 |             (Circle one number.)
```

(12%)   1   "BOILERPLATE MATERIALS" COMPRISE 75-100% OF A TYPICAL DOCUMENT

(38%)   2   "BOILERPLATE MATERIALS" COMPRISE 50%-74% OF A TYPICAL DOCUMENT

(0%)   3   "BOILERPLATE MATERIALS" COMPRISE 25%-49% OF A TYPICAL DOCUMENT

(50%)   4   "BOILERPLATE MATERIALS" COMPRISE 0%-24% OF A TYPICAL DOCUMENT

9b. How productive do you find the use of such in-house or "boilerplate" materials? (Circle one number.)

(38%)   1   VERY PRODUCTIVE
(12%)   2   PRODUCTIVE
(50%)   3   NOT TOO PRODUCTIVE
(0%)   4   NOT AT ALL PRODUCTIVE

9c. Do you have any additional comments about the use or productivity of in-house or "boilerplate" materials in group writing?

10. How often do the group or groups with which you work assign duties for completing a project according to a set plan? (The set plan might specify, for instance, that the group will plan and outline a proposed document together, then divide writing tasks so that each member drafts a part, and then reconvene so that the group can compile and revise the entire document.) (Circle one number.)

```
   1   NEVER      (PLEASE SKIP TO QUESTION #11)   (20%)
-- 2   SELDOM                                     ( 0%)
-- 3   OFTEN                                      (20%)
-- 4   VERY OFTEN                                 (50%)
-- 5   ALWAYS                                     (10%)
```

-------> 10a. When your group or groups follow a set plan to divide duties, who typically assigns the tasks each member of the group will accomplish? (Circle one number.)

```
(78%)   1   GROUP LEADER
( 0%)   2   SUPERIOR OUTSIDE THE GROUP
(11%)   3   GROUP MEMBER OTHER THAN LEADER
( 0%)   4   THE ENTIRE GROUP
(11%)   5   OTHER (Please specify_____)
```

10b. When your group or groups follow a set plan, how productive do you find its use? (Circle one number.)

```
(44%)   1   VERY PRODUCTIVE
(56%)   2   PRODUCTIVE
( 0%)   3   NOT TOO PRODUCTIVE
( 0%)   4   NOT AT ALL PRODUCTIVE
```

10C. Please briefly describe the set plan your group or groups most often use in assigning duties, or attach a copy of the plan with this questionnaire. (After describing this set plan, please skip to question #12.)

11. If the group or groups you write with do <u>not</u> follow a set plan to assign duties, how do you decide how those duties will be divided?

12. When you write as part of a group, how is authorship or credit most often assigned? (Circle one number.)

(10%)	1	TO ALL THOSE WHO PARTICIPATED IN THE PROJECT
(10%)	2	TO THE MAIN WRITER(S)
(0%)	3	TO THE GROUP LEADER
(0%)	4	TO THE WRITERS OF EACH SECTION OF THE DOCUMENT
(0%)	5	TO A SUPERIOR OUTSIDE THE GROUP
(70%)	6	TO THE COMPANY ONLY (NO PERSON IS CITED AS THE AUTHOR)
(10%)	7	OTHER (Please specify_____)

13. Are you satisfied or dissatisfied with the way authorship or credit is typically assigned in group writing projects in which you participate?

      | --   1   SATISFIED   (100%)
      | --   2   DISSATISFIED
      |
      |----> 13a. Please explain why you are satisfied
      | or dissatisfied with the way
      | authorship or credit is typically
      | assigned in group writing projects in
      | which you participate.

14. In your experience, to what extent are members of the group or groups with which you work likely to agree about each of the following areas? If you are generally not involved with one or more of these areas, please circle 5 for not applicable. (Circle one number for each.)

	VERY LIKELY TO AGREE	LIKELY TO AGREE	LIKELY TO DISAGREE	VERY LIKELY TO DISAGREE	NOT APPLIC-ABLE
a. Division of duties . .	1 (20%)	2 (80%)	3 (0%)	4 (0%)	5 (0%)
b. Research methodology . .	1 (30%)	2 (40%)	3 (20%)	4 (0%)	5 (10%)
c. Content or substance . .	1 (10%)	2 (90%)	3 (0%)	4 (0%)	5 (0%)
d. Format or organization of document . . .	1 (10%)	2 (90%)	3 (0%)	4 (0%)	5 (0%)
e. Style . .	1 (0%)	2 (50%)	3 (50%)	4 (0%)	5 (0%)
f. Grammar, punctuation or usage . . .	1 (30%)	2 (50%)	3 (10%)	4 (0%)	5 (10%)

g. credit or
responsibility
for document   1 (40%) 2 (30%) 3 (0%) 4 (0%) 5 (30%)
h. other
Please specify 1   2   3   4   5

_____

_____

15. When the group or groups with which you work come to
     the revision stage of a project, who most often does
     the actual revision? (Circle one number.)

     (20%)   1   GROUP LEADER
     (0%)   2   GROUP MEMBER OTHER THAN LEADER
     (10%)   3   ENTIRE GROUP
     (0%)   4   SEVERAL MEMBERS OF THE GROUP
     (50%)   5   TECHNICAL WRITER OR EDITOR
                     WITHIN THE GROUP
     (10%)   6   TECHNICAL WRITER OR EDITOR
                     OUTSIDE THE GROUP
     (10%)   7   OTHER (Please specify _____)

16. Please briefly describe the stages of review a group-
     written document typically goes through from the time
     the initial draft is complete to the time it is
     delivered to the intended receiver. (Please include
     all levels of review--legal, editorial, scientific,
     technical, etc.)

17. When you are working on a group writing project, how
     often do you use the following technologies? (Circle
     one number for each.)

	VERY OFTEN	OFTEN	OCCASION- ALLY	NEVER
a. Photocopying . . .	1 (70%)	2 (20%)	3 (0%)	4 (10%)
b. Conference phone calls	1 (0%)	2 (0%)	3 (40%)	4 (60%)
c. Teleconferencing . .	1 (0%)	2 (0%)	3 (10%)	4 (90%)
d. Electronic mail . .	1 (10%)	2 (0%)	3 (40%)	4 (50%)
e. Computer links . . .	1 (30%)	2 (0%)	3 (50%)	4 (20%)
f. Word processing . . .	1 (90%)	2 (10%)	3 (0%)	4 (0%)
g. Dictaphones	1 (0%)	2 (0%)	3 (10%)	4 (90%)
h. Other (Please specify _____)	1	2	3	4

18. Have any of the technologies listed in the preceding question affected the writing you typically do as part of a group? (Circle one number.)

```
      1    NO        (10%)
|--   2    YES       (90%)
|
|------> 18a.  Please describe how any of these
               technologies have affected your writing.
```

19. In your experience, what are the three greatest <u>advantages</u> of group writing in your profession?

20. In your experience, what are the three greatest <u>disadvantages</u> of group writing in your profession?

21. Please comment on how your participation in group writing contributes or does not contribute to your overall job satisfaction.

22. What advice would you give to someone in your field about how to write effectively as part of a group?

23. Were you given any on-the-job training to prepare you for the group writing you do? (Circle one number.)

```
      1    NO    (70%)
|--   2    YES   (30%)
|
|------> 23a.  Please describe this training and comment on
               its effectiveness.
```

24. Do you feel that your high school and college English classes adequately prepared you for the group writing you do in your profession? (Circle one number.)

```
    1    YES  (30%)
--  2    NO   (70%)

------>  24a.  Please comment on how your high school or
              college English classes might have better
              prepared you for professional group writing
              tasks.
```

25. What degrees, if any, do you hold? Please list the degree (BA, MA, etc.), the major, the year awarded, and the awarding institution.

DEGREE	MAJOR	YEAR	INSTITUTION
_____	_____	____	_____
_____	_____	____	_____
_____	_____	____	_____

26. Please add any additional comments that will help us better understand group writing in your profession.

(THANK YOU FOR YOUR COOPERATION)

Appendix C / Interview Prompts: Stage Three

COLLABORATIVE WRITING IN THE PROFESSIONS

Interview Questions

1.   Please describe your job and the kind of writing it requires.

2.   Do you consider yourself typical of the membership of your professional organiza-
     tion? What can you tell us about the membership?

3.   Please describe the kind of document you most frequently write as part of a group
     (referring to question 6 on Survey 1). Could we see an example of such a document?

4.   Please describe in detail the process you and the group go through in producing
     a typical document.

5.   Do your group-written documents follow a standard format? If so, could we see an
     example of such a format?

6.   Could we see samples of any boilerplate materials you use?

7.   Please elaborate on what you see as the major advantages and disadvantages of
     group writing.

8.   What characterizes an excellent group-written product? A poor one?

9.   Are these characteristics in any way different from those distinguishing a singly
     written product?

10. Please describe an ideal group project.

11. Please compare the process of producing a group-written product with the process
     of producing a product alone. Can you identify any differences in these processes?

12. Can you identify any difference in the way you feel about a group-written product
     as opposed to one you have written alone?

13. Is revision of a group-written product easier, harder, or the same as revision of one
     written alone? Why? (Same question for idea gathering, for organizing, and for
     drafting, if appropriate.)

14. What is the most serious problem you have encountered in a group writing project? How was it resolved?

15. Please describe the most personally satisfying group project you have been involved with.

16. If you were to design a training program for people who do the kind of writing you do, what would it comprise?

17. What one factor most accounts for the effectiveness of the group projects you work on?

Appendix D / Collaborative Writing Assignments

At Purdue University, these researchers developed and tested the following collaborative writing sequence in a business writing class:

Preproposal Memo

Each member of a three- to four-person group must write a preproposal memo directed to members of his or her group describing a problem in an organization familiar to that student. Typical organizations include fraternities or sororities, businesses where students have been or are presently employed, and on- or off-campus social and volunteer organizations. In this memo the student describes the problem and possible research methods to fellow group members and persuades them to accept this problem for the group's project. An additional copy of the memo is turned in to the instructor for grading as an individually written memo assignment.

Proposal

The group reviews each member's preproposal memo and chooses one problem that they think will function most successfully as a report project, using the criteria for choosing problems that they discussed in class earlier. The group then collaboratively writes a proposal to an appropriate representative of the organization describing the problem that they perceive within that organization and detailing the methods the group proposes to use in researching solutions.

Because the group may choose a problem in an organization associated with only one group member, the potential exists for the other members of the group to lose interest in the group project. In our experience group members have generally agreed that the problem they chose through consensus was a good one for a group project and felt committed to completing it. They were also motivated by their grade consciousness, and they thought being associated with a good project topic was more likely to produce a good grade. Occasionally, though, some students have had strong preferences for another project topic. In these instances, we have allowed students to trade places with a willing member of another group so that each can work on a problem that engages their interests. Any such exchange of group members should be completed before proposals are prepared.

The process of choosing and defining a problem and writing a proposal generally takes about three weeks. These proposals may or may not be sent to the organization, though we believe the report sequence functions best when at least the final reports are sent to the organizational audience. Some instructors schedule a conference with each group to discuss research procedures and other details of the specific project during or after preparation of the proposal. A copy of the proposal is always turned in to the instructor for grading and for approval of the project.

Progress Reports

The progress report portion of the assignment consists of two reports: one written by individuals, the other by the group.

Approximately two weeks after submitting the proposal, or about halfway through the research process, each group member submits an individually written progress report to the group, with an additional copy submitted to the instructor for an individual grade. In this report the student details progress on his or her portion of the research assignment and outlines the specific tasks that remain. The group then uses the information from the individual progress reports to prepare a group progress report, which is graded as a group assignment. Any useful attachments, such as interview summaries, sample questionnaires, or diagrams, are included with the report.

Final Report

While preparing the progress reports and during the following week, the groups should be able to finish their research and begin drafting. At this time instructors often schedule a conference with each group to discuss their draft and how it will be organized to meet the organization's needs. Finally, about two weeks after submitting its progress report, the group submits two copies of a collaboratively written final problem-solving report that presents conclusions, recommendations, or a usable product to the organizational audience. One copy goes to the organization and the other copy is graded by the instructor.

Memo Describing Logs to Students

TO: English 420 Students

FROM: English 420 Instructors

SUBJECT: Collaborative Report Logs: Why and How

To help all of you become comfortable with, enjoy, and learn from your collaborative writing experience, each individual student will keep a private log about group meetings. My objectives for this assignment and guidelines for fulfilling the assignment are detailed below.

Objectives for Keeping Individual Logs

Your log entries about your group's meetings can facilitate the group's success—and yours—in four ways. The entries provide opportunities for you to

    1. reflect upon, understand, and develop both your writing skills and your working-with-others skills;

2. explore and determine how to solve any problems that might handicap the group's productivity and your development as a writer/collaborator;
3. express freely your feelings about the group and about collaborating;
4. help me help you make the collaborative writing project a success.

<u>Guidelines for Writing Individual Logs</u>

So that your log entries do facilitate your collaborating, you'll need to make one entry per each group meeting. Each entry, written as soon as possible after a group meeting, should include:

1. Contextual Information
    —Date and Location of Meeting
    —List of Members Present
    —Purpose of Meeting
    —Starting and Stopping Times

2. Analysis and Response: This part of your entry—the heart of it—should address
    —Members' Writing Procedures
        Who did what? What was accomplished? What problems or obstacles arose?
    —Members' Interactions
        How did members tend to interact? What were the positive and negative aspects of those interactions?
    —Your Feelings
        How do you feel about the group and your place within it?
        What goals might you set for yourself to improve how you and the group function?

3. Contextual Information About Next Meeting
    —Date, Location, and Time
    —Purpose of Meeting
    —Assignments Made to Group Members

Please remember that these log entries are *your private record*. I will ask to see them after the proposal, progress report, and long report. Anything I read, however, will be between you and me. And, of course, your collaborative assignment grades will reflect how faithfully you maintained your log.

<u>Assessment Sheet Designed as a Memo</u>
<u>to the Instructor from the Student</u>

TO: English 420 Instructor

FROM:

SUBJECT: Assessment of Group Members

DATE:

You asked for my assessment of the members of my group. I have completed the form below which is my best assessment of participation in and contribution to the group.

Assignment:_____

Name of the Group:_____

Group Member:_____

PARTICIPATION/CONTRIBUTION:	HIGH 4	3	2	LOW 1
Planning: (contributes ideas, makes suggestions, offers constructive criticism)	( )	( )	( )	( )
Research: (does primary/secondary research, designs instruments, analyzes data)	( )	( )	( )	( )
Writing: (drafts parts of the reports)	( )	( )	( )	( )
Revising: (reads and revises initial draft, types draft)	( )	( )	( )	( )

COMMENTS:

At McGill University, Anthony Paré and his colleagues use another form of group-authored assignment. The assignment and a brief discussion of it appear below:

The Assignment
(used in writing courses with first, second, and third year electrical and mechanical engineering students)

Mr. Dedeke, a science teacher at FACE High School, has asked us to prepare some materials for his Secondary I (grade seven) science students. He is particularly interested in brief explanations of certain relatively simple mechanical and electrical devices.

Mr. Dedeke will be using the information we provide to teach his students. Although he may supplement what we give him with material of his own, it is best to assume that the information you supply will be all that these twelve- to fourteen-year-old students receive on the topic you choose. After we have submitted the papers to Mr. Dedeke, we will receive plenty of feedback, in person and in writing.

You will be working in groups of four to complete this task. Much of the work will be done in class. How your group cooperates on the writing of this paper is up to you; however, remember it is a *group project*.

The following is a list of topics Mr. Dedeke has suggested. If you wish to write about something which is not on the list, check with me first.

lightbulb	x-ray machine	hydraulic cylinder
flashlight	neon light	block and tackle
thermostat	battery	universal joint

Discussion

The situation described [in this assignment] is real. Ted Dedeke is an actual (and an excellent) teacher, and he does use the papers with his students. My own students receive feedback, both written and oral, from Ted and his class.

What happens? Well, first, my students display a much greater knowledge of and facility with writing than I, or my pedagogy, had given them credit for. The communicative reality of the task causes them to draw on impressive linguistic and rhetorical abilities. And the demands of group work force them to be explicit and to extend themselves. They argue, defend, explain, agree, share, and debate. They must constantly and publicly struggle with all aspects of the rhetorical situation. They brainstorm, set goals, talk about possible formats and structure, and consider their readers. . . .

The students pool their knowledge and abilities. The creative and voluble but disorganized student is balanced by the quiet but more logical student concerned with sequence and form. The student whose explanations are too abstract and technical is reined in by the group member with a fourteen-year-old sister. And, unlike most peer-editing conferences, in which the editor has no vested interest, students working on this assignment show a high degree of commitment in responding to the work of their colleagues. After all, their names must go on the paper too. In my experience, the finished group paper is better (more correct, accurate, and interesting) than it would be for the majority of individual students.

The emerging perspective on writing as a social act challenges much current theory and practice. Pedagogies resulting from variations on the process theory of writing continue to treat composition as the endeavour of a solitary individual. Invention is taught as self-discovery, the creative or cognitive exercise of a single person outside of a social context. This misrepresents to students the actual ways in which writing often occurs and robs them of the value of interaction. Given authentic readers and reasons to write and the rich dynamics of collaboration, students can produce something better than the tired term paper we so often lament.

Bibliography

Abercrombie, M[innie] L[ouie] Johnson. *Aims and Techniques of Group Teaching*. London: Society for Research into Higher Education, 1970.

———. *The Anatomy of Judgment: An Investigation into the Processes of Perception and Reasoning*. London: Hutchinson, 1960. Harmondsworth: Penguin, 1969.

Aers, David, Jonathan Cook, and David Punter. Introduction. *Studies in English Writing 1765–1830*. London: Routledge, 1981. 1–6.

Albright, Evelyn May. "Authorship and Ownership of Plays as Affecting Publication." *Dramatic Publication in England 1580–1640: A Study of Conditions Affecting Content and Form of Drama*. New York: Heath; London: Oxford UP, 1927. 202–49.

Allen, Judson Boyce. *The Friar as Critic: Literary Attitudes in the Later Middle Ages*. Nashville: Vanderbilt UP, 1971.

Allen, Nancy J. "Crossing Disciplinary Boundaries: Hermeneutics and Collaborative Writing." Unpublished paper delivered at Conference on College Composition and Communication. St. Louis, Mar. 1988.

Allen, Nancy J., Dianne Atkinson, Meg Morgan, Teresa Moore, and Craig Snow. "Shared-Document Collaboration: A Definition and Description." Unpublished paper delivered at Conference on College Composition and Communication. New Orleans, Mar. 1986.

———. "What Experienced Collaborators Say About Collaborative Writing." *Iowa State Journal of Business and Technical Communication* 1 (Sept. 1987): 70–90.

Altick, Richard D. *The English Common Reader: A Social History of the Mass Reading Public 1800–1900*. Chicago: U of Chicago P, 1957.

Anderson, Paul V. "What Survey Research Tells Us About Writing at Work." *Writing in Nonacademic Settings*. Ed. Lee Odell and Dixie Goswami. New York: Guilford, 1985. 3–83.

Angier, Natalie. "Nice Guys Don't Win Nobel Prizes." Rev. of *Science as a Process: An Evolutionary Account of the Social and Conceptual Development of Science*, by David L. Hull. *New York Times Book Review* 6 Nov. 1988: 14–16.

Artistic Collaboration in the Twentieth Century. Announcement for Hirshhorn Museum Exhibit. Smithsonian Inst., June 9–Aug. 19, 1984.

Astin, Alexander. "Competition or Cooperation? Teaching Teamwork as a Basic Skill." *Change* 19 (Sept.–Oct. 1987): 12–19.

Atkinson, Dianne. "Experimental Research: Is Collaboration Effective Pedagogy?" Unpublished paper delivered at Conference on College Composition and Communication. St. Louis, Mar. 1988.

———. "When and How to Collaborate: Some Suggestions." Unpublished paper delivered at Assn. for Business Communication Midwest Regional Meeting. Milwaukee, Apr. 1985.

Atwood, Margaret. "An End to Audience." Dorothy J. Killam Lecture. Halifax, NS: Dalhousie U, 8 Oct. 1980. Rpt. in *Dalhousie Review* 60 (Autumn 1980): 415–33. Rpt. in *Second Words: Selected Critical Prose*. Toronto: Toad, 1982. 334–57.

"Authorship from the Reader's Side." *Annals of Internal Medicine* 97 (1982): 613–14.

Bain, Alexander. *On Teaching English*. New York: Appleton, 1887.

Bakhtin, Mikhail. *The Dialogic Imagination*. Ed. Michael Holquist. Trans. Caryl Emerson and Michael Holquist. Austin: U of Texas P, 1981.

———. (P. N. Medvedev). *The Formal Method in Literary Scholarship: A Critical Introduction to Sociological Poetics*. Trans. Albert J. Wehrle. Baltimore: Johns Hopkins UP, 1978.

———. (V. N. Vološinov). *Freudianism: A Critical Sketch*. Trans. I. R. Titunik. Ed. I. R. Titunik and Neal H. Bruss. New York: Academic, 1976.

———. (V. N. Vološinov). *Marxism and the Philosophy of Language*. Trans. Ladislav Matejka and I. R. Titunik. New York: Seminar, 1973. Rpt. Cambridge, MA: Harvard UP, 1986.

Barritt, Loren. "Writing/Speaking: A Descriptive Phenomenological View." *Exploring Speaking-Writing Relationships: Connections and Contrasts*. Ed. Barry M. Kroll and Roberta J. Vann. Urbana, IL: NCTE, 1981. 124–33.

Barthes, Roland. "Authors and Writers." *Critical Essays*. Evanston, IL: Northwestern UP, 1972. Rpt. in *A Barthes Reader*. Ed. Susan Sontag. New York: Hill, 1982. 185–93.

———. "The Death of the Author." *Image—Music—Text*. New York: Hill, 1977. 142–48.

Bartholomae, David. "Inventing the University." *When a Writer Can't Write: Studies in Writer's Block and Other Composing-Process Problems*. Ed. Mike Rose. New York: Guilford, 1985. 134–65.

Baumeister, Roy F. "How the Self Became a Problem: A Psychological Review of Historical Research." *Journal of Personality and Social Psychology* 52 (1987): 163–76.

Bazerman, Charles. "Scientific Writing as a Social Act: A Review of the Literature of the Sociology of Science." *New Essays in Technical and Scientific Communication: Research, Theory, Practice*. Ed. Paul V. Anderson, R. John Brockman, and Carolyn R. Miller. Baywood's Technical Communication Series 2. Farmingdale, NY: Baywood, 1983. 156–84.

Beaven, Mary H. "Individualized Goal Setting, Self-Evaluation, and Peer Evaluation." *Evaluating Writing: Describing, Measuring, Judging*. Ed. Charles R. Cooper and Lee Odell. Urbana, IL: NCTE, 1977. 135–56.

Beebe, Steven A., and John T. Masterson. *Communicating in Small Groups: Principles and Practices*. Glenview, IL: Scott, 1982.

Belenky, Mary Field, Blythe McVicker Clinchy, Nancy Rule Goldberger, and Jill Mattuck Tarule. *Women's Ways of Knowing: The Development of Self, Voice, and Mind*. New York: Basic, 1986.

Beljame, Alexandre. *Men of Letters and the English Public in the Eighteenth Century 1660–1744*. Ed. Bonamy Dobree. Trans. E. O. Lorimer. London: Kegan Paul, 1948.

Bellah, Robert N., Richard Madsen, William M. Sullivan, Ann Swidler, and Steven M. Tipton. *Habits of the Heart: Individualism and Commitment in American Life*. Berkeley: U of California P, 1985.

Belsey, Catherine. *Critical Practice*. London: Methuen, 1980.

Bendixen, Alfred. "It Was a Mess! How Henry James and Others Actually Wrote a Novel." *New York Times Book Review* 27 Apr. 1986: 28.

Benjamin, Walter. "The Author as Producer." *Reflections: Essays, Aphorisms, Autobiographical Writings*. Trans. Edward Jephcott. Ed. Peter Demetz. New York: Harcourt, 1978. 220–38.

Bentley, Gerald Eades. "Authenticity and Attribution in the Jacobean and Caroline Drama." *Evidence for Authorship: Essays on Problems of Attribution*. Ed. David V. Erdman and Ephim G. Fogel. Ithaca: Cornell UP, 1966. 179–87.

Bereiter, Carl, and Marlene Scardamalia. "From Conversation to Composition: The Role of Instruction in a Developmental Process." *Advances in Instructional Psychology*. Ed. Robert Glaser. Vol 2. Hillsdale, NJ: Erlbaum, 1982. 1–64. 3 vols. 1978–87.

Berkenkotter, Carol. "Student Writers and Their Sense of Authority Over Texts." *College Composition and Communication* 35 (1984): 312–19.

Berlin, James A. "Contemporary Composition: The Major Pedagogical Theories." *College English* 44 (1982): 765–77.

———. "Rhetoric and Ideology." *College English* 50 (Sept. 1988): 477- 94.

———. *Rhetoric and Reality: Writing Instruction in American Colleges, 1900–1985*. Carbondale: Southern Illinois UP, 1987.

———. *Writing Instruction in Nineteenth-Century American Colleges*. Carbondale: Southern Illinois UP, 1984.

Bernhardt, Stephen, and Brice Appleby. "Collaboration in Professional Writing with the Computer." Unpublished paper delivered at Conference on College Composition and Communication. Minneapolis, Mar. 1985.

Bizzell, Patricia. "Cognition, Convention, and Certainty: What We Need to Know About Writing." *Pre/Text* 3 (1982): 213–43.

———. "Foundationalism and Anti-Foundationalism in Composition Studies." *Pre/Text* 7 (1986): 37–56.

Black, Edwin. "Secrecy and Disclosure as Rhetorical Forms." *Quarterly Journal of Speech* 74 (1988): 133–50.

Bleich, David. *The Double Perspective: Language, Literacy, and Social Relations*. New York: Oxford UP, 1988.

Bolter, J[ay] David. "Information and Knowledge: The Computer as a Medium of Humanistic Communication." *Federation Reports: The Journal of the State Humanities Councils* 8 (Jan.–Feb. 1985): 1–8.

Bonham-Carter, Victor. *Authors by Profession*. Vol. 1. London: Soc. of Authors, 1978. 2 vols. 1978–84.

Booth, Wayne C. *Critical Understanding: The Powers and Limits of Pluralism*. Chicago: U of Chicago P, 1979.

———. *Modern Dogma and the Rhetoric of Assent*. Ward-Phillips Lectures in English Language and Literature 5. Notre Dame: U of Notre Dame P; Chicago: U of Chicago P, 1974.

Bosley, Deborah. "A National Study of the Uses of Collaborative Writing in Business Communications Courses Among Members of the ABC." Diss. Illinois State U, 1989.

Bouton, Clark, and Russell Y. Garth, eds. *Learning in Groups*. New Directions for Teaching and Learning 14. San Francisco: Jossey-Bass, 1983.

——. "Students in Learning Groups: Active Learning Through Conversation." *Learning in Groups*. Ed. Clark Bouton and Russell Y. Garth. San Francisco: Jossey-Bass, 1983. 73–82.

Bowker, Richard Rogers. *Copyright: Its History and Its Law*. Boston: Houghton, 1912.

Boyer, Ernest L. "Cooperation, Not Competition." *Chronicle of Higher Education* 20 Apr. 1988: B2.

Brandt, Deborah. "Toward an Understanding of Context in Composition." *Written Communication* 3 (1986): 139–57.

Braunwald, Eugene. "On Analyzing Scientific Fraud." *Nature* 15 Jan. 1987: 215–16.

Bridgwater, Carol Austin, Philip H. Bornstein, and John Walkenbach. "Ethical Issues and the Assignment of Publication Credit." *American Psychologist* 36 (1981): 524–25.

Britton, James N. *Language and Learning*. Coral Gables: U of Miami P; Harmondsworth: Penguin, 1970.

Britton, James N., et al. *The Development of Writing Abilities (11–18)*. Schools Council Research Studies. London: Macmillan Educ., 1975.

Broad, William J. "Crisis in Publishing: Credit or Credibility?" *BioScience* 32 (1982): 645–47.

——. "The Publishing Game: Getting More for Less." *Science* 13 Mar. 1981: 1137–39.

Brodkey, Linda. *Academic Writing as Social Practice*. Philadelphia: Temple UP, 1987.

——. "Modernism and the Scene(s) of Writing." *College English* 49 (1987): 396–418.

Brown, Cynthia Stokes, ed. *Alexander Meiklejohn: Teacher of Freedom*. Meiklejohn Civil Liberties Inst. Studies in Law and Social Change 2. Berkeley: Meiklejohn Civil Liberties Inst., 1981.

Bruffee, Kenneth A. "The Brooklyn Plan: Attaining Intellectual Growth Through Peer-Group Tutoring." *Liberal Education* 64 (1978): 447–68.

——. "Collaborative Learning and the 'Conversation of Mankind.' " *College English* 46 (1984): 635–52.

——. "Collaborative Learning: Some Practical Models." *College English* 34 (1973): 634–43.

——. "Learning to Live in a World Out of Joint: Thomas Kuhn's Message to Humanists Revisited." *Liberal Education* 70 (1984): 77–81.

——. "Liberal Education and the Social Justification of Belief." *Liberal Education* 68 (1982): 95–114.

——. "On Not Listening in Order to Hear: Collaborative Learning and the Rewards of Classroom Research." *Journal of Basic Writing* 7 (Spring 1988): 3–12.

——. *A Short Course in Writing*. 2nd ed. Cambridge, MA: Winthrop, 1980.

——. "Social Construction, Language, and the Authority of Knowledge: A Bibliographical Essay." *College English* 48 (1986): 773–90.

——. "The Structure of Knowledge and the Future of Liberal Education." *Liberal Education* 67 (1981): 177–86.

——. "Teaching Writing Through Collaboration." *Learning in Groups*. Ed. Clark Bouton and Russell Y. Garth. New Directions for Teaching and Learning 14. San Francisco: Jossey-Bass, 1983. 23–29.

——. "The Way Out: A Critical Survey of Innovations in College Teaching. . . ." *College English* 33 (1972): 457–70.

———. "Writing and Reading as Collaborative or Social Acts." *The Writer's Mind: Writing as a Mode of Thinking*. Ed. Janice N. Hays, et al. Urbana, IL: NCTE, 1983. 159–69.

Buck, Gertrude. "Recent Tendencies in the Teaching of English Composition." *Educational Review* 22 (1901): 371–82.

Burke, Carolyn. "Parenting, Teaching, and Learning as a Collaborative Venture." *Language Arts* 62 (1985): 836–43.

Burke, Kenneth. *Counter-Statement*. Berkeley: U of California P, 1968.

———. *A Grammar of Motives*. Berkeley: U of California P, 1969.

———. *The Philosophy of Literary Form*. 3rd ed. Berkeley: U of California P, 1973.

———. *A Rhetoric of Motives*. Berkeley: U of California P, 1969.

———. "Terministic Screens." *Language as Symbolic Action: Essays on Life, Literature, and Method*. Berkeley: U of California P, 1966. 44–62.

Burman, Kenneth D. "Hanging from the Masthead: Reflections on Authorship." *Internal Medicine* 97 (1982): 602–5.

Burrows, Alvina Treut, Doris C. Jackson, and Dorothy O. Saunders. *They All Want to Write: Written English in the Elementary School*. 4th ed. Hamden, CT: Library Professional, 1984.

Buys, Christian J. "Humans Would Do Better Without Groups." *Personality and Social Psychology Bulletin* 4 (1978): 123–25.

Cantwell, Joan. "In the Ointment, A Few Flies." *English Journal* 72 (Apr. 1983): 55–56.

Carlson, Margaret B. "Making Book." *New Republic* 17 Mar. 1986: 12–13.

Carpenter, Michael. *Corporate Authorship: Its Role in Library Cataloguing*. Westport, CT: Greenwood, 1981.

Carry, L. Ray. "Dissertation Publication: The Issue of Joint Authorship." *Journal for Research in Mathematics Education* 11 (1980): 391–93.

Caywood, Cynthia L., and Gillian R. Overing, eds. *Teaching Writing: Pedagogy, Gender, and Equity*. Albany: State U of New York P, 1987.

Chapman, R.W. "Authors and Booksellers." *Johnson's England: An Account of the Life and Manners of His Age*. Ed. A. S. Turberville. Vol. 2. Oxford: Clarendon, 1933. 310–30.

Chaytor, H. J. *From Script to Print: An Introduction to Medieval Vernacular Literature*. Cambridge: Cambridge UP, 1945.

Chodorow, Nancy. *The Reproduction of Mothering: Psychoanalysis and the Sociology of Gender*. Berkeley: U of California P, 1978.

Chodorow, Nancy, Deirdre English, Arlie Hochschild, Karen Paige, Lillian Rubin, Ann Swidler, and Norma Wikler. "Feminism 1984: Taking Stock on the Brink of an Uncertain Future." *Ms.* Jan. 1984: 102.

Church, Susan M. "Blossoming in the Writing Community." *Language Arts* 62 (1985): 175–79.

Cixous, Helene. "The Laugh of the Medusa." Trans. Keith Cohen and Paula Cohen. *Signs* 7 (Summer 1976): 875–93. Rpt. in *New French Feminisms: An Anthology*. Ed. Elaine Marks and Isabelle de Courtivron. Amherst: U of Massachusetts P, 1980. 245–64.

Clanchy, M. T. *From Memory to Written Record: England, 1066–1307*. Cambridge, MA: Harvard UP, 1979.

Clark, Katerina, and Michael Holquist. *Mikhail Bakhtin*. Cambridge, MA: Belknap-Harvard UP, 1984.

Clemente, Frank. "Measuring Sociological Productivity: A Review and a Proposal." *The American Sociologist* 7 (1972): 7–8.

Clifford, James L., ed. *Man Versus Society in Eighteenth-Century Britain: Six Points of View.* Cambridge: Cambridge UP, 1968.

Clifford, John. "Composing in Stages: The Effects of a Collaborative Pedagogy." *Research in the Teaching of English* 15 (1981): 37–53.

Coe, Richard M. *Toward a Grammar of Passages.* Conference on College Composition and Communication Studies in Writing and Rhetoric Series. Carbondale: Southern Illinois UP, 1988.

———. "Writing in Groups." *Working Together* 2 (1979): 29–31.

Coles, William E., Jr. *The Plural I: The Teaching of Writing.* New York: Holt, 1978.

Collins, A. S. *The Profession of Letters: A Study of the Relation of Author to Patron, Publisher, and Public, 1780–1832.* London: Routledge, 1928.

Conley, Rance. "Talk About Writing in an Off-Campus Writing Group." Unpublished paper delivered at Conference on College Composition and Communication. Seattle, Mar. 1989.

Cooper, Marilyn M. "The Ecology of Writing." *College English* 48 (1986): 364–75.

Corder, Jim W. "Hunting for Ethos Where They Say It Can't Be Found." *Rhetoric Review* 7 (Spring 1989): 299–316.

Cross, Geoffrey Arthur. "Editing in Context: An Ethnographic Exploration of Editor-Writer Revision at a Midwestern Insurance Company." Diss. Ohio State U, 1988.

Curtius, Ernst Robert. *European Literature and the Latin Middle Ages.* Trans. Willard R. Trask. Bollingen Series 36. New York: Pantheon, 1953.

Daiute, Colette. "Do 1 and 1 Make 2?: Patterns of Influence by Collaborative Authors." *Written Communication* 3 (1986): 382–408.

———. *Writing and Computers.* Reading, MA: Addison Wesley, 1985.

Daiute, Colette, and Bridget Dalton. "Let's Brighten Up a Bit: Collaboration and Cognition in Writing." *The Social Construction of Writing.* Ed. B. Rafoth and D. Rubin. Norwood, NJ: Ablex, in press.

Davis, William E., Jr., and George F. Estey. "Research and Writing by Student Groups—Difficult But Rewarding." *College Composition and Communication* 28 (1977): 204–6.

Debs, Mary Beth. "Collaboration and Its Effects on the Writer's Process: A Look at Engineering." Unpublished paper delivered at Conference of College Composition and Communication. Detroit, Mar. 1983.

DeRieux, Robin. "Brewing Up a Great Group Project." *Campus Voice* 1 (Aug.–Sept. 1984): 10–14.

DeVries, D., and K. Edwards. "Student Teams and Learning Games: Their Effect on Cross-Race and Cross-Sex Interaction." *Journal of Educational Psychology* 66 (1974): 741–49.

Dewey, John. *Experience and Education.* New York: Macmillan, 1938; New York: Collier, 1963.

———. *The Public and Its Problems.* Denver: Swallow, 1927.

DiPardo, Anne, and Sarah Warshauer Freedman. *Historical Overview: Groups in the Writing Classroom.* Technical Report 4. Center for the Study of Writing. Berkeley: U of California; Pittsburgh: Carnegie Mellon U, 1987.

Doheny-Farina, Stephen. "Writing in an Emerging Organization: An Ethnographic Study." *Written Communication* 3 (1986): 158–85.

Dressel, Paul L., and Dora Marcus. *On Teaching and Learning in College.* San Francisco: Jossey-Bass, 1982.

D'Zurilla, Thomas J., and Marvin R. Goldfried. "Problem Solving and Behavior Modification." *Journal of Abnormal Psychology* 78 (1971): 107–26.

Eagleton, Terry. "A Small History of Rhetoric." *Walter Benjamin, or Towards a Revolutionary Criticism.* London: NLB-Verso, 1981. 101–13.

———. "The Subject of Literature." *Cultural Critique* 2 (Winter 1985–86): 95–104.

Eaton, Joseph W. "Social Processes of Professional Teamwork." *American Sociological Review* 16 (1951): 707–13.

Ede, Lisa S. "The Concept of Authorship: An Historical Perspective." Unpublished paper delivered at NCTE Convention. Philadelphia, Nov. 1985.

Ede, Lisa S., and Andrea A. Lunsford. "Collaborative Learning: Lessons from the World of Work." *Writing Program Administrators* 9 (Spring 1986): 17–27.

———. "Let Them Write—Together." *English Quarterly* 18 (Winter 1985): 119–27.

———. "Why Write . . . Together?" *Rhetoric Review* 1 (Jan. 1983): 150–58.

Eisenstein, Elizabeth. *The Printing Press as an Agent of Change: Communications and Cultural Transformations in Early Modern Europe.* Cambridge: Cambridge UP, 1979.

Elbow, Peter. "Closing My Eyes as I Talk: An Argument against Audience Awareness." *College English* 49 (Jan. 1987): 50–69.

———. *Embracing Contraries: Explorations in Learning and Teaching.* New York: Oxford UP, 1973.

———. *Writing Without Teachers.* New York: Oxford UP, 1973.

———. *Writing with Power: Techniques for Mastering the Writing Process.* New York: Oxford UP, 1981.

Elbow, Peter, and Pat Belanoff. *A Community of Writers: A Workshop Course in Writing.* New York: Random, 1989.

Elbow, Peter, and Jennifer Clark. "Desert Island Discourse: The Benefits of Ignoring Audience." *The Journal Book.* Ed. Toby Fulwiler. Portsmouth, NH: Boynton, 1988. 19–32.

Eldridge, Elaine. *Solving Problems in Technical Writing.* Ed. Lynn Beene and Peter White. New York: Oxford, 1988.

Elsasser, Nan, and Vera P. John-Steiner. "An Interactionist Approach to Advancing Literacy." *Harvard Educational Review* 47 (1977): 355–59.

Emerson, Caryl. "The Outer Word and Inner Speech: Bakhtin, Vygotsky, and the Internalization of Language." *Critical Inquiry* 10 (1983): 245–64.

Emig, Janet. *The Web of Meaning.* Upper Montclair, NJ: Boynton, 1983.

Faigley, Lester, and Thomas P. Miller. "What We Learn from Writing on the Job." *College English* 44 (1982): 557–69.

"Fears of Collaboration Among Scientists Examined." *Chronicle of Higher Education* 14 Aug. 1985: 6.

Febvre, Lucien, and Henri-Jean Martin. *The Coming of the Book: The Impact of Printing, 1450–1800.* Trans. David Gerard. Ed. Geoffrey Nowell-Smith and David Wooton. London: NLB, 1976.

Ferguson, Mary Anne. "Review: Feminist Theory and Practice, 1985." *College English* 48 (Nov. 1986): 726–35.

Feuillerat, Albert. *The Composition of Shakespeare's Plays: Authorship, Chronology.* New Haven: Yale UP, 1953.

Fields, Cheryl M. "Professors' Demands for Credit as 'Co-Authors' of Students' Research Projects May Be Rising." *Chronicle of Higher Education* 14 Sept. 1983: 7, 10.

Finkel, Donald L., and G. Stephen Monk. "Teachers and Learning Groups: Dissolution of the Atlas Complex." *Learning in Groups.* Ed. Clark Bouton and Russell Y. Garth. New Directions for Teaching and Learning 14. San Francisco: Jossey-Bass, 1983. 83–97.

Fish, Stanley. *Is There a Text in This Class?* Cambridge, MA: Harvard UP, 1980.

Fisher, B. Aubrey. *Small Group Decision Making: Communication and the Group Process.* 2nd ed. New York: McGraw, 1980.

Fisher, John Hurt. "Assertion of the Self in the Works of Chaucer." Unpublished paper delivered at Ohio State U Conference on "The Emergence of the Individual in the Fourteenth Century." Columbus, Feb. 1988.

Flower, Linda, and John R. Hayes. "A Cognitive Process Theory of Writing." *College Composition and Communication* 32 (1981): 365–87.

———. "Images, Plans, and Prose: The Representation of Meaning in Writing." *Written Communication* 1 (1984): 120–60.

Ford, Ford Madox. *The Ford Madox Ford Reader.* Ed. Sondra J. Stang. London: Paladin, 1987.

Forman, Janis. "Computer-Mediated Group Writing in the Workplace." *Computers and Composition* 5 (Nov. 1987): 19–30.

———. "The Design of Writing Instruction as Planned Change." *The Writing Instructor* 5 (1985): 5–13.

———. "The Discourse Communities and Group Writing Practices of Management Students." *Worlds of Writing.* Ed. Carolyn Matalene. New York: Random, forthcoming.

Forman, Janis, and Patricia Katsky. "The Group Report: A Problem in Small Group or Writing Processes?" *Journal of Business Communication* 23 (Fall 1986): 23–35.

Forsyth, Donelson R. *An Introduction to Group Dynamics.* Monterey: Brooks, 1983.

Foucault, Michel. "What Is an Author?" *Textual Strategies: Perspectives in Post-Structuralist Criticism.* Ed. Josué V. Harari. Ithaca: Cornell UP, 1979. 141–60.

Frank, Ronald E. "Coexisting with Corporate Classrooms." *Chronicle of Higher Education* 14 August 1985: 31.

"Fraud, Libel, and the Literature." *Nature* 15 Jan. 1987: 181–82.

Freire, Paolo. *Pedagogy of the Oppressed.* Trans. Myra Bergman Ramos. New York: Seabury, 1970.

Gardner, John. Interview. By Pat Ensworth and Joe David Bellamy. *The New Fiction: Interviews with Innovative American Writers.* Ed. Joe David Bellamy. Urbana: U of Illinois P, 1974.

Garfield, Eugene. *Citation Indexing: Its Theory and Application in Science, Technology, and Humanities.* New York: Wiley, 1979.

Gebhardt, Richard. "Teamwork and Feedback: Broadening the Base of Collaborative Writing." *College English* 42 (1980): 69–74.

Geertz, Clifford. "Common Sense as a Cultural System." *Local Knowledge: Further Essays in Interpretive Anthropology.* New York: Basic, 1983. 73–93.

Gellrich, Jesse M. *The Idea of the Book in the Middle Ages: Language Theory, Mythology, and Fiction.* Ithaca: Cornell UP, 1985.

Genovese, Eugene D. *Roll, Jordan, Roll: The World the Slaves Made.* New York: Pantheon, 1974.

George, Diana. "Working with Peer Groups in the Composition Classroom." *College Composition and Communication* 35 (1984): 320–26.

Gere, Anne Ruggles. *Writing Groups: History, Theory, and Implications.* Carbondale: Southern Illinois UP, 1987.

Gere, Anne Ruggles, and Robert D. Abbott. "Talking About Writing: The Language of Writing Groups." *Research in the Teaching of English* 19 (1985): 362–85.

Gere, Anne Ruggles, and Ralph S. Stevens. "The Language of Writing Groups: How Oral Response Shapes Revision." *The Acquisition of Written Language: Response and Revision.* Ed. Sarah Warshauer Freedman. Norwood, NJ: Ablex, 1985. 85–105.

Gilbert, G. Nigel. "Referencing as Persuasion." *Social Studies of Science* 7 (1977): 113–22.

Gilligan, Carol. *In a Different Voice: Psychological Theory and Women's Development.* Cambridge, MA: Harvard UP, 1982.

Goleman, Daniel. *Vital Lies, Simple Truths: The Psychology of Self-Deception.* New York: Simon, 1985.

Goodman, Ellen. "Eloquence to Order: What Reagan's Speechwriters Say." *Vancouver Sun* 15 Feb. 1986: A6.

Gordon, William J. J. *Synectics: The Development of Capacity.* New York: Collier, 1961.

Graff, Gerald. *Professing Literature.* Chicago: U of Chicago P, 1987.

Graner, Michael H. "Revision Workshops: An Alternative to Peer Editing Groups." *English Journal* 76 (Mar. 1987): 40–45.

Graves, Nancy B., and Theodore D. Graves. "Creating a Cooperative Learning Environment: An Ecological Approach." *Learning to Cooperate, Cooperating to Learn.* Ed. Robert Slavin, et al. New York: Plenum, 1985. 403–36.

Greenblatt, Stephen. *Renaissance Self-Fashioning: From More to Shakespeare.* Chicago: U of Chicago P, 1980.

Hall, Jay, and Martha S. Williams. "Group Dynamics Training and Improved Decision Making." *Journal of Applied Behavioral Science* 6 (1970): 39–68.

Halloran, S. Michael. "On the End of Rhetoric, Classical and Modern." *College English* 36 (Feb. 1975): 621–31.

———. "Rhetoric in the American College Curriculum: The Decline of Public Discourse." *Pre/Text* 3 (Fall 1982): 245–69.

Halmos, Paul R. "Nicolas Bourbaki." *Scientific American* May 1957: 88–89.

Halpern, Diane F. *Sex Differences in Cognitive Abilities.* Hillsdale, NJ: Erlbaum, 1986.

Hamilton-Wieler, Sharon. "Awkward Compromises and Eloquent Achievements." *English Education* 21 (Oct. 1989).

———. "How Does Writing Emerge from the Classroom Context? (A Naturalistic Study of the Writing of Eighteen-Year-Olds in Biology, English, Geography, History, History of Art, and Sociology)." ERIC, 1983. ED 284 209.

———. "Writing as a Thought Process: Site of a Struggle." Unpublished paper delivered at NCTE Convention. San Antonio, Nov. 1986. ERIC, 1986. ED 277 045. Rpt. in *Journal of Teaching Writing* 7 (Fall-Winter 1988): 167–80.

Harari, Josué V. "Critical Factions/Critical Fictions." *Textual Strategies: Perspectives in Post-Structural Criticism.* Ed. Josué V. Harari. Ithaca: Cornell UP, 1979. 17–72.

Hardcastle, John, Alex McLeod, Bronwyn Mellor, John Richmond, and Helen Savva. "Growth, Community and Control in Secondary School Writers." *Explorations in the Development of Writing: Theory, Research, and Practice.* Ed. Barry M. Kroll and Gordon Wells. New York: Wiley, 1983. 209–47.

Hare, A. Paul. *Creativity in Small Groups.* Beverly Hills: Sage, 1982.

———. *Handbook of Small Group Research.* 2nd ed. New York: Free, 1976.

Haring-Smith, Tori. "Is Peer Tutoring Collaborative?" Unpublished essay.

———. "When Collaborative Learning Backfires." Unpublished paper delivered at Conference on College Composition and Communication. St. Louis, Mar. 1988.

―――. *Writing Together: Collaborative Learning in the Writing Classroom*. Glenview, IL: Scott, 1990.

Harris, Joseph. "The Idea of Community in the Study of Writing." *College Composition and Communication* 40 (Feb. 1989): 11–22.

Harris, Wendell V. "Toward an Ecological Criticism: Contextual Versus Unconditioned Literary Theory." *College English* 48 (1986): 116–31.

Haskins, Caryl P. "Cooperative Research." *American Scholar* 13 (1944): 210–23.

Hawkins, Thom. *Group Inquiry Techniques for Teaching Writing*. Urbana, IL: ERIC Clearinghouse on Reading and Communication Skills, National Institute of Education, 1976.

Healy, Mary K. *Using Student Writing Response Groups in the Classroom*. Curriculum Publ. 12. Berkeley: Bay Area Writing Project, 1980.

Heath, Shirley Brice. *Ways with Words: Language, Life, and Work in Communities and Classrooms*. Cambridge: Cambridge UP, 1983.

Heffner, Alan G. "Authorship Recognition of Subordinates in Collaborative Research." *Social Studies of Science* 9 (1979): 377–84.

Heilbrun, Carolyn. *Toward a Recognition of Androgyny*. New York: Knopf, 1973.

Heller, Scott. "Collaboration in the Classroom Is Crucial if Teaching Is to Improve, Educators Say." *Chronicle of Higher Education* 11 Mar. 1987: 17.

―――. "Humanities Institutes Signal Resurgent Interest in Field." *Chronicle of Higher Education* 18 May 1988: A4-A5, A8.

Heller, Thomas C., Morton Sosna, and David E. Wellbery, eds. *Reconstructing Individualism: Autonomy, Individuality, and the Self in Western Thought*. Stanford: Stanford UP, 1986.

Henriques, Julian, Wendy Hollway, Cathy Urwin, Couze Venn, and Valerie Walkerdine. *Changing the Subject: Psychology, Social Regulation, and Subjectivity*. London: Methuen, 1984.

Hermann, Andrea W. "Collaboration in a High School Computers and Writing Class: An Ethnographic Study." Unpublished paper delivered at Conference on College Composition and Communication. Minneapolis, Mar. 1985.

Higley, Jerry. "The New Comp." *College English* 37 (1976): 682–83.

Hikins, James W., and Kenneth S. Zagacki. "Rhetoric, Philosophy, and Objectivism: An Attenuation of the Claims of the Rhetoric of Inquiry." *Quarterly Journal of Speech* 74 (1988): 201–28.

Hilgers, Thomas L. "On Learning the Skills of Collaborative Writing." Unpublished paper delivered at Conference on College Composition and Communication. New Orleans, Mar. 1986.

Hillocks, George, Jr. *Research on Written Composition: New Directions for Teaching*. Urbana, IL: ERIC Clearinghouse on Reading and Communication Skills, National Conference on Research in English, 1986.

Holt, Mara. "Collaborative Learning From 1911–1986: A Sociohistorical Analysis." Diss. U of Texas at Austin, 1988.

―――. "Collaborative Pedagogy in the 1930's and 1950's." Unpublished paper delivered at Conference on College Composition and Communication. Atlanta, Mar. 1987.

Hurlbert, C. Mark. "Rhetoric, Possessive Individualism, and Beyond." *The Writing Instructor* 8 (Fall 1988): 8–14.

Illich, Ivan, and Barry Sanders. *ABC: The Alphabetization of the Popular Mind*. San Francisco: North Point, 1988.

Irigaray, Luce. *Speculum of the Other Woman.* Trans. Gilliam C. Gill. Ithaca: Cornell UP, 1985.

Jacko, Carol M. "Small-Group Triad: An Instructional Mode for the Teaching of Writing." *College Composition and Communication* 29 (1978): 290–92.

Jacobs, Gloria. "Work/Life: Going into Business—Have You Considered a Partnership?" *Ms.* Jan. 1983: 74–77.

Jacques, David. *Learning in Groups.* London: Croom Helm, 1984.

Janda, Mary Ann. "Talk into Writing: How Collaborative Writing Works." Diss. U of Illinois at Chicago, 1988.

Janis, Irving L. *Groupthink: Psychological Studies of Policy Decisions and Fiascoes.* 2nd ed. Boston: Houghton, 1983.

———. *Victims of Groupthink: A Psychological Study of Foreign Policy Decisions and Fiascoes.* Boston: Houghton, 1972.

Jauss, Hans Robert. "The Alterity and Modernity of Medieval Literature." *New Literary History* 10 (1979): 181–229.

Jewell, Linda N., and H. Joseph Reitz. *Group Effectiveness in Organizations.* Glenview, IL: Scott, 1981.

Johnson, David W., and Frank P. Johnson. *Joining Together: Group Theory and Group Skills.* 3rd. ed. Englewood Cliffs: Prentice, 1987.

Johnson, David W., and Roger T. Johnson. "Instructional Goal Structure: Cooperative, Competitive, or Individualistic." *Review of Educational Research* 44 (1974): 213–40.

———. "The Internal Dynamics of Cooperative Learning in Groups." *Learning to Cooperate, Cooperating to Learn.* Ed. Robert Slavin, et al. New York: Plenum, 1985. 103–24.

———. "Learning Together and Alone: Cooperation, Competition, and Individualization." Unpublished paper delivered at Cooperative Learning Center, U of Minnesota, n.d.

Johnson, Richard. "What Is Cultural Studies Anyway?" *Social Text* 16 (Winter 1986–87): 38–80.

Juliebo, Moira Fraser. "To Mediate or Not to Mediate: That Is the Question." *Language Arts* 62 (1985): 849–56.

Kadushin, Charles. "The Managed Text: Prose and Qualms." *Change* 11 (Mar. 1979): 30–35, 64.

Kail, Harvey. "Collaborative Learning in Context: The Problem with Peer Tutoring." *College English* 45 (1983): 594–99.

Kamuf, Peggy. *Signature Pieces: On the Institution of Authorship.* Ithaca: Cornell UP, 1988.

Katz, Robert. "Gore Goes to War." *American Film* Nov. 1987: 43–46.

Keller, Evelyn Fox, and Helene Moglen. "Competition and Feminism: Conflicts for Academic Women." *Signs: Journal of Women in Culture and Society* 12 (1987): 493–511.

Keller, Rodney D. "Collaborative Composition: Peer Papers." Unpublished paper delivered at Conference on College Composition and Communication. New Orleans, Mar. 1986.

Kernan, Alvin. "Shakespeare's Essays on Dramatic Poesy: The Nature and Function of Theater Within the Sonnets and the Plays." *The Author in His Work: Essays on a Problem in Criticism.* Ed. Louis L. Martz and Aubrey Williams. New Haven: Yale UP, 1978. 175–96.

Kimball, Jack. "A Rationale for Unevaluative, Group Invention in Writing." Qualifying Paper. Harvard Graduate School of Educ. Nov. 1988.

Kolb, David A. "Learning Styles and Disciplinary Differences." *The Modern American College: Responding to the New Realities of Diverse Students and a Changing Society.* Ed. Arthur W. Chickering, et al. San Francisco: Jossey-Bass, 1981. 232–55.

Bibliography

269

Kolodny, Annette. "Respectability Is Eroding the Revolutionary Potential of Feminist Criticism." *Chronicle of Higher Education* 4 May 1988: A52.

Kristeva, Julia. *Desire in Language: A Semiotic Approach to Literature and Art.* Ed. Leon S. Roudiez. Trans. Alice Jardine, Thomas Gora, and Leon Roudiez. Oxford: Blackwell, 1980.

———. "The System and the Speaking Subject." *The Tell-Tale Sign: A Survey of Semiotics.* Ed. Thomas Sebeok. Lisse, Neth.: Ridder, 1975. 45–55.

Kroll, Barry M. "Why Is Plagiarism Wrong?" Unpublished paper delivered at Greencastle, IN: DePauw U, 11 Nov. 1987.

Kuhn, Thomas S. *The Structure of Scientific Revolutions.* Chicago: U of Chicago P, 1962.

———. *The Structure of Scientific Revolutions.* 2nd ed. Chicago: U of Chicago P, 1970.

Lakatos, Imre. *The Methodology of Scientific Research Programmes.* Ed. John Worrall and Gregory Currie. Cambridge: Cambridge UP, 1978.

Lanham, Richard A. "Self, Society, and the Rhetorical Paideia." Unpublished paper delivered at Conference on "Interpretive Communities and the Undergraduate Writer." U of Chicago, Mar. 1987.

Larsen, Elizabeth. "A History of the Composing Process." Diss. U of Wisconsin at Milwaukee, 1983.

Laumer, Keith. "How to Collaborate Without Getting Your Head Shaved." *Turning Points: Essays on the Art of Science Fiction.* Ed. Damon Knight. New York: Harper, 1977. 215–17.

Lay, Mary M. "Interpersonal Conflict in Collaborative Writing: What We Can Learn from Gender Studies." Unpublished essay.

Lay, Mary M., and William M. Karis, eds. *Collaborative Writing in Industry: Investigations in Theory and Practice.* Farmingdale, NY: Baywood, 1990.

Ledbetter, James. "Racter, the Poetic Computer: The Case of the Disappearing Author." *New Republic* 11 and 18 Aug. 1986: 39–41.

Leerhsen, Charles. Rev. of *The Talisman,* by Stephen King and Peter Straub. *Newsweek,* 24 Dec. 1984: 62.

LeFevre, Karen Burke. *Invention as a Social Act.* Carbondale: Southern Illinois UP, 1987.

Lemon, Hallie S. "Collaborative Strategies for Teaching Composition: Theory and Practice." Unpublished paper delivered at Conference on College Composition and Communication. St. Louis, Mar. 1988.

———. "A Practical Application of Collaborative Writing." Unpublished paper delivered at Pennsylvania State Conference on Rhetoric and Composition. University Park, July 1985.

Leonard, Sterling Andrus. "The Correction and Criticism of Composition Work." *English Journal* 5 (1916): 598–604.

———. *English Composition as a Social Problem.* Boston: Houghton, 1917.

Levine, Lawrence. "Slave Songs and the Slave Consciousness." *American Negro Slavery: A Modern Reader.* Ed. Allen Weinstein and Frank Gatell. New York: Oxford UP, 1973. 153–82.

Lindsey, Duncan. "Production and Citation Measures in the Sociology of Science: The Problem of Multiple Authorship." *Social Studies of Science* 10 (1980): 145–62.

Long, J. Scott, Robert McGinnis, and Paul D. Allison. "The Problem of Junior-Authored Papers in Constructing Citation Counts." *Social Studies of Science* 10 (1980): 127–43.

Lu, Min-zhan. "From Silence to Words: Writing as Struggle." *College English* 49 (1987): 437–48.

Luhmann, Niklas. "The Individuality of the Individual: Historical Meanings and Contemporary Problems." *Reconstructing Individualism: Autonomy, Individuality, and the Self.* Ed. Thomas C. Heller, Morton Sosna, and David E. Wellbery. Stanford: Stanford UP, 1986. 313–24.

Lunsford, Andrea A. "Assignments for Basic Writers: Unresolved Issues and Needed Research." *Journal of Basic Writing* 5 (Spring 1986): 87–99.

Lunsford, Andrea A., and Lisa S. Ede. "Collaboration and Compromise: The Fine Art of Writing with a Friend." *Writers on Writing.* Ed. Tom Waldrep. Vol. 2. New York: Random, 1987. 121–28.

———. "On Distinctions Between Classical and Modern Rhetoric." *Essays on Classical and Modern Discourse.* Ed. Robert J. Connors, Lisa S. Ede, and Andrea A. Lunsford. Carbondale: Southern Illinois UP, 1984.

———. "Rhetoric in a New Key: Women and Collaboration." *Rhetoric Review* 8 (Spring 1990).

———. "Why Write Together: A Research Update." *Rhetoric Review* 5 (Fall 1986): 71–84.

Lykes, M. Brinton. "Gender and Individualistic vs. Collectivist Bases for Notions about the Self." *Journal of Personality* 53 (1985): 356–83.

McClelland, Ben W., and Timothy R. Donovan, eds. *Perspectives on Research and Scholarship in Composition.* New York: MLA, 1985.

McDonald, Kim. "Ethical Offenses by Scholars Said to Harm Science and Its Journals." *Chronicle of Higher Education* 5 June 1985: 5, 9.

McFarland, Thomas. *Originality and Imagination.* Baltimore: Johns Hopkins UP, 1985.

Macrorie, Ken. *Telling Writing.* New York: Hayden, 1970.

———. *Telling Writing.* 2nd ed. Rochelle Park, NJ: Hayden, 1976.

———. *Telling Writing.* 4th ed. Upper Montclair, NJ: Boynton, 1985.

Maimon, Elaine P. "Graduate Education and Cooperative Scholarship." *Learning in Groups.* Ed. Clark Bouton and Russell Y. Garth. New Directions for Teaching and Learning 14. San Francisco: Jossey-Bass, 1983. 57–63.

Mangan, Katherine S. "Undergraduates, Professors Collaborate on Research at More and More Colleges." *Chronicle of Higher Education* 27 May 1987: 1, 26.

Marks, Elaine, and Isabelle De Courtivron, eds. *New French Feminists: An Anthology.* New York: Schocken, 1981.

Marrett, C. B., and Louise Cherry Wilkinson, eds. *Gender Influences in Classroom Interaction.* Orlando: Academic, 1985.

Marshall, Eliot. "Copyrights Obsolete in an Electronic Age, OTA Finds." *Science* 2 May 1986: 572.

———. "Textbook Credits Bruise Psychiatrists' Egos." *Science* 20 Feb. 1987: 835–36.

Mason, Edwin. *Collaborative Learning.* London: Ward Lock Educ., 1970.

May, Miriam, and Jamie Shepherd. "Collaboration as Subversion." Unpublished paper delivered at Second Annual Graduate Student Conference in English Studies. Milwaukee, Oct. 1988.

Mead, George Herbert. *Mind, Self and Society from the Standpoint of a Social Behaviorist.* Ed. Charles W. Morris. Chicago: U of Chicago P, 1934.

Meadows, A. J. *Communication in Science.* London: Butterworths, 1974.

Meese, George P. E. "Interdepartmental Collaborative Projects in Research and Teaching." Unpublished paper delivered at ADE Midwestern Meeting, Houghton, MI, June 1987.

Memory, J. D., J. F. Arnold, D. W. Stewart, and R. E. Fornes. "Physics as a Team Sport." *American Journal of Physics* 53 (1985): 270–71.

Merton, Robert K. Foreword. *Citation Indexing—Its Theory and Application in Science, Technology, and Humanities*. Ed. Eugene Garfield. New York: Wiley, 1979. vii–xi.

Michaels, James W. "Classroom Reward Structures and Academic Performance." *Review of Educational Research* 47 (1977): 87–98.

Michaelson, Larry K. "Team Learning in Large Classes." *Learning in Groups*. Ed. Clark Bouton and Russell Y. Garth. New Directions for Teaching and Learning 14. San Francisco: Jossey-Bass, 1983. 13–29.

Miller, J. W. *Modern Playwrights at Work*. New York: Samuel French, 1968.

Miller, Jacqueline T. *Poetic License: Authority and Authorship in Medieval and Renaissance Contexts*. New York: Oxford UP, 1986.

Miller, James E. "How Newton Discovered the Law of Gravitation." *American Scientist* Jan. 1951: 134–40.

Miller, J[ean] B[aker]. "The Development of Women's Sense of Self." Work in Progress Paper 12. Wellesley, MA: Wellesley College, The StoneCenter.

Minnis, A. J. *Medieval Theory of Authorship: Scholastic Literary Attitudes in the Later Middle Ages*. London: Scolar, 1984.

———. *Medieval Theory of Authorship: Scholastic Literary Attitudes in the Later Middle Ages*. 2nd ed. Philadelphia: U of Pennsylvania P, 1988.

Mitchell, Mildred B. "Trends Toward Multiple Authorship in Scientific Publications." *Journal of Psychology* 52 (1961): 125–31.

Moffett, James. *Teaching the Universe of Discourse*. 1968. Boston: Houghton, 1983.

Moffett, James, Charles Cooper, and Miriam Baker. *Active Voices IV*. Upper Montclair, NJ: Boynton, 1986.

Moi, Toril. *Sexual/Textual Politics: Feminist Literary Theory*. London: Methuen, 1985.

Monk, G. Stephen. "Student Engagement and Teacher Power in Large Classes." *Learning in Groups*. Ed. Clark Bouton and Russell Y. Garth. New Directions for Teaching and Learning 14. San Francisco: Jossey-Bass, 1983. 7–12.

Morgan, Bob. "Three Dreams of Language; Or, No Longer Immured in the Bastille of the Humanist Word." *College English* 49 (1987): 449–58.

Morgan, Meg. "Case Study Methods and Collaborative Writing." Unpublished paper delivered at Conference on College Composition and Communication. St. Louis, Mar. 1988.

———. "So What? . . . How Can We Apply What We Learn as Researchers to the Business Writing Classroom?" Unpublished paper delivered at Assn. for Business Communication Midwest Regional Meeting, Milwaukee, Apr. 1985.

Morgan, Meg, Nancy Allen, Teresa Moore, Dianne Atkinson, and Craig Snow. "Collaborative Writing in the Classroom." *Bulletin of the Association for Business Communication* 50 (Sept. 1987): 20–26.

Morris, Colin. *The Discovery of the Individual 1050–1200*. New York: Harper, 1972.

Morson, Gary Saul. "Who Speaks for Bakhtin? A Dialogic Introduction." *Critical Inquiry* 10 (1983): 225–43.

Morton, Herbert C., and Anne Jamieson Price. "The ACLS Survey of Scholars: Views on Publications, Computers, Libraries." *Scholarly Communication: Notes on Publishing, Library Trends, and Research in the Humanities* 5 (Summer 1986): 1–15.

Murphy, James J. *Rhetoric in the Middle Ages: A History of Rhetorical Theory from Saint Augustine to the Renaissance*. Berkeley: U of California P, 1974.

Murray, Donald M. *Learning by Teaching: Selected Articles on Writing and Teaching*. Montclair, NJ: Boynton, 1982.

————. "Writing as Process: How Writing Finds Its Own Meaning." *Eight Approaches to Teaching Composition*. Eds. Timothy R. Donovan and Ben W. McClelland. Urbana, IL: NCTE, 1980. 3–20.

Myers, Greg. "Reality, Consensus, and Reform in the Rhetoric of Composition Teaching." *College English* 48 (1986): 154–74.

Newcomb, Theodore, and Everett Wilson. *College Peer Groups*. Chicago: Aldine, 1966.

Newkirk, Thomas. "Direction and Misdirection in Peer Response." *College Composition and Communication* 35 (1984): 301–11.

————. "How Students Read Student Papers: An Exploratory Study." *Written Communication* 1 (1984): 283–305.

Nilsen, Alleen Pace. "Men and Women: Working Together in Changing Times." *School Library Journal* 27 (Sept. 1980): 29–32.

Noddings, N. *Caring: A Feminine Approach to Ethics and Moral Education*. Berkeley: U of California P, 1984.

Nudelman, Arthur E., and Clifford E. Landers. "The Failure of 100 Divided by 3 to Equal 33–1/3." *American Sociologist* 7 (Nov. 1972): 9.

Odell, Lee. "Beyond the Text: Relations between Writing and Social Context." *Writing in Nonacademic Settings*. Ed. Lee Odell and Dixie Goswami. New York: Guilford, 1985. 249–80.

Odell, Lee, and Dixie Goswami, eds. *Writing in Nonacademic Settings*. New York: Guilford, 1985.

O'Donnell, Angela M., et al. "Cooperative Writing." *Written Communication* 2 (1985): 307–15.

Ohmann, Richard. *English in America: A Radical View of the Profession*. New York: Oxford UP, 1976.

Ohmann, Richard. *Politics of Letters*. Middletown, CT: Wesleyan UP, 1987.

Ong, Walter J. *Interfaces of the Word: Studies in the Evolution of Consciousness and Culture*. Ithaca: Cornell UP, 1977.

————. "Reading, Technology, and Human Consciousness." *Literacy as a Human Problem*. Ed. James Raymond. University: U of Alabama P, 1982. 170–99.

————. "The Writer's Audience Is Always a Fiction." *PMLA* 90 (1975): 9–22. Rpt. in *Interfaces of the Word: Studies in the Evolution of Consciousness and Culture*. Ithaca: Cornell UP, 1977. 53–81.

Oromaner, Mark. "Career Contingencies and the Fate of Sociological Research." *Social Science Information* 12 (Apr. 1973): 97–111.

Over, Ray. "Collaborative Research and Publication in Psychology." *American Psychologist* 37 (1982): 996–1001.

Over, Ray, and Susan Smallman. "Maintenance of Individual Visibility in Publication of Collaborative Research by Psychologists." *American Psychologist* 28 (1973): 161–66.

Palmer, Stacy E. "Age of Computers Poses Challenge to Copyright Law." *Chronicle of Higher Education* 23 Jan. 1985: 15, 17.

Paradis, James, David Dobrin, and Richard Miller. "Writing at Exxon ITD: Notes on the Writing Environment of an R&D Organization." *Writing in Nonacademic Settings*. Ed. Lee Odell and Dixie Goswami. New York: Guilford, 1985. 281–307.

Paré, Anthony. "How It Works: A Group-Authored Assignment." *Inkshed* 7 (Sept. 1988): 5–7.

Patel, Narsi. "Quantitative and Collaborative Trends in American Sociological Research." *American Sociologist* 7 (1972): 5–6.

Patterson, Lyman Ray. *Copyright in Historical Perspective*. Nashville: Vanderbilt UP, 1968.

Patton, Bobby R., and Kim Griffin. *Decision-Making Group Interaction*. 2nd ed. New York: Harper, 1978.

Perelman, Les. "The Context of Classroom Writing." *College English* 48 (1986): 471–79.

Perkins, Jean A. *The Concept of the Self in the French Enlightenment*. Geneva: Librarie Droz, 1969.

Perloff, R. "Self-interest and Personal Responsibility Redux." *American Psychologist* 42 (1987): 3–11.

Perry, Ruth, and Martine Watson Brownley, eds. *Mothering the Mind: Twelve Studies of Writers and Their Silent Partners*. New York: Holmes, 1984.

Peterson, Penelope L., Louise Cherry Wilkinson, and Maureen Hallinan, eds. *The Social Context of Instruction: Group Organization and Group Processes*. Orlando: Academic, 1984.

Petry, Glenn H., and Halbert S. Kerr. "Pressure to Publish Increases Incidence of Co-Authorship." *Phi Beta Kappa* 63 (Mar. 1982): 495.

Phelan, James. *Reading People, Reading Plots*. Chicago: U of Chicago P, 1989.

Piaget, Jean. *The Construction of Reality in the Child*. Trans. Margaret Cook. New York: Basic, 1954.

Piazza, Carolyn, and Carl M. Tomlinson. "A Concert of Writers." *Language Arts* 62 (1985): 150–58.

Piternick, Anne Brearley. "Authors Online: A Searcher's Approach to the Online Author Catalog." Unpublished paper delivered at UCLA Conference on Conceptual Foundations of Cataloguing. Los Angeles, Feb. 1987.

———. "Traditional Interpretations of 'Authorship'and 'Responsibility' in the Description of Scientific and Technical Documents." *Cataloguing and Classification Quarterly* 5 (Spring 1985): 17–33.

Poe, Edgar Allan. "The Purloined Letter." *The Complete Works of Edgar Allan Poe*. Ed. J. A. Harrison. New York: Ames, 1965. 28–52.

Polack, Andrew. "Scholars Reconsider Role of Trendy High-Tech Entrepreneurs." *The Columbus Dispatch* 17 June 1988: F3.

Poovey, Mary. *The Proper Lady and Woman Writer: Ideology as Style in the Works of Mary Wollstonecraft, Mary Shelley, and Jane Austen*. Chicago: U of Chicago P, 1984.

Popper, Karl Raimund. *Objective Knowledge: An Evolutionary Approach*. Oxford: Clarendon, 1972; Oxford: Oxford UP, 1979.

Porter, Alan L. "Citation Analysis: Queries and Caveats." *Social Studies of Science* 7 (1977): 257–67.

Porter, James E. "Intertextuality and the Discourse Community." *Rhetoric Review* 5 (1986): 34–47.

Posner, Ari. "The Culture of Plagiarism." *New Republic* 18 April 1988: 19–24.

Potter, David. "The Literary Society." *History of Speech Education in America: Background Studies*. Ed. Karl R. Wallace. New York: Appleton, 1954. 238–58.

Price, Derek J. de Solla. *Little Science, Big Science*. New York: Columbia UP, 1963.

Price, Derek J. de Solla, and Donald D. Beaver. "Collaboration in an Invisible College." *American Psychologist* 21 (1966): 1011–18.

Reiss, Timothy J. *The Discourse of Modernism*. Ithaca: Cornell UP, 1982.

Reither, James A. "Writing and Knowing: Toward Redefining the Writing Process." *College English* 47 (1985): 620–28.

Richards, I. A. *The Philosophy of Rhetoric*. Mary Flexner Lectures on Humanities 3. New York: Oxford UP, 1965.

Rogers, Michael, with Richard Sandza. "Computers of the '90s: A Brave New World." *Newsweek* 24 Oct. 1988: 52–57.

Romer, Karen T. "Collaboration: New Forms of Learning, New Ways of Thinking." *Forum for Liberal Education* 8 (Nov.–Dec. 1985): 2–4.

Rorty, Richard. *Philosophy and the Mirror of Nature*. Princeton: Princeton UP, 1979.

Rotter, George S., and Stephen M. Portugal. "Group and Individual Effects in Problem Solving." *Journal of Applied Psychology* 53 (1969): 338–41.

Said, Edward W. *Beginnings: Intention and Method*. New York: Basic, 1975. Rpt. New York: Columbia UP, 1985.

Sampson, Edward. "The Debate on Individualism." *American Psychologist* 43 (1988): 15–22.

Saunders, J[ohn] W[hiteside]. *The Profession of English Letters*. London: Routledge, 1964.

Schmuck, Richard. "Learning to Cooperate, Cooperating to Learn: Basic Concepts." *Learning to Cooperate, Cooperating to Learn*. Ed. Robert Slavin, et al. New York: Plenum, 1985. 1–4.

Schoenbaum, S. "A Note on Dramatic Collaboration." *Internal Evidence and Elizabethan Dramatic Authorship: An Essay in Literary History and Method*. Evanston, IL: Northwestern UP, 1966. 223–31.

Scholes, Robert. *Textual Power: Literary Theory and the Teaching of English*. New Haven: Yale UP, 1985.

Schuster, Charles I. "The Un-Assignment: Writing Groups for Advanced Expository Writers." *Freshman English News* 13 (Winter 1984): 4–14.

Scott, F[red] N[ewton]. "What the West Wants in Preparatory English." *The School Review* 17 (1909): 10–20.

Scott, Fred Newton, and Joseph Villiers Denney. *Elementary English Composition*. Boston: Allyn and Bacon, 1900.

Sears, Cynthia L. "What Counts as Work?" *Working It Out*. Ed. Sara Ruddick and Pamela Daniels. New York: Pantheon, 1977.

Selfe, Cynthia L. "Collaborating Across the Curriculum: Writing Research and Evaluation in Other Disciplines." Unpublished paper delivered at Conference on College Composition and Communication. Minneapolis, Mar. 1985. Rpt. as "Confessions of a Collaborator: Classroom Research and Writing-Across-the-Curriculum Programs." *The English Record* 37 (1986): 3–7.

Selfe, Cynthia L., and Billie Wahlstram. "An Emerging Rhetoric of Collaboration: Computers and the Composing Process." *Collegiate Microcomputer* 4 (Nov. 1986): 289–95.

Shapiro, Laura. "Gilbert and Gubar." *Ms.* 14 (Jan. 1986): 59–60, 103, 106.

Sharan, Shlomo. "Cooperative Learning in Small Groups: Recent Methods and Effects on Achievement, Attitudes, and Ethnic Relations." *Review of Educational Research* 50 (1980): 241–71.

Sharan, Shlomo, and Yael Sharan. *Small-Group Teaching*. Englewood Cliffs: Educ. Tech. Publ., 1976.

Shaw, Harry E. "Grandison and His Discontents: Narrative Recollection and the Self in Richardson." Unpublished paper delivered at Narrative Literature Conference. Columbus, May 1988.

Shaw, Marjorie E. "A Comparison of Individuals and Small Groups in Rational Solution of Complex Problems." *American Journal of Psychology* 44 (1932): 491–504.

Shor, Ira, ed. *Freire for the Classroom: A Sourcebook for Liberatory Teaching*. Portsmouth, NH: Boynton, 1987.

Showalter, Elaine, ed. *The New Feminist Criticism: Essays on Women, Literature, and Theory*. New York: Pantheon, 1985.

Simon, Julian L. "A Plan to Improve the Attribution of Scholarly Articles." *American Sociologist* 5 (1970): 265–67.

Slavin, Robert E. *Cooperative Learning*. New York: Longman, 1983.

———. "Cooperative Learning." *Review of Educational Research* 50 (1980): 315–42.

———. "Effects of Biracial Learning Teams on Cross-Racial Friendship Interaction." *Journal of Educational Psychology* 71 (1979): 381–87.

———. "An Introduction to Cooperative Learning Research." *Learning to Cooperate, Cooperating to Learn*. Ed. Robert Slavin, et al. New York: Plenum, 1985. 5–15.

Slavin, Robert, et al. *Learning to Cooperate, Cooperating to Learn*. New York: Plenum, 1985.

Sloane, Sarah. Letter to Andrea Lunsford. June 1989.

Smith, Louise Z. "Independence and Collaboration: Why We Should Decentralize Writing Centers." *Writing Center Journal* 7 (Fall-Winter 1986): 3–10.

Smith, M. B. "Perspectives on Selfhood." *American Psychologist* 33 (1978): 1053–63.

Smith, Nicholas D. "Collaborating Philosophically." *Rhetoric Society Quarterly* 17 (1987): 247–62.

Snow, Craig. "Towards a Non-Definition of Collaboration." Unpublished essay, 1985.

Somerville, E. OE. [Edith Oenone], and Martin Ross [Violet Florence Martin]. *The Big House of Inver*. London: Heinemann, 1925.

Spear, Karen. *Sharing Writing: Peer Response Groups in English Classes*. Portsmouth, NH: Boynton, 1988.

Spence, J. T. "Achievement American Style: The Rewards and Costs of Individualism." *American Psychologist* 40 (1985): 1285–95.

Spender, Dale. *Man Made Language*. 2nd ed. London: Routledge, 1985.

Spiegel, Don, and Patricia Keith-Spiegel. "Assignment of Publication Credits: Ethics and Practices of Psychologists." *American Psychologist* 25 (1970): 738–47.

Spitzer, Leo. "Note on the Poetic and Empirical 'I' in Medieval Authors." *Traditio* 4 (1946): 414–22.

Stanger, Carol A. "The Sexual Politics of the One-To-One Tutorial Approach and Collaborative Learning." *Teaching Writing: Pedagogy, Gender, and Equity*. Ed. Cynthia L. Caywood and Gillian R. Overing. Albany: State U New York P, 1987. 31–44.

Steiner, Ivan D. *Group Process and Productivity*. New York: Academic, 1972.

Stewart, Donald C. "Collaborative Learning and Composition: Boon or Bane?" *Rhetoric Review* 7 (Fall 1988): 58–83.

———. Rev. of *Invention as a Social Act*, by Karen Burke LeFevre. *Rhetoric Review* 6 (1987): 107–11.

Stewart, Walter W., and Ned Feder. "The Integrity of the Scientific Literature." *Nature* 15 Jan. 1987: 207–14.

Stravinsky, Igor, and Robert Craft. *Conversations with Igor Stravinsky*. Berkeley: U of California P, 1958.

Street, Brian V. *Literacy in Theory and Practice*. Cambridge: Cambridge UP, 1984.

Sullivan, Patricia A. "From Student to Scholar: A Contextual Study of Graduate Student Writing in English." Diss. Ohio State U, 1988.

Swearingen, C. Jan. "Between Intention and Inscription: Toward a Dialogical Rhetoric." *Pre/Text* 4 (1983): 257–71.

Tait, James A. *Authors and Titles*. London: Bingley, 1969.

Taylor, Mark C. *Kierkegaard's Pseudonymous Authorship: A Study of Time and the Self*. Princeton: Princeton UP, 1975.

Tocqueville, Alexis de. *Democracy in America*. Trans. George Lawrence. Ed. J. P. Mayer. New York: Doubleday-Anchor, 1969.

Tompkins, Jane. "Me and My Shadow." *New Literary History* 19 (Autumn 1987): 169–78.

Toulmin, Stephen. *Human Understanding: The Collective Use and Evolution of Concepts*. Princeton: Princeton UP, 1972.

———. "The Inwardness of Mental Life." *Critical Inquiry* 6 (1979): 1–16.

Trimbur, John. "Collaborative Learning and Teaching Writing." *Perspectives on Research and Scholarship in Composition*. Ed. Ben W. McClelland and Timothy R. Donovan. New York: MLA, 1985. 87–109.

———. "Consensus and Difference in Collaborative Learning." Unpublished paper delivered at MLA Convention, San Francisco, Dec. 1987. Rpt. in *College English,* forthcoming.

———. Letter to authors. 1989.

Tritt, Michael. "Collaboration in Writing: From Start to Finish and Beyond." *English Quarterly* 17 (Spring 1984): 82–86.

Ullman, Walter. *The Individual and Society in the Middle Ages*. Baltimore: Johns Hopkins UP, 1966.

Van Pelt, William, and Alice Gillam-Scott. "Peer Collaboration and the Computer-Assisted Classroom: Bridging the Gap between Academia and the Workplace." Unpublished essay, 1988.

Vincinus, Martha. *The Industrial Muse: A Study of Nineteenth Century British Working-Class Literature*. New York: Barnes, 1974.

Wall, Susan V., and Anthony R. Petrosky. "Freshman Writers and Revision: Results from a Survey." *Journal of Basic Writing* 3 (Fall-Winter 1981): 120–21.

Wallace, Karl R., ed. *History of Speech Education in America: Background Studies*. New York: Appleton, 1954.

Webb, Noreen M. "Student Interaction and Learning in Small Groups." *Review of Educational Research* 52 (1982): 421–45.

Webber, Samuel. *Institution and Interpretation*. Theory and History of Literature 31. Minneapolis: U of Minnesota P, 1987.

Weston, Ralph E. "A Modest Proposal." *Physics Today* 15 (June 1962): 79–80.

"What Revolution?" *Corvallis Gazette-Times* 27 June 1981: 1.

Whyte, William H., Jr. *The Organization Man*. New York: Simon, 1956.

Wiener, Harvey. "Collaborative Learning in the Classroom: A Guide to Evaluation." *College English* 48 (1986): 52–61.

Wilkinson, Louise Cherry, and Cora B. Marrett, eds. *Gender Influences in Classroom Interaction*. Educ. Psych. Series. Orlando: Academic, 1985.

Williams, Raymond. *Marxism and Literature*. Oxford: Oxford UP, 1977.

Winsor, Dorothy A. "An Engineer's Writing and the Corporate Construction of Knowledge." *Written Communication* 6 (July 1989): 270–85.

Witte, Stephen P. "Some Contexts for Understanding Written Literacy." Unpublished paper delivered at Right to Literacy Conference. Columbus, Sept. 1988.

Woodmansee, Martha. "The Genius and the Copyright: Economic and Legal Conditions of the Emergence of the 'Author.'" *Eighteenth-Century Studies* 17 (1984): 425–48.

———. "The Interest in Disinterestedness: Karl Phillip Moretz and the Emergence of the Theory of Aesthetic Autonomy in Eighteenth-Century Germany." *Modern Language Quarterly* 45 (Mar. 1984): 22–47.

Woods, William F. "Nineteenth-Century Psychology and the Teaching of Writing." *College Composition and Communication* 36 (1985): 20–41.

Woolf, Virginia. *A Room of One's Own.* London: Woolf, 1929. Rpt. London: Hogarth, 1929. Rpt. New York: Harcourt, 1981.

Wordsworth, William. "Essay, Supplementary to the Preface." *Literary Criticism of William Wordsworth.* Ed. Paul M. Zall. Lincoln: U of Nebraska P, 1966. 158–87.

Yarnoff, Charles. "Contemporary Theories of Invention in the Rhetorical Tradition." *College English* 41 (1980): 552–60.

Young, Edward. *Conjectures on Original Composition. In a Letter to the Author of Sir Charles Grandison [i.e. Samuel Richardson].* Dublin: Wilson, 1759. Rpt. Leeds, Eng.: Scholar, 1966. Rpt. Folcroft, PA: Folcroft, 1970.

Young, Iris Marion. "The Ideal of Community and the Politics of Difference." *Social Theory and Practice* 12 (Spring 1986): 1–26.

Young, Richard. "Arts, Crafts, Gifts, and Knacks: Some Disharmonies in the New Rhetoric." *Reinventing the Rhetorical Tradition.* Ed. Aviva Freedman and Ian Pringle. Ontario: Canadian Council of Teachers of English; Conway, AR: L & S, 1980. 53–60.

Zavarzadeh, Mas'ud, and Donald Morton. "Theory Pedagogy Politics: The Crisis of 'The Subject' in the Humanities." *Boundary 2: A Journal of Postmodern Literature and Culture* 15 (Fall-Winter 1986–87): 1–22.

Ziman, J. M. *Public Knowledge: An Essay Concerning the Social Dimension of Science.* London: Cambridge UP, 1968.

Zoellner, Robert. "Talk-Write: A Behavioral Pedagogy for Composition." *College English* 30 (1969): 267–320.

Zuckerman, Harriet A. "Patterns of Name Ordering among Authors of Scientific Papers: A Study of Social Symbolism and Its Ambiguity." *American Journal of Sociology* 74 (1968): 276–91.

Name Index

Abbott, George, 68
Abercrombie, M. L. J., 111, 112
Allen, Judson Boyce, 77–78
Allen, Nancy J., 15, 119, 125
Allison, Paul D., 11, 76
Anderson, Paul V., 15
Andrews, Mary R. Shipman, 70
Angier, Natalie, 3
Arendt, Hannah, 126
Arnold, J. F., 19
Atkinson, Dianne, 15, 125
Atwood, Margaret, 69

Bain, Alexander, 109
Bakhtin, Mikhail, 91–92, 101, 134, 142
Bangs, John Kendrick, 70
Barritt, Loren, 6
Barthes, Roland, 87–89, 140
Bartholomae, David, 107, 115
Bazerman, Charles, 74, 115
Beebe, Steven A., 10, 11
Belenky, Mary Field, 1, 104, 132, 135
Bellah, Robert N., 109, 129
Bellamy, Joe David, 129
Belsey, Catherine, 89
Bendixen, Alfred, 71
Bereiter, Carl, 7
Berlin, James A., 113–15
Bernstein, Albert, 27–30, 38, 42, 43, 134, 137
Bizzell, Patricia, 113, 115
Bleich, David, 115
Boccaccio, 84

Bolter, J. David, 68, 101
Bonham-Carter, Victor, 78, 80–81
Booth, Wayne C., 113, 137, 138
Bornstein, Philip H., 99
Bosley, Deborah, 15, 118
Boswell, James, 94
Bourbaki, Nicolas, 70
Bouton, Clark, 10, 11, 116
Bowker, Richard Rogers, 84
Boyer, Ernest L., 103
Bridgwater, Carol Austin, 99
Britton, James N., 112
Broad, William J., 98
Brodkey, Linda, 20
Brown, Alice, 70
Bruffee, Kenneth A., 7, 9, 20, 114–17, 142
Buber, Martin, 110
Buck, Gertrude, 109
Burke, Kenneth, 5, 21, 72, 101, 130, 134, 136, 142

Carey, Henry C., 84
Carpenter, Michael, 93–95, 97
Carry, L. Ray, 9
Cavenar, Jesse O., Jr., 3–4
Chaytor, H. J., 78
Chiogioji, Eleanor, 38–41, 43, 134, 137
Chodorow, Nancy, 132
Chopin, Kate, 91
Cicero, 109
Cixous, Helene, 91, 127
Clark, Katerina, 92

Subject Index

Active learning. *See* Cooperative learning

Act of Queen Anne, 1710. *See* Copyright laws: history of

American Consulting Engineers Council (ACEC), 8, 22, 45

American Institute of Chemists, 8, 32, 45, 60

American Psychological Association, 8, 27, 45

Audience, 30–31, 32, 66

Author: concept of, 93, 140; as construct, 73, 76–77, 85–87, 92, 101; destabilizing of concept of, 87–93, 97, 101; eighteenth-century, 81–85; medieval, 77–79; modern, 86–90; nature of, 78, 80–87, 90–92; as problem, 87–91, 93, 95, 140; redefining, 89; Renaissance, 79–81; Romantic, 85–86; Victorian, 86

Authorship: attribution of, 99–100; concept of, 101–2, 112, 122; effects of technology on, 139; electronic media and, 97, 101; exclusion of women from, 91; feminist concerns with, 91; history of the concept of, 76–88, 93; multiple, in the sciences, 11–12, 73–76; nature of, 12–13, 72, 75–77, 85–88, 137; origination theory of, 77–87, 95; pride of, 25–26, 29, 30, 37, 40, 62; redefining, 89, 101; renouncing, 98; responsibility for, 92, 98–100; student, in the sciences, 107

Backgrounding, 141–42

Bakhtinian theory of "voice," 43–44, 91–92

Book: definition of, 82

Citation: analysis, 11; counts, 11–12, 74–76, 138; ethics of, 12; name-ordering in, 12

Collaboration: achieving consensus in, 119; advantages of, 33, 41, 62, 64–65; attitudes towards, 6, 26, 29, 31, 39; challenge to traditional pedagogy, 119–21, 140; characteristics of effective, 10, 25–26, 29–30, 32, 34–37, 40–41, 64; characteristics of ineffective, 10, 28–29; constraints against, 120–21; definition of, 14–16; disadvantages of, 33, 41, 43–44, 60–62; ethics of, 9; frequency of, 8, 63; gender issues and, 100, 138; group size and, 29; groupthink and, 10; guidelines to, 121–22; images of, 20–21, 41–42, 72; issues of power and, 120, 137–38, 140–42; methods of, 8, 33–34, 37, 39; motivation for, 22; pedagogy of, 7–9, 13, 107–26; politics of, 115; race issues and, 100, 138

Collaboration, research on: in composition, 7, 9, 44, 118–19; in education, 10; in psychology, 131–32; in sciences, 11–12, 73–76; in social sciences, 9–10; types of documents, 63; unanswered questions about, 125–26

Collaboration, work-related, 118; characteristics of, 21; in chemistry, 32–35; in city management, 35–38; critical perspective of, 137–38; in engineering, 21–27; in government, 38–41; in psychology, 27–30; in technical writing, 30–32; work-related writing processes and, 7, 14

Collaborative groups: degree of satisfaction in, 64–65; organization of, 63–64, 124

Collaborative learning: in Britain, 111–12; criticisms against, 136; history of, 108–12; purposes of, 11

Collaborative pedagogy: history of, 109–12

Collaborative writing: assignments, 115–16, 123–25; dialogic mode of, 67, 112, 132–36, 140, 142; effects of, 11; hierarchical mode of, 67, 132–34, 136; teacher's authority and, 120. *See* Collaboration: definition of

Collaborators: qualities of effective, 21–23, 65–66

Commonsense wisdom, 5, 7, 73, 87, 89, 101

Composition theory: in collaborative learning, 113–15; current, 112–13; research in, 116

Cooperative learning: advantages of, 117; assignments, 116–17; research in, 10–11, 116–18

Copyright laws: history of, 81–87

Corporate authorship, 95–97

Critical Qualls Method: description of, 23–24; functions of, 24–25; popularity of, 25–27

Critics, role of, 86

Disjunction of theory and practice, 139–40

Examinations, 120–21

Feminist issues, 132–35, 140

Group processes and dynamics, 61; research in, 10

Group writing. *See* Collaborative writing

Heteroglossia, 44, 92, 122

Honorary authorship, 98–99

Humanism, Western male, 91

Individualism, 79, 89–90, 108–10, 118, 131

International City Management Association, 8, 35, 45, 65

Knowledge, construction of, 107–8; nature of, 12, 78–79, 83–85, 89, 108, 114–15, 133

Learning groups. *See* Collaborative learning

Library cataloguing of authors, 93–97

Modern Language Association, 8, 38, 42, 45

Overstanding, 137–41

Patriarchal academic mode, 13

Peer tutoring, 114

Plagiarism: history of, 78

Printing: development of, 79–80

Professional Services Management Association, 8, 45, 61

Purloined letter, 5, 9, 43, 143

Reader: devalued, 88–89

Research, FIPSE-funded project: conclusions, 130–32; generalizations, 141; goals, 44, 60; interviews, 8, 21; limitations of interviews, 42–44; methods, 45–67; questions, 7; results of interviews, 21; subjects of: Bernstein, Albert, 27–30; Chiogioji, Eleanor, 38–41; Irving, George, 32–35; Miller, Dick, 35–38; Qualls, Bill, 21–27; Warrior, Allan, 30–32

Research, FIPSE-funded project, Survey 1: description of, 8; goals, 8, 46; methods, 45–46; results, 47–51, 63–67; subjects of, 8

Research, FIPSE-funded project, Survey 2: definition of collaborative writing used in, 14; description of, 8; goals, 62; issues of, 8; methods, 46; responses to, 27; results, 46–67; subjects of, 8

Scientific collaboration. *See* Collaboration, research on: in sciences

Society for Technical Communication, 8, 30, 42, 45, 61

Subject: questioning the status of, 13, 73, 89–90, 131–32

Teaching practice, theoretical implications of, 139–40

Text editor program, 31–32

Texts: authorless, 88; reviewing of, 88–89; status of, 89, 92

Theory: practical implications of, 138–39

Vocabulary, controlled, 30–32

Writing: as collaboration, 5, 7, 20, 31, 60, 114–15; deconstructed, 94–95; image of solitary author in, 73, 85, 109, 140; as solitary, 5–7, 9, 12, 60, 113–14, 118

Lisa Ede is Associate Professor and Director of the Communication Skills Center at Oregon State University; *Andrea Lunsford* is Professor and Vice Chair of English at The Ohio State University. With Robert J. Connors, they edited *Essays on Classical Rhetoric and Modern Discourse*, which won the 1985 MLA Mina Shaughnessy Prize. In 1984, their coauthored article "Audience Addressed/Audience Invoked: The Role of Audience in Composition Theory and Pedagogy" received the CCCC Braddock Award.